PERFORMANCE BUDGETING FOR STATE AND LOCAL GOVERNMENT

PERFORMANCE BUDGETING FOR STATE AND LOCAL GOVERNMENT

JANET M. KELLY AND
WILLIAM C. RIVENBARK

M.E.Sharpe
Armonk, New York
London, England

Library of Congress Cataloging-in-Publication Data

Kelly, Janet M.
   Performance budgeting for state and local government / Janet M. Kelly and William C.
Rivenbark.
      p. cm.
   Includes bibliographical references and index.
   ISBN 0-7656-1129-5 (cloth: alk. paper)   ISBN 0-7656-1130-9 (pbk.: alk. paper)
      1. Budget—United States—States. 2. Program budgeting—United States—States.
   3. Local budgets—United States. I. Rivenbark, William C. II. Title.

HJ2053.A1K45 2003
352.4'8213'0973—dc21   2003050597

Printed in the United States of America

The paper used in this publication meets the minimum requirements of
American National Standard for Information Sciences
Permanence of Paper for Printed Library Materials,
ANSI Z 39.48-1984.

BM (c)   10   9   8   7   6   5   4   3   2   1
BM (p)   10   9   8   7   6   5   4   3   2   1

Contents

List of Illustrations

Tables

Figures

Boxes

Appendices

Preface

Interested practitioners and students of public administration can review a general literature on performance budgeting that uses survey research or case studies to describe governments' experience with implementing performance budgeting and the impact on budget outcomes. The federal experience with performance budgeting has been the most thoroughly documented, though state-level studies are emerging as more states adopt performance budgeting systems. These readers would probably conclude that performance budgeting is not a stand-alone budgeting technique, nor a change in budget format, and that organizational factors beyond performance are just as important to resource allocation decisions, even in organizations where performance budgeting is mandated. They might wonder, given the results of their literature review, why states and localities continue to adopt performance budgeting and why public professional organizations continue to promote it when the record of success is mixed.

Alternatively, the interested reader might choose one of the texts that offers a technical perspective of performance budgeting and come away with a very different impression. Guides on the construction and implementation of performance measurement programs typically advocate performance measurement as a way to improve the quality of management decisions, to increase program efficiency and effectiveness, to enhance program and service performance, and to leave citizens more satisfied and confident that their service providers are holding themselves accountable for results. These texts are a valuable source of information for any practitioner or student, describing how to construct meaningful performance measures and how to present them in the most useful form for decision making. However, they rarely link performance measurement to the budget process or address the elements of capacity for performance-based management.

This book bridges the gap between the general literature and technical treatments, summarizing the techniques that support performance budgeting in the political, historical, economic, managerial, and institutional context of its application. We hammer a few themes throughout the book. The first is that performance budgeting, like other budgetary reforms, has been adopted with more enthusiasm than understanding. The second is that the prudent manager should fit performance budgeting into the existing managerial and budget process, not fit other processes into performance budgeting. Third, a good performance measurement and reporting system is the foundation for performance budgeting, but reporting performance results in the budget document does not constitute performance budgeting. Finally, performance budgeting can never be determinate. It cannot decide "who gets what" because, in the words of Aaron Wildavsky, that would amount to a theory of politics. Performance budgeting functions within the political system, informing allocation decisions with performance results but accommodating political and legal mandates.

We apologize to the reader who would prefer the consistency of tone associated with either of these two views. Three of the chapters are clearly "broad view." Chapter 1 frames the question about the value of performance budgeting for public organizations, and chapter 2 describes its ancestry and current impact, reviewing the record of performance budgeting in federal, state, and local government. Chapter 8 concludes the book by describing the managerial capacity needed for performance budgeting, with special emphasis on the leadership needed from elected officials, senior managers, and line managers to make performance budgeting successful.

Chapter 3 is almost exclusively technical, devoted to the budget preparation and adoption process in state and local government, including the major stages of how budgets are developed, implemented, and evaluated. The three examples we selected for this chapter (Washington State; Fairfax County, Virginia; and the city of Hickory, North Carolina) show how the budget process can be expanded to accommodate the tangible and intangible elements of performance budgeting. Chapter 3 shows that management tools promoting the performance agenda can be directly linked to the budgetary process. This component of performance budgeting is often missing from discussions about how performance results can inform resource allocation decisions.

The remaining chapters are dedicated to exploring the management tools that promote the success of performance budgeting, including planning (chapter 4), performance measurement (chapter 5), benchmarking (chapter 6), and evaluation (chapter 7). They are both general and technical. The elements of "how" are intertwined with the questions of "why" to fashion a managerial approach to performance budgeting. We use examples from states and localities throughout these chapters to show how planning determines the selection of the measure and how an appropriate, verifiable measure links back to the budget process. Because our emphasis is managerial, we focus on how goals and objectives drive measures and how changes in the economic, political, or social climates of the government force good managers to update their measures, just as they update their goals and objectives.

We hope students of public administration come away with a clearer understanding of the promise of performance budgeting by seeing how it can enhance operational accountability for programs and services without sacrificing political accountability for how resources are spent. We also hope that this book serves as a resource guide for practitioners of state and local government as they continue their quest for informing the budget preparation and adoption process with accurate and reliable information derived from the performance of service delivery.

We would like to thank the staff of M.E. Sharpe for their attention to detail, the timeliness of their work, and their suggestions throughout the publication process.

We are indebted to the Maxine Goodman Levin College of Urban Affairs at Cleveland State University and the School of Government at the University of North Carolina at Chapel Hill for their continuing support of this book and our other research endeavors. We are fortunate to work for organizations with such a strong applied research and public service ethic. Special thanks also goes to David N. Ammons, Carla M. Pizzarella, and Gregory S. Allison who provided feedback and offered suggestions on several of the chapters.

It is impossible to name all the state and local government officials who gave generously of their time and expertise to inform this project. We are grateful to them for their belief that sharing innovation and experience elevates the profession of public budgeting and finance. Our professional organization—the Government Finance Officers Association (GFOA)—reflects that same ideal and assisted us with the implementation of the survey. We appreciate GFOA's interest in this project.

On days when this book seemed like a particularly bad idea, our families counseled perseverance and offered encouragement. The most heartfelt thanks to Roy and Hazel Kelly and to Rebecca, Will, and Jay Rivenbark.

PERFORMANCE BUDGETING FOR STATE AND LOCAL GOVERNMENT

— Chapter 1 —

Performance Budgeting: Combining Operational and Financial Accountability

The quest for governmental accountability is as old as the country and reflects our national skepticism about the size of government and its propensity to grow. The problem is that there is no consensus on what constitutes accountability to citizens. Is it giving them what they want? Yes and no. Citizenship is more than a financial transaction between a buyer and a seller, but governments must tailor their tax-service mix to citizen preferences, just as the private sector tailors its price-quality mix to customers. We use an electoral system to filter citizen preferences and formulate policy that creates public services. That process is not efficient. We could give citizens a list of public services and the tax cost and ask them to select the mix they prefer every five years or so, avoiding the inevitable delays and haggling that comes with the way we make service provision decisions now. Economic theory tells us that the optimal level of government service exists at the point at which the marginal value of the service provided equals the marginal cost to the median taxpayer. It is a great theory, but difficult to implement when citizens value services differently and have varying tolerations for taxes.

Until we come up with a new system that is both efficient and responsive, we will have to parse accountability along several dimensions. The first is political accountability, or the responsiveness of government to the needs and desires of citizens. Elected officials have to shoulder the burden of political accountability as they craft public policy in the public interest. They must choose which services to provide and establish broad priorities for them. They also must decide which services are most important to the government and provide them more resources than services that they consider less important. Elected officials may delegate some power to make resource allocations to public managers, but the managers do not have to defend their allocation decisions (or the service provision changes that the decision caused) at the next election.

Public managers have another kind of accountability. Operational accountability goes to the economy and effectiveness dimensions of public services.

3

While managers may not choose the mix of services provided nor the priority in the set of all services provided, they must monitor the delivery of those services for economy and effectiveness. By economy we mean the most efficient use of public tax dollars; effectiveness is the degree to which the service is accomplishing the purpose for which it was created. Performance management is an approach to operational accountability that uses information systems to monitor services for economy and effectiveness. It cannot tell managers *what* services to provide, but it can suggest *how* they should be provided subject to the time, resource, and political constraints attached to public organizations.

The third type of accountability is financial accountability. It requires public finance officers to answer for how every dollar of tax money was collected and spent. Financial accountability is much more than protection against fraud or embezzlement, though financial controls do serve that purpose. The larger purpose is to accurately reflect where tax money comes from and where it goes, and in the process provide an accurate assessment of the overall financial condition of the government. The finance or budget division of a government is responsible to both the chief administrative officer and to elected officials, but most in the profession would say that we owe financial accountability primarily to citizens, and to our own professional standards.

This book describes an approach to public management that integrates operational accountability and financial accountability while accommodating political accountability. Performance budgeting offers a way to make budget decisions about the allocation of limited resources based on the performance of service delivery. It starts with *performance measurement*, requiring mission statements, service delivery goals, objectives, and mix of performance measures at the programmatic level. It then moves to *performance management*, which requires the actual use of performance information for informing the decision-making processes within the core functions of management. It culminates when public officials embrace performance management during the annual budget preparation process. Therefore, we use the following definition as the foundation for this text. Performance budgeting is a budget preparation and adoption process that emphasizes *performance management*, allowing allocation decisions to be made *in part* on the efficiency and effectiveness of service delivery.

Facts and Values in Budget Decisions

When we were budget officers, we believed our job was to inform resource allocation decisions. We offered a recommendation about how much money a service should be allocated based on a set of facts. It was up to others to accept or reject our recommendation. The set of facts we assembled influenced the recommendation we made. Always relevant was last year's appropriation, actual spending in the current budget year, organization-wide salary and benefit changes, and the requests that service managers made for additional resources. Those facts are still relevant to the decision today, but many governments have formally added performance to the list of facts that are always relevant to allocation decisions. They have instructed program managers to use performance in their budget requests and required their budget officers to make budget recommendations based on performance. Chief administrative officers in those governments are committed to reviewing budget recommendations based on performance, and elected officials are committed to considering service performance when they approve or deny a budget recommendation. Those governments are engaged in performance budgeting.

We believe that those who are charged with making budget decisions can make better ones when deliberating the performance of service delivery, even if they ultimately make the final decision based on other values (such as political accountability). Budget decisions are informed by both facts and values. Performance budgeting presupposes that the best budget decisions are based on consideration of facts, but it leaves room for value-based budget decisions so that political accountability is not sacrificed for the sake of financial or operational accountability.

Our cultural tradition holds science and analysis in high regard, even when the decision at hand is ultimately one about values. We do not need to sacrifice values for facts in performance budgeting, as some critics have charged. The two have coexisted in public policy for centuries. Performance measures might indicate that the animal shelter has not been as successful at realizing its mission as the visitor's center, but that information does not trump other considerations in budget decisions. It certainly does not require that the animal shelter take a budget cut while the visitor's center gets a budget increase. Budget officers and elected representatives deliberate budgets for the two services separately, but with a sense of their relative priority to the government's mission, the preferences of citizens, and the financial condition of the government in the new budget year. They also may consider relevant performance measures for both services, to advance operational accountability without sacrificing either political or financial accountability.

The "Key" Question

Sixty years ago, political scientist V.O. Key asked *the* budgeting question, "On what basis shall it be decided to allocate x dollars to activity A instead of activity B?"[1] Key was complaining that we do not seem to allocate dollars to activities in any rational, predictable way. His lament reflects the "facts" position; that our decisions about who gets what would be better if we based them on facts and analysis. Twenty years later, Aaron Wildavsky summarized the "values" position. He said, in response to Key's lament, that if we had a theory to answer who gets what, it would amount to a political theory.[2]

We believe Wildavsky was right. Any budgetary theory that determines who gets what is fundamentally undemocratic. Performance budgeting is not a budgeting theory. It does not determine whether x dollars go to the animal shelter instead of the visitor's center. We can predict the next question: If performance budgeting does not change who gets what, what good is it? We answer this way: performance budgeting expands managerial capacity in the organization. It unifies the two dimensions of accountability that pertain to public services in a way that enhances productivity and encourages innovation without sacrificing political accountability. When operational accountability and financial accountability are separated, the organization suffers.

Performance and Citizen Satisfaction

Performance measurement as a tool of operational accountability has been around long enough to permit some generalizations about whether citizen attitudes toward government change after a government adopts a performance program. Despite optimistic predictions about how citizens would regain their confidence in government when they saw public organizations holding themselves accountable for service quality, there is no objective evidence that public confidence in government has improved. More specifically, there is no evidence that high-performing organizations have higher citizen satisfaction with services or higher confidence in government than lower-performing organizations.[3] The few attempts to demonstrate a correlation between citizen satisfaction and service performance have not been persuasive.[4]

In fact, the relationship might go exactly the other way. Citizens may support performance improvement programs because they hope good performance will maintain or improve services at a lower tax cost. The assumption about high performance leading to cost savings was central to the federal government's National Performance Review (NPR) plan. The NPR assumed a high-performing federal government costs less than a poorly performing one, hence the title *From Red Tape to Results: Creating a Government That Works Better and Costs Less*. It also advanced the notion that the performance improvement allows governments to maintain or improve services at a lower tax cost.[5]

We can anticipate another question: If performance budgeting does not guarantee improved citizen satisfaction with services and does guarantee cost savings, what good is it? Here are a few reasons to adopt a performance budgeting system, despite a future that promises more pressure to do more with less for citizens who suspect government wastes money. First, as public employees, we are compelled to give the public we serve the best value we can create, and to employ whatever management/budgeting system creates value in our services. This is the public service ethic familiar to the reader, whether student or administrator. It requires no elaboration. Second, performance budgeting links resources with outcomes, and that is currently how public professional organizations define accountability to citizens. Regardless of what conclusions citizens may draw from the performance information we provide, we provide it fully and freely to account for the use of public money. Finally, our profession has operated on one overarching belief since its founding: The best decision is the informed decision. We believe performance information is most relevant for decision making. This last point ties the first two together, as performance budgeting helps create value in public services by setting meaningful performance targets and measuring progress toward them, then offering decision makers this information for their deliberations about service priorities and limited resources.

Performance Budgeting and Functions of Management

Performance budgeting is not a budgeting technique or format. It integrates operational accountability into the budget process, because the budget process unifies the functions of management. Luther Gulick and Lydall Urwick were the first to identify what a manager does; public administration students recognize the shorthand for their description as POSDCORB (planning, organizing, staffing, developing, coordinating, reporting, and budgeting).[6] The budget process forces managers to plan, both for current and future spending. They must organize their programs, make staffing and compensation decisions, direct and coordinate the delivery of services, and report their service or program effectiveness as well as report how resources were used in the delivery of those services as a part of the traditional budgeting function.

We would add a few more managerial functions to Gulick and Urwick's list. Modern managers use the budget process for short- and long-range capital planning, auditing, and program evaluation. Maybe the one-year cycle of most state and local budgets (a few have biennial budgets) forces policy decisions to be made more quickly than they should be, but the cycle itself is an important feature of the policy process.[7] Many budget decisions are automatic; they comply with federal or state mandates or are conditions of aid for grants. Other budget decisions are continuations of or small adjustments to existing programs. But a minority of budget decisions adjusts existing policy or sets new policy, which managers will justify on some basis. Performance budgeting requires that the justification include performance information. Whatever is decided in the budget process determines what the organization can do in each of these realms of managerial action. Performance budgeting influences managerial action because the manager knows that performance data will be part of the deliberation process.

Realities of Performance Budgeting

Performance budgeting rests on the assumptions that improving service performance is what we should be doing as public managers, and that progress toward improving service performance is a necessary, but not sufficient, basis for making budgetary decisions. Just that, nothing more.

* *Performance budgeting is not a budgetary theory*

It does not answer the "Key" question of who gets what. In fact, it usually raises more questions than it answers. What aspects of the animal shelter's performance do not meet expectations? Compared to what, past performance or other animal shelters? Are there special circumstances that help explain the performance data? Can the manager at the animal shelter control the aspects of performance that are below performance expectations (e.g., can the manager reduce the number of stray animals in the community)? And finally, do citizens care about how unwanted animals are treated in the community and expect that the shelter will be funded adequately to reflect those values, regardless of performance?

* *Performance budgeting is not a new budget format*

The line-item budget is here to stay. Reasonable people can disagree about whether the line-item format is the best presentation for decision making. We acknowledge that the format lends itself to scrutiny of inputs rather than consideration of outputs, and so emphasizes control rather than planning. We explore the point in more detail later, but for now we simply draw on our experience in state and local budgeting to assert that most decision makers demand line-item budgets during their deliberations. Budget officers who call their process performance or program budgeting say that they use information in the line-item budget as the basis for evaluating next year's request.[8] Performance budgeting can be used with any budget format, but is particularly suited for combining the program budget with the traditional line-item budget.

- *Performance budgeting is not a new budgeting or management technique*

The history of public administration shows how management ideas from the private sector have often been appropriated and modified to improve public sector management. Again, reasonable people can argue philosophy, but our interpretation of the history is that these new ideas were appealing because they seemed to offer ways of taking the politics out of public management. That notion founded the discipline of public administration and sustains it. However unattainable (or undesirable) it might be in practice, it is consistent with our cultural value that public decisions should be grounded in expertise rather than political considerations. Performance budgeting makes no such promise. Just as we presume it will be applied to the traditional line-item budget, we presume it will be applied to traditional managerial functions.

Limitations of Performance Budgeting

Before we summarize the rest of the book, in the interest of full disclosure, we caution the reader that performance budgeting has never been shown to solve any political or economic problem. In addition to our confidence in science and analysis to render good decisions, Americans are inclined to believe that there is a solution to every problem—a magic bullet—and that government could find it if it really wanted to. A student recently revealed this attitude in a senior-level state budgeting course when he wrote an essay on performance budgeting. In part, he says:

> The state of Tennessee is facing a budget deficit because there is no accountability for how tax dollars are spent. They closed down the state parks because there is not enough money to keep them open, while the Tennessee Department of Transportation has millions in surplus funds from the gasoline tax, which it uses to build roads that nobody wants. A performance budget would keep things like this from happening. If decisions were made on performance rather than political cronyism, there would be no budget crisis and there would be plenty of money for state parks and higher education. Performance budgeting would keep money from going to wasteful and inefficient services, which means there would be enough money for other services without having to raise taxes.

Several aspects of this essay are remarkable. First, the student believes that a change in the process of budgeting will alter the "who gets what" equation. Simplistic and naive perhaps, but not uncommon, as leaders of governments and organizations both public and private often try to cope with serious problems by tinkering with the budget process. Next, the student believes that taking public service decisions out of the hands of politicians (and presumably giving it to budget officers) will result in spending decisions that the public will find more appropriate. Taking the politics out of government is always a good stump speech, but few serious people believe that budget analysts are better positioned to serve the public interest than the public's elected representatives. Then the student asserts that wastefulness revealed and eliminated by performance budgeting will be of a magnitude to support or even expand other, preferred, services. The student is in good company here; recall that the federal performance initiative (NPR) made the same assumption. Finally, the student makes a mistake that demonstrates that he understands performance budgeting only as a slogan. He assumes that a reallocation of tax dollars based on performance would result in fewer roads and more parks and education. In fact, a performance budgeting system as he envisions it would probably have exactly the opposite effect. Road construction and repair is more likely to show gains in efficiency and effectiveness than recreation or education, simply because it is much easier to measure progress toward road-building than education or recreation. The student should be careful about what he wishes for, as he might not like the outcome.

Before discussing the considerable advantages of adopting a performance budgeting system, we describe the limitations of performance budgeting. The student essay hinted at most of them:

• *Performance budgeting cannot solve a fiscal crisis*

Fiscal crises are rarely the result of poor budgetary decision making. They are the natural consequence of increasing demands for services and rising service costs and reluctance to raise taxes to pay for those services. Performance budgeting will not change citizen demands or produce new tax revenue. There may not even be any savings associated with implementing performance budgeting systems. If a high-performing service department gets a budget cut as a reward for its efforts, how long do you imagine that department would stay motivated to constantly improve its performance?

• *Performance budgeting cannot take the politics out of budgeting*

Without politics, there would be no budget. In fact, some budget scholars see the budget as a political manifesto—an expression of the government's priorities. The decision about what services to provide may be the product of law or custom, but the decision about how to fund them and at what level is the result of elected officials responding to community values. Some communities prefer high taxes and high levels of service and are willing to pay for them. Others prefer lower taxes and are willing to accept lower levels of service. Some communities are focused on safety and others on recreation and other amenities. The only way for citizen priorities to be reflected in the budget is through the political process.

- *Performance budgeting cannot reduce the influence of interest groups*

We all know that interest groups have different levels of power and influence in the political process, and that they work to secure benefits for their members. In a performance budgeting system, information about service performance may be presented to elected officials, but it will not reduce those elected officials' need to be sensitive to interest group concerns. The citrus growers have a powerful voice in Florida and the auto manufacturers have a powerful voice in Michigan. In local government, neighborhood groups may lobby for expanded police patrols or twice-a-week curbside garbage pickup. Economic interests are also powerful at the state and local level. The Chamber of Commerce will generally carry more weight in an economic development decision than a performance report from the local economic development authority.

- *Performance budgeting cannot prevent poor managerial decisions*

Sometimes the path of least resistance is just too tempting to resist. We are all guilty of taking it from time to time, and public managers are not immune to it by virtue of their position. It is much easier to continue to fund a program that is not working than to discontinue the program. We recently saw an example of the path of least resistance in a public school drug education program known by its acronym DARE (Drug Abuse Resistance Education). Despite evidence that the incidence of drug use among children who participated in the DARE program was not statistically different from those children who did not participate, the program continues because certain antidrug interest groups believed that to discontinue it would "send the wrong message."

- *Performance budgeting cannot refocus citizen priorities*

One of the goals of any performance system is to communicate to citizens how well their services are performing, but there is no guarantee that citizens will agree with the criteria used to assess performance or care about the results. If citizens are concerned about safety issues, a police department with a poor performance record is going to be a higher priority than a parks department with a superior performance record. Those preferences are going to be reflected in the decisions made by their elected representatives, and in the budget. Performance information can give those elected officials another perspective, which they can balance with their constituency preferences. Performance information also can give interest groups ammunition to use for or against certain service departments, which is one reason managers give for their reluctance to make unfavorable performance information available to the public.

Possibilities of Performance Budgeting

We believe that performance budgeting can improve public management.

- *Performance budgeting can align service priorities and service spending*

Performance budgeting, in combination with a planning/management process like strategic planning or balanced scorecard, requires programs to periodically prioritize their service delivery goals consistent with changing service missions and realign their spending to reflect those changes. As existing responsibilities are altered and new responsibilities are added, as old problems abate and new problems emerge, programs have to reevaluate how they use their financial and human resources. A performance-based system that asks "what should we be doing?" and "how well are we doing it?" can only improve service quality.

• *Performance budgeting can add an information dimension to budget deliberations*

Sometimes elected officials are accused of making budgetary decisions on the basis of political expediency without consideration of whether other, reliable information was at their disposal when they reached their conclusion. A good performance budgeting process can put timely, reliable, relevant data in the hands of decision makers, who can then decide how to weigh the information in the budget decision. Decision makers do not have to rely exclusively on performance information as the basis of their decision, nor do they have to make the decision that the data would indicate. In a performance budgeting system, they must have access to the information and use it in their deliberations.

• *Performance budgeting can motivate program managers and employees by recording their progress toward service delivery goals*

The public personnel literature established long ago that public employees are motivated by a commitment to their service mission, not simply by financial rewards or the promise of advancement. But public employees, like private sector employees, respond to incentives. Performance budgeting, in conjunction with a planning and management process that focuses on outcomes, can help employees define their service delivery goals and measure their program's progress toward them. Though we do not cover it here, performance systems also can be useful in evaluating individual performance where the employee's personal performance is assessed in relation to the program's performance goals.

• *Performance budgeting can help demonstrate to citizens that their public service providers are interested in improving service quality*

Making relevant performance information available to citizens shows that program managers are focused on reaching performance goals and are willing to be held accountable for their progress toward attaining them. Performance budgeting is a poor outreach tool, and should never be undertaken for public relations purposes. But a commitment to performance budgeting can challenge suspicion that government programs are wasteful or that government employees do not want to be accountable for results.

Plan of the Book

Chapter 2 is about the history of budgetary reform in the past century. We debated including it in a text that is primarily about how to design and implement a performance budgeting program. We kept coming back to two seemingly incompatible ideas and one ridiculous proposition. The first idea is that budgeting reform has been driven by the notion that budget decisions should be based on objective (i.e., nonpolitical) information and that better information and better analysis make for better decisions. The second idea is that for any government to survive, it must make budget decisions that reflect public opinion about services and service priorities, and these opinions and priorities are always changing. The ridiculous proposition is that some change in budget process or format will reconcile the two ideas—that there is some way to take the politics out of budgeting that will allow the budget to still reflect public opinion. If we were to assert the merits of performance budgeting in a context where politics and values matter, we figured we had better make these arguments early. We chose a public budgeting survey through the twentieth century as our way of making the point.

Chapter 3 begins to focus more narrowly on the budget process in state and local government. We describe a process for incorporating performance budgeting into an established budget process by looking at examples from Washington State, Fairfax County, Virginia, and the city of Hickory, North Carolina. In chapter 3 we also defend our position on the line-item budget format and discuss how to work with it—not around it—in a performance budgeting system.

Chapter 4 puts performance budgeting into a popular management system to show how it is compatible with most any system, by demonstrating how the budget brings together the functions of management. Using the balanced scorecard approach, we look at the four quadrants of financial accountability, internal processes, employees, and customers (citizens) to show how performance budgeting can enhance managerial decision making in each of these areas. The city of Charlotte, North Carolina, has used performance budgeting in its balanced scorecard management plan to great success. We trace its experience from strategic planning down to the collection and analysis of performance data for decision making.

Chapter 5 steps back to look at some issues associated with performance measurement. It is hoped that previous chapters have demonstrated the process and promise of performance budgeting. Now we turn our attention to getting the kind of information needed to make decisions based on performance. We answer some typical questions about performance measurement, such as who is doing it, what they are measuring, and what they are doing with the results. We offer some detail about the different kinds of measures by using examples of a local sanitation department and a state children's services agency to explain why "cookbook" or standardized measures are of limited value in a performance budgeting system. We also discuss some of the problems with performance measurement, including what can go wrong if the manager is not careful when selecting and using performance measures.

We present a particular approach to performance measurement in chapter 6 that is very useful for performance budgeting—benchmarking. Benchmarking compares the service provider's actual performance-to-performance targets, to past performance, or to providers in other governments to give decision makers an idea of how well that service is performing. The kind of information that comes from a benchmarking process is useful, but only if the benchmarking process is carefully constructed and monitored for relevance and accuracy. There has been one national benchmarking project, and also several state projects. We talk about them, and look at one state project in detail.

Performance budgeting is only as good as the performance data that support it. There is a terrible temptation to keep measuring and monitoring the same aspects of service performance, even when the demands on the program or the service environment change. We discuss how to review performance data periodically for relevance and accuracy, and how to make the changes necessary to achieve both in chapter 7. We look at how performance data auditing is done in a state system in Texas, and in the cities that participate in a benchmarking project in North Carolina.

We return to the idea we introduced in this chapter about how performance budgeting can expand a government's capacity in chapter 8. We describe two kinds of capacity, organizational and managerial, and suggest how they fit together. We also describe how public professional organizations encourage members to expand their capacity by adopting new management tools, paying special attention to the organizations that have taken a position on performance measurement. The organization that sets standards for government financial reporting may be preparing to add performance measures to the list of financial information governments are required to provide in their annual reports. The prospect of auditing for operational accountability as well as financial accountability has implications for public managers and for performance budgeting. We conclude the book by asking if the reader's organization is ready for performance budgeting, summarizing the requirements for a successful performance budgeting program.

Conclusion

One fair criticism of public budgeting reforms is that they rarely deliver what they promise. Budgeting reforms usually go something like this: "Assume the budget decision will be made based on data; what kind of data are needed to make the decision?" Despite a faulty first premise, that approach advanced public budgeting as a subfield in public administration. It has not, however, given us a way to deal with decisions that are going to be made on a basis other than data. Performance budgeting does not assert that the decision to increase, decrease, eliminate, or create spending items will be made exclusively on the basis of performance data. Adoption of performance budgeting is a commitment to bring performance data to each decision and to include it in the deliberation process. Managers believe that decision makers will discuss performance data during budget deliberations, so they care about their performance record. Employees know that managers care about performance because it will be discussed at budget deliberations. External actors like the media and interest groups learn that performance is a part of every budget decision. Hopefully, citizens learn that performance matters and that their service providers are committed to it, even though there is room in every decision for other kinds of information, especially public values and priorities.

Despite its promise to integrate operational and financial accountability while accommodating political accountability, performance budgeting is no panacea for the myriad difficulties of public budgeting. Citizens still resist taxation but demand high quality services. State and local officials still groan under the weight of rules and mandates that limit their discretion, and thus their ability to be responsive to citizens' preferences. Through it all, state and local government commitment to performance budgeting grows, because the definition of public service is changing to reflect new, higher expectations for public service providers. The challenge we face is to meet those higher expectations without sacrificing responsiveness.

— Chapter 2 —

The Lineage of Performance Budgeting

The general idea of performance budgeting surfaced when the field of public budgeting emerged almost 100 years ago. It flickered after the Great Depression, and then returned in earnest after World War II. In the 1950s, some leading thinkers in public administration described the actual budget process of government and pointed out the mismatch between theory and practice. Performance budgeting was one of the casualties of this "realism" period. The modern re-introduction of performance budgeting traces back to roughly the mid-1990s. How long will this latest version of performance budgeting last? No one knows for sure, but before you conclude that performance budgeting is just another "flash in the pan," let us affirm that every major budget reform movement has lasting impacts even when the next, new thing has overtaken it. Because it advocates using data analysis to link inputs (expenditures) with outcomes (results), performance budgeting is a concept with staying power.

We believe that this iteration of performance budgeting has greater staying power than the one fifty years ago because it is an information-driven reform, and information technology is widely available today to every government, regardless of size. Still, we need to examine the reasons why performance budgeting may be a fragile reform. Our political system allocates resources based on values, not administrative performance. Attempts to force a rational framework on a value-based system is doomed to fail and should fail, because it is fundamentally undemocratic. Second, performance budgeting may not have enjoyed a fair implementation in its prior appearance because there was no accompanying commitment to support high-performing programs and services. We face the same challenge today. A commitment to performance budgeting implies that we will give agencies and departments the resources they need to accomplish their mission effectively and compensate employees adequately for meeting performance expectations. We cannot seriously expect public agencies and employees to stay motivated to be high performers without offering some incentives. Third, all budget reforms come and go to some degree, reflecting the prevailing public opinion toward government and the priorities of elected officials and senior managers. Sometimes the budget reform is theoretically appealing but not very practical (zero-based budgeting comes to mind), but its feasibility could only be tested after implementation, not before. The field of public budgeting learned something from trying each new process, regardless of its success. Our faith in any one reform to change budget outcomes may be a bit unrealistic, but the spirit to try a succession of reforms in good faith is what makes the field dynamic and responsive.

We try to present a balanced history of budget reform that celebrates Americans' confidence in the ability of science to improve government even as they remain skeptical about politics and cautious about the expanding scope of government. We place performance budgeting in this lineage of budget reform and look for things it shares with previous reforms and aspects of it that are unique. We then turn our attention exclusively to performance budgeting and what we know about how it works from our limited experience with it over the past decade or so. We return to an old argument in public budgeting toward the end of the chapter, one that questions whether there is a theory of budgeting and whether there ought to be one.

Finally, we go back to the hard questions that arise from our list of allegations about the staying power of performance budgeting.

1. Is performance budgeting democratic; that is, can it accommodate public preferences for programs and activities while keeping a performance focus?
2. Are there some credible results to review from a fair test of performance budgeting?
3. Is performance budgeting another in a series of budget reforms, representing current leadership priorities?
4. Is performance budgeting a way to look reformed without changing budget outcomes?

Public Administration and Performance Budgeting

Our interpretation of the history of performance budgeting, and of budget reform generally, is informed by our training as public administrators. When public administrators look back on the history of the discipline, they can relate movements in public administration theory and practice to points in history where citizens have wanted government to be more efficient (typically in times of peace and prosperity) or to be more responsive (typically in times of economic or social upheaval). Historians have suggested that there is a cycle of sorts between a national focus on public purposes and private interests.[1] During times of peace and prosperity, citizens prefer a less active government and look to the private sector for leadership. The public sector may adopt private sector management practices during these times. However, during times of social turmoil or economic hardship, especially when private markets are weak, citizens look to government for leadership and public sector management practices are more likely to be focused on responsiveness.

Our review of the history of budget reform and the emergence of performance budgeting suggests that efficiency-based budget reforms were more likely to gain ground during times of relative prosperity, though the belief that a "science" of budgeting would improve budget outcomes is a historical constant. Of course, public administration traces its origins to the belief that a science of management could be applied to public endeavors to advance the public interest. The most quoted statement of these ideas must certainly be Woodrow Wilson's essay on a science of public administration.[2] We return to it often in public administration, not just because it defined us, but also because we still hold to Wilson's beliefs that politics and science are at odds with each other in the public sector. Like Wilson and the Progressives of the early part of the twentieth century, there is a part of us that wants to liberate public administration from politics through science. At the same time, we hold the seemingly incompatible belief that our political system is just and good and that it should guide our actions. We have historically parsed the inconsistency this way: elected officials make budget decisions and administrators faithfully execute them. But, as Norton Long said, "For good or ill, we know the fund of knowledge in the bureaucracy will be a source of power."[3] We know that the way facts are presented influences decisions. And we also know that budget officials are sensitive to the political, social, and legal environment in which they operate.

Just as public administration in general has shown sensitivity to changes in what people wanted from their government, public budgeting has reflected changes in what citizens want from government. Right now, they seem to want government to run like a business, so we adapt a budgeting technique from the private sector to public budgeting. And we look to citizens we serve to define success. Any definition of success that budgeting professionals create for themselves is likely to fail if it is contrary to what citizens want their government to accomplish.

Budgeting theory and practice respond to changes in the national mood because budgeting is an "open system." That is, budgeting does not proceed on some independent path toward technical refinement independent of the political environment. It fashions and refashions itself to reflect that environment. Steven Koven made the case well, "Responsiveness to the external environment will . . . enhance organizational survival, increase agency legitimacy, and heighten public satisfaction with government."[4] To pursue internal rationality and efficiency criteria without regard to the political environment—to act as if the system were closed—would jeopardize the future of the very endeavor that the budget is supposed to advance.

So when citizens call on government to lead, they are less interested in how efficiently the government performs the budget function and more interested in whether the desired outcome is achieved. An example that affects all of us who use over-the-counter medications provides a good illustration. In 1982, during the Reagan administration, a few bottles of the over-the-counter pain reliever Tylenol were laced with cyanide. Seven people died. Citizens were understandably concerned about the safety of foods and drugs and demanded action from the federal government. Even though President Reagan was philosophically committed to reducing the size and scope of government, and especially to curtailing government regulation of private industry, he directed the Food and Drug Administration to take swift action. The tamper-proof packaging we are all familiar with was the result of federal regulation on the private sector—quite a costly one, but one that satisfied the public's need for assurance that their drugs were safe.

A federal budget analyst working during that period would probably not have recommended an expansion of the regulatory agency's authority into the private market for over-the-counter drugs prior to the Tylenol incident, but would have been imprudent to argue against it afterward, even to a president whose commitment to a reduced regulatory role was unquestioned. President Reagan realized that his orientation toward regulation was subject to change when a crisis or problem required it, and could be resumed once the crisis passed or the problem was resolved. The budget officer, aware of and responsive to a change in the external environment, would adjust his or her recommendations accordingly.

By and large, citizens prefer a less active government and lower taxes until something happens to cause them to set aside that preference in exchange for prompt and effective government action. When the problem is solved, they resume their general preference for limited government. A budget officer would not advocate dramatic budget cuts during periods of public demand for government action. Budget officers cannot operate in a closed budget system, immune to the political environment, any more than elected officials can. Therefore, politics cannot be separated from financial administration because Americans demand open systems. Citizens can, and do, prefer a government that is both responsive and efficient. The fact that citizen preferences may sometimes be contradictory does not mitigate the necessity for respecting them. Our history of budgeting suggests that reform has been driven more by the need for responsiveness to public opinion than to advances in analytical techniques that would facilitate efficiency-based decision making.

This paradox of budgeting, the public demand for responsiveness and efficiency, emerged at the same time as the idea of budgeting back in the early twentieth century. Even as the founding fathers of public budgeting argued for keeping the budget value neutral, they brought their own values about separability of politics and administration. Yet when there is a policy crisis, the budget does not separate politics and administration. It merges them to achieve a response to the crisis. Even when there is no policy crisis, the budget brings politics and administration together. As we will see, the separation_of the political function and the administrative function was the founding assumption of the field of public budgeting, and the way that the professionalization of public budgeting was sold to the public.

Budgeting Begins in the City

America's transformation from an agrarian economy to an industrial economy in the nineteenth century brought people to the cities to work. It was in those cities that we really began our experiment with modern government; so budgeting for service provision started in cities rather than in the federal or state government. As migrants and immigrants moved to the cities to take factory jobs, municipal government was left to deal with matters practical and political.

One of the first practical matters was moving the merchandise produced by the factories to consumers. Getting merchandise from one harbor to another was a relatively simple matter, but getting merchandise from the harbor inland to where the buyers were located was considerably tougher. Municipal governments could not think of a way to recover their cost for road construction, which amounted to clearing away tree stumps and rocks. Sometimes shopkeepers paid for their own road construction. Sometimes people in jail for nonpayment of debts worked off their sentence by constructing roads. And farmers maintained their own trails to their property so that they could get back and forth from town with supplies.

Another practical matter was related to transportation. Getting around inside the city was still done on foot, making proximity to the workplace necessary as well as desirable. That meant urban space closer to the city center was more valuable than space farther away. The result was housing density, as high land values dictated using every square foot of urban land. High rents in the city center forced laborers to pack several families in apartment space designed for a single family. Families crowded into tenement houses lit by candles after dark. Fires were common, and spread quickly to the closely built, wood frame houses. Proximity also gave rise to crime. The watchman system common to rural communities was not adequate for the urban setting.

Concentrated living gave rise to sanitation problems. Humans (and animals) need water; all produce waste and generate garbage. Because cities were located near water, one might think that access to water for cooking and bathing would not be a problem. In fact, the problem was not access to water, but separating water fouled by waste from water used for drinking. Household garbage was typically dumped outside the door of the building that produced it, and roving packs of rats, dogs, goats, and hogs consumed at least some of it. But they carried disease, for which there were no effective treatments. The city was a dismal, dangerous place to live for the working classes.

A plethora of civic reform groups emerged in cities like New York, Chicago, and Boston to address these social and economic ills. To say that they were fashionable in the day does not disparage their effort, their results, or the motives of typically upper-class citizens who took up causes as their own. There were reform groups for child labor, education, sanitation, housing, health, and parks and playgrounds. Now called public goods and delivered by government, in the early days of the century it was unclear whether these were the proper sphere of the public sector or charities. Perplexing problems caused by prosperity and growth were not ameliorated by the economic forces that gave rise to them. Charitable organizations could not deal with the safety needs of the city, and reform efforts such as public education for all children were simply too massive for charities to provide. City government grew out of necessity, out of recognition that if government did not solve these problems, the economic viability of the city would be threatened. Cities taxed property and used the revenues to deal with the consequences of city life. But like the federal government in the early twentieth century, their approach to revenues and expenditures was ad hoc, spending what they had for what they needed, and providing some rudimentary accounting for expenditures at the end of the year.

Machine Politics

America lacked experience with the political problems that arise when revenues are collected and services distributed. Our early attempts at political organization have been characterized as crude, but they were generally effective. Depending on your perspective, the first urban political systems in places like New York and Chicago had both positive and negative features. Political "machines" associated with the two parties were good in that voter turnout was high—sometimes over 75 percent—and citizens were attuned to local politics, even though many of them could not read. Machines held community meetings and sponsored special events that brought more people into the party and to the polls. They sometimes provided emergency food and shelter for immigrants, widows, and orphans.

Of course, the expectation was that those who benefited would turn out to support the party in the next election. The secret ballot often was not; machine bosses knew who voted and had a pretty good idea of how they voted. Political participation was induced by the promise of some tangible reward such as the prospect of a government job for a family member, a better chance of getting the pothole in front of the apartment filled, a turkey at Christmas, or even cold, hard cash on election day. A quarter for a vote could look like a good deal to a poor citizen. And there was genuine criminality associated with machines in some cities.

Urban political reformers took up the cause of good government just as the urban social reformers took up the cause of poverty, housing, and sanitation. The goal of the Progressives was to take government from machine politicians and turn it over to high-minded men who would practice the "science" of public administration that Woodrow Wilson described. They advocated nonpartisan municipal elections, a council-manager system of government, and the civil service system as an antidote to machine politics. They were successful in most cities, and their legacy explains much about public administration and provides the backdrop for the emergence of public budgeting. Their zeal to take the politics out of public administration defined the reform agenda for the next century, and continues to define it today.

The Progressive Era

In the early years of the twentieth century, the citizens were enthralled with the changes that science and technology could make in the economy and in their quality of life. Improvements in transportation, industry, and manufacturing were made possible through a revolutionary approach to production typified by Henry Ford's assembly line for the mass production of automobiles. Notable thinkers of the day included Frederick Taylor, whose "scientific management" promised to improve management efficiency through the application of scientific principles.[5] This optimism about science to improve business and government was tempered by concern for workers. The Federal Trade Commission Act of 1914 regulated working hours and working conditions and protected consumers from unfair business practices. The American labor movement grew and became institutionalized. These years can be best characterized by tremendous optimism about the ability of science to provide prosperity, and caution about the excesses of private sector prosperity.

The Progressive movement is deservedly credited with advancing the cause of public management for the common good by applying scientific principles of administration. It would be remiss not to mention that some of the concern for a science of budgeting, a model for who gets what, was stimulated by the fear that the rapidly increasing immigrant population might use the electoral process to secure outcomes consistent with their values, which were thought by many Progressives not to be consistent with traditional Anglo values. Universal participation in the political system might be followed by universal representation in the emerging administrative system, and that might threaten elite interests in municipal affairs. To be fair, the Progressives also supported consumer protections and social reforms that benefited immigrants and the working classes even as they railed against the corruption in cities that resulted from machine politics.

Historians can parse how much of the desire for reform of municipal political systems came from fear about the political power of immigrants and the working class and how much from a genuine belief that a cadre of professionals trained in the science of management could bring about a more efficient and effective city government. One of the founders of the field of public administration, Frank Goodnow, saw the two as separable and desirable.[6] Political reform like nonpartisan elections would bring an end to the political machines and administrative reform would produce decisions in the public interest. This separation between politics and administration was embodied in the National Municipal League's Model City Charter of 1916.

The New York Bureau of Municipal Research

The origination of modern public budgeting is considered one of the most noteworthy of the reform institutions of the Progressive era. Like the National Municipal League, the bureaus of municipal research were citizens' organizations formed by citizens with the goal of local government reform, or, as Jane Dahlberg describes, "to get good men in government."[7] The New York Bureau of Municipal Research was the first of this kind; it was incorporated in 1907. Its founders were Henry Bruere, director, Frederick A. Cleveland, technical director, and William H. Allen, secretary (which included publicity and fundraising). Cleveland and Allen held doctorates from the Wharton School of Business at the University of Pennsylvania. Bruere had a bachelor's degree from the University of Chicago and a track record as a social reformer. Their relationship was sometimes tense, but each brought to the Bureau some talent essential for the kind of lasting impact they would have on government and public finance.[8]

The New York Bureau identified the following purposes for its work:

1) to promote efficient and economical government, 2) to promote the adoption of scientific methods of accounting and of reporting the details of municipal business, with a view to facilitating the work of public officials, 3) to secure constructive publicity in matters pertaining to municipal problems, 4) to collect, 5) to classify, 6) to analyze, 7) to correlate, 8) to interpret, and 9) to publish facts as to the administration of municipal government.[9]

The Bureau did not create the concept of the budget; private businesses had been reconciling accounts for years and calling the result a budget. What the Bureau did was to take the practice of accounting, modify it by including the ideas of planning and management, identify it as an executive function, provide a methodology by which the "science" of budgeting could advance, and offer it as a government reform. They established the difference between an accounting at the end of the year, and a plan for revenues and expenditures at the beginning of the year, a prospective approach to financial management rather than a retrospective one. The prospective nature of budgeting intertwined the funds with the policy goals to which they were directed, and made the budget document a plan for management to achieve those goals.

The contribution of the Bureau to budgeting cannot be overstated, but these men were fully human and capable of mixed motives. They believed that these changes would improve government, but they had to be aware at some level that they were advocating taking government out of the hands of ordinary men and delivering it into the hands of "experts." It is not unfair to consider the complicated motives of the founders of the enterprise. Looking beyond the surface tells us something about how the founding fathers of budgeting thought about the relationship between budget specialists, elected officials, interest groups, and citizens. A closer inspection of the stated functions of the Bureau reveals something about the values that underlay the profession and the practice at its founding.

The first purpose, promotion of a more efficient and economical government, was the heart of the reform movement. Cleveland articulated the emerging shift in the role of government in his book *Organized Democracy*.[10] The spoils system of the nineteenth century primarily served the needs of a few well-placed citizens and had to be replaced with a new system that served all citizens.[11] Bureau founders believed that "wasteful, ineffective government could not serve democracy well"[12] and that responsibility for ensuring an effective government should be shared by elected officials and the citizens that elected them. Cleveland was careful not to disparage the political machines, perhaps because they were still powerful, as he insisted that their way was simply not adequate for the new century where science could show men a better way to govern. Allen went a step further, equating efficiency with goodness in his writings, and setting out the value of efficiency as morality.[13] Bruere wrote that efficiency could advance the social welfare, but did not go so far as Allen to raise efficiency as the goal of government.[14]

The Bureau's second purpose was promoting the adoption of scientific methods of accounting and reporting. The Bureau wanted to make government more like a business applying the same kind of scientific management principles that were revolutionizing the private sector. Very likely Cleveland and Bruere's training in finance predisposed them to look at the function they understood best as a target for reform, even though their diagnosis of the problem involved governance issues rather than financial mismanagement. Readers may recall the description of turning elective office into private economic gain by Tammany Hall's George Washington Plunkitt:

> Everybody is talkin' these days about Tammany men growin' rich on graft, but nobody thinks of drawin' the distinction between honest graft and dishonest graft. There's all the difference in the world between the two. Yes, many of our men have grown rich in politics. I have myself. . . I might sum up the whole thing by sayin': I seen my opportunities and I took 'em. . . . Let me tell you that most politicians who are accused of robbin' the city got rich the same way. They didn't steal a dollar from the city treasury. . . . The Tammany heads of departments looked after their friends, within the law, and gave them what opportunities they could to make honest graft. . . . Every good man looks after his friends, and any man who don't isn't likely to be popular. . . . Tammany was beat in 1901 because the people were deceived into believin' that it worked dishonest.[15]

Plunkitt described an ethical problem more than a budget problem, but the Bureau, especially Allen, was equating budgetary efficiency with ethical management, and so the budget was identified as a target for reform.

The next item on the reform agenda, securing constructive publicity, is a necessity of any public organization, but the Bureau paid especially close attention to it and it paid off in widespread legitimacy being attached to their cause. The Bureau chose its reform targets carefully, pulling back when political considerations dictated.[16] It cultivated friends in the machine, in labor, in the media, and most especially in the business community. It enjoyed the support of J.P. Morgan, Andrew Carnegie, and John D. Rockefeller, and not necessarily because they applauded the concept of bringing business efficiency to government. Kahn noted that these barons of business feared government regulation at the hands of politicians representing interests of the working class. They were eager to support a reform effort that kept the public and private spheres separate, and kept the public sphere focused on internal standards of efficiency rather than their business activities.[17]

The next group of Bureau functions reveals something about the nature of the budget that it promoted. First, it believed a budget process started with a scientific and unbiased survey of existing activities and expenditures. After collecting facts, activities and expenditures would be classified. The classification of activities has been interpreted as the first program budget,[18] but that might give a bit more credit than is deserved. The Bureau did group activities together by function, though, and that was quite an advance over the previous practice of lump-sum accounting. This grouping was the precursor to the object-of-expenditure budget format that we now call the traditional or line-item budget. Within each functional classification, expenditures for related items are grouped together. For example, the line-item for the budget director's office supplies appears under the subheading of "office of director" under the heading of the "department of finance." The Bureau's early success is demonstrated by the New York City budget of 1908, which was the first to use the functional classification system.[19] The first reform was probably the most important, as object-of-expenditure classification is still the most common format in public budgeting.

Finally, the Bureau would analyze, correlate, interpret, and publish its "facts." As modern budget officers know, facts may be weak, but the interpretation of facts is very powerful. The foundation assumption that efficiency is the standard to which government should aspire is problematic in itself. A related assumption that an expert can determine the extent to which efficiency exists by surveying activities without imparting his own values to the activities also is questionable. The Bureau was nonpartisan and independent, serving different administrations equally (though not always equally regarded by different administrations), but it was not value-neutral. Perhaps the best way to describe the lasting impact of this set of functions is to say it changed the nature of political debate. Partisan politics were replaced with the language of expertise. Lack of facility with the language of expertise silenced the average citizen, and shifted control over the debate to government officials and away from the parties. This was perfectly consistent with the reform era and its belief that science would serve the public interest better than politics, but it was exclusive and not very democratic.

> Through the budget process, government could define the terms and set the boundaries for all political debate. Insofar as citizens accepted the Bureau's model of budget reform, they delegitimized the free flow of public discussion among citizens unmediated by the state. In the political world of budget reform, before one citizen could speak authoritatively to another on a matter of public concern, he or she first had to consult the budget for relevant information.[20]

The budget ultimately emerged as an instrument that facilitated, rationalized, and legitimated the expansion of government. It was not intended primarily to constrain government expenditures or to force hard choices about distributing services. On the contrary, by identifying waste and distinguishing "legitimate" programs from graft, budget reform would enable an activist government to expand to meet all true social needs as defined by the budgetmakers.[21]

The New York Bureau deserves so much attention because it changed the way we talk about government and established the budget as the document of accountability. Many attribute the federal budget reforms coming after the 1910 Taft Commission on Economy and Efficiency to ideas planted by the Bureau. Frederick Cleveland chaired the Taft Commission, and its report on the executive budget reflected the Bureau's position on the executive's responsibility for administration, and recommended an executive-level department, Bureau of the Budget, to produce and implement the federal budget.[22] The Taft Commission report described the first unified federal budget, bringing expenditures for all federal operations into one document, and putting responsibility for that document under the executive's control. Congress fiercely resisted the relocation of its control to the executive branch, and so it was a decade later until the Budget and Accounting Act of 1921 could be hammered out and passed, and signed by President Harding.

World War I redirected public attention from the Progressive agenda, for obvious reasons, but Progressive era ideals have never lost their appeal. The confidence in science and rationality to lift the public interest above partisan politics remains constant, even as public support for the men and women in the bureaucracy who bring those skills to policy making wavers. The enthusiasm for a science of administration that developed during the Progressive era of public administration was not really driven by public demand for a more activist government, but by an appetite for reform fueled by a suspicion that public dollars might be wasted, or worse. The New York Bureau's system of line-item expenditures was conducive to cost control and resistant to trickery, and so it endures to this day even though the process reforms we are about to describe have expanded the budget's function beyond cost control. Modern budget officers know the presentation of the budget frames the debate. Classification by expenditure type leads to discussion of cost control, an easy format to manage when one has limited information, a time deadline, and a political system that favors incremental changes in resource allocations.

Performance Budgeting Emerges

To understand the dawn of performance budgeting, one has to understand the expansion of government that followed the Great Depression. America suffered depressions regularly throughout the nineteenth century, but the first depression of the twentieth century was devastating not just because of its duration and severity, but also because of a change in the American workforce. The rise of the manufacturing sector and migration to the cities for work precluded the "wait it out" policy that government had employed during previous depressions. Farmers were acquainted with hard times and were able to maintain subsistence until economic conditions improved. Factory workers were not.

Post–World War I prosperity restored American confidence in business. Confidence in a self-regulating economy was high, which makes the stock market crash of 1929 easier to understand. The crash was a complicated event with multiple causes, but the basic problem was excessive speculation in an overheated market with few institutional or governmental controls. But the political response to the crash and the depression that followed was slow. Even as unemployment climbed toward one-quarter of the workforce in late 1931, President Herbert Hoover still maintained that government had no business interfering in private economic matters. But public opinion had already begun to turn in favor of an active government, as hardship and fear replaced unbridled confidence in capitalism.

The first hundred days of Franklin Delano Roosevelt's administration were spent creating social insurance programs, work for welfare, regulation of financial markets, and bank and workplace regulations. Traditional notions of dual federalism were suspended as the national government worked in partnership with states for development projects and antipoverty programs.

> The early days of the "first" New Deal violated almost every idea in the gospel of the disciples of the management movement in public administration. New agencies were established for new programs independent of established departments and agencies already operating in the same field. Personnel for the new agencies were employed without reference to the established civil service. Funds for new programs were appropriated outside the regular budget process in what became known as the "double budget" system. The time-honored division between policy and administration was repeatedly violated, since most policy initiatives came from the Administration. For orthodox students of public administration, the "first" New Deal was chaos.[23]

Late in Roosevelt's first term he appointed a committee composed of Louis Brownlow, Charles Merriam, and Luther Gulick to study the management of the executive branch. These men were arguably the brightest lights in the young field of public administration. The need for "study" was necessitated by the seriousness of economic circumstances and the difficulty Roosevelt had marshaling Congress to join his administration in concerted action. The committee's report, issued in 1937, is one of the more significant documents in public administration, despite the fact that Congress rejected all of the proposals it contained. It set a standard of expertise and neutrality that would be copied by succeeding presidential committees on administrative reform. In general, the Brownlow Committee Report argued for a strong executive to whom all agencies owe policy accountability. Retrospective analyses of the Commission note that the principals were strongly motivated by the desire to establish public administration as a "science," and that their quest for disciplinary credibility may have trumped loyalty to President Roosevelt and a goal of reforms that had some practical chance for surviving Congress.[24]

The Brownlow Committee did more for public administration than it did for President Roosevelt, so it was ironic that its successor, the Hoover Commission, would continue the theme of reorganizing the executive branch to create a clear line of executive authority. A Republican Eightieth Congress, more than a little resistant to the expansion of federal programs, created its own committee headed by former president Herbert Hoover, whose position on Roosevelt's New Deal agenda was well known. The Republicans planned on enjoying the benefits of a strong executive after the next presidential election, but Harry Truman's election in 1948 dashed those hopes. After the election, Hoover decided to refocus the Commission on accountability in the executive branch, setting aside partisanship in pursuit of genuine administrative reform.[25] Truman agreed to let the Commission's work proceed. The Hoover Commission Report, issued in 1949, echoed the Brownlow Committee's call for centralized executive control, but also decentralized administrative discretion over managerial functions like budgets, accounting, and financial management.[26] It is in the consideration of how agencies should conduct their financial function that performance budgeting emerges as a general concept.

Recall that the first kind of budget reform was cost control and prevention of malfeasance, facilitated by the line-item format advocated by the Bureau of Municipal Research. The second wave of budget reform emphasized financial management in pursuit of program performance. A more expansive definition of financial accountability was emerging, and it was linked to the management function. Performance budgeting was advocated as a form of accounting for results, not just inputs and expenditures as in the line-item budget.

Two ideas from these two presidential committees warrant special attention. First, the Brownlow Report called for a system of linking inputs to outputs through the budget process, so credit for a vision of a system that might accomplish the link goes to the early report. The Hoover Commission Report focused on how resource allocation decisions are made at the departmental level, and began to articulate how a system to link inputs and outputs might work. Using the private sector as an efficiency standard, the Hoover Commission was especially critical of the government's focus on inputs. The Commission recommended a performance-based budget where allocations could be made to activities and projects based on the volume of work and the cost of resources in the same fashion as the private sector made allocation decisions. Such a system, the members declared, would improve managerial control over the budget function. "Control" still meant a check on spending and guarding against misappropriation of public funds, but also included expansion to 'programmatic control. In Paul Appleby's classic essay, "The Role of the Budget Office," he expressly acknowledged that the discretion involved in saying no to some requests and yes to others was policy making on the part of the budget officer, and made no apology for it. The budget office was not intended to substitute for executive and legislative decisions, but to inform them. Like its private sector counterpart, the public budget office served a management function.[27]

A final noteworthy development of the period was the elevation of the profession of budgeting from accounting to management, a feature for which we have special fondness as we define performance budgeting as a management system about seventy years later. Postwar public administration was seeking an identity separate from private administration, and Luther Gulick was advancing the cause by defining what it is that managers do. Gulick believed the division of work that had made Henry Ford prosperous could be used to advance the public interest through the more efficient (new definition) discharge of the public's business, but still within the reform agenda of the Progressives. Gulick's concern with the separation of politics and administration, a Progressive era article of faith, is revealed in his writings on the nature of the managerial function.

> As Dr. Frank Goodnow pointed out a generation ago, we are faced here by two heterogeneous functions, "politics" and "administration," the combination of which cannot be undertaken within the structure of the administration without producing inefficiency.[28]

As one of the elements of Gulick's POSDCORB, the budget function included detail of the activities still associated with budgeting today—fiscal planning, execution, research, accounting, and auditing. Gulick can be credited with an early description of the modern budget office.

Budget Process Reforms

We begin a quick review of the "modern" period of budget reform with two ideas firmly planted in public administration. (1) The budget should perform the control and oversight function first, but can be used to implement management reforms that fundamentally change outcomes in a way that advance the public interest. (2) The appropriate way to reform the budget process is to add more rationality to it, usually by adapting whatever science methods are popular at the time to the budget process.

Modern presidents still used the select committee of "experts" as a vehicle for achieving their desired budget reforms. Some patterns in the use of these committees trace back to the Brownlow Committee and the Hoover Commission. First, they claimed independence and neutrality though each would offer recommendations that were in concert with the president's budgetary priorities. Second, they helped align administrative budget practice with popular opinion about the role of government. This second feature illustrates the point made earlier that budgeting is an "open" system, capable of adapting to the demands and expectations of citizens and their elected representatives.

Planning-Programming-Budgeting System

President Lyndon Johnson's Task Force on Governmental Reorganization (1964) recommended a "scientific" approach to policy analysis, one that would apply operations research and economic theory to link programmatic inputs to outputs. Budgeting had been borrowing from the economic literature for decades, but now budgeting was treated as a policy tool for program planning and for judging program performance. The best example is the Planning-Programming-Budgeting System (PPBS), where competing expenditure options are evaluated for their marginal benefit to the program. Implemented in 1961 by the Department of Defense, and mandated for all federal agencies by President Johnson in 1965, PPBS was hailed as a way to integrate planning and budgeting by using systems theory and cost-benefit analysis. It was superior to performance budgeting, its proponents claimed, because the work activities being measured in a performance budget are simply the process by which inputs are converted into outputs. In PPBS, substitutable alternatives are evaluated for their contribution to the program objective, yielding high quality budgetary decisions. The problems with PPBS were predictable. First, even its proponents acknowledged that the process created "enormous information and analytical burdens."[29] Other agencies lacked the clear and singular objectives and technical expertise enjoyed by the Department of Defense. Second, and related, policy objectives were to be defined from the top down, but the location of the "top" for an agency is as elusive as consensus on program objectives. Even if "top level" officials could agree on the definition of a desirable program outcome, they were unlikely to leave decisions about the means by which it could be achieved to a process incapable of reflecting their values and priorities.

PPBS formally ended with an Office of Management and Budget (OMB) memo in 1971. Some mourned the surrender of policy analysis to politics[30] and some applauded it.[31] Agency adoption of PPBS was variable depending on factors such as the interest in the process by the congressional oversight committee, the Bureau of the Budget oversight group's interest, the availability of analytic data, the age of the agency or program, and the support of top officials.[32] In other words, the bureaucracy could not function to keep politics out of budgetary policy, regardless of the elegance of the formal decision process. In fact, as the seventies began, some had started to believe that the proper role of the bureaucracy was to embody values, not reject them in favor of ever more scientific methods of policy analysis.

Management-by-Objectives

Richard Nixon's committee on government reorganization and reform, the Advisory Council on Governmental Organization, reflected Nixon's desire for greater executive control over agency functions. The Council's 1970 report recommended reorganizing the Bureau of the Budget (BOB) into the Office of Management and Budget (OMB), expanding its size and scope, and maintaining its sensitivity to executive priorities by increasing the number of appointed officials relative to career officials.[33] The result was more than a cosmetic change in federal budgeting. Schick related the story of a BOB official describing how the Bureau's job evolved during this period from saying "no" to expenditures to finding ways to accomplish presidential objectives.[34]

Nixon was less interested in budgeting techniques than in the extent to which budget expenditures reflected his policy priorities. Management-by-objectives (MBO), loosely based on the 1954 book by Peter Drucker, *The Practice of Management*,[35] looked promising to Nixon for two reasons. First, it offered a way to align activities with objectives, and second, it seemed to address the widely perceived "management problem" in the federal government. Nixon's desire to respond to popular sentiment that the Great Society programs had created an unwieldy bureaucracy coincided nicely with his desire to exercise more executive control over spending. However, MBO was doomed upon implementation.

> The initial OMB directive to the agencies welcomed the submission of objectives of any type, as long as they conformed to three broad criteria: the issue is important to the President; there is a means of determining whether it has been achieved; and no additional financial or legislative resources would be required.[36]

At the risk of pointing out the obvious, an objective important to the president might not be important to Congress, an objective that easily lends itself to quantification is not necessarily the most important to achieve, and there are precious few cost-free objectives.

Zero-Based Budgeting

Nixon's departure from office was surrounded by economic as well as political upheaval. The previous years had tested some of the assumptions of Keynesian economics and found them wanting. A loss of confidence in government initiated by Vietnam and deepened by the Watergate scandals was intensified by a seeming inability to make fiscal policy. Jimmy Carter was elected on the heels of the 1974–75 recession, on a pledge to restore integrity to the White House, and stability to the economy. But fiscal stress had come to stay in the American economy, at least in the short term. Carter's interest in reform of the federal civil service and the federal budget process was consistent with the reform-minded temper of the American public. Arnold noted that the tone and substance of presidential commissions shifted at this point in modern history, from reorganizing the bureaucracy to make it stronger to reorganizing the bureaucracy to make it less objectionable.[37] Reform efforts were offered as bureaucratic punishment more than bureaucratic improvement, consistent with a public that had lost confidence in the federal government. Carter's Reorganization Act of 1977 was far-reaching and significant, though it had very little salience to a dispirited public.

Carter's legacy to public budgeting, the zero-based budget, was attractive as a concept. Rather than making incremental adjustments to what had been done in the previous budget year, the zero-based budget (ZBB) would force agencies to examine their activities anew each year and consider new ways to deliver benefits at the least cost. This reform started in state government as Carter implemented ZBB in Georgia when he was governor. The record of ZBB in Georgia was mixed. The process did not substantially reduce program costs or change program activities, though it may have facilitated redistribution of resources among state programs.[38]

Vestiges of ZBB remain at all levels of government: the "bare-bones" budget, the maintenance budget, the intermediate budget, and the improvement budget. Some ideas about budget process are associated with, if not attributable to ZBB. Under ZBB the top managers send lower-level managers a set of policy objectives and the lower-level managers consider different alternatives to meet those objectives, ranking them for presentation to upper management. The process is both bottom-up and top-down, but lower-level managers have a stronger role to play than in a traditional budget process.

The epitaph for ZBB at the federal level was not particularly laudatory, though Carter and the OMB hailed it as a success. Preparation of three budgets took more agency time than preparation of one, and the two alternatives were simply a percentage increase and/or decrease over the current budget. Budget justification replaced budget preparation as the dominant activity. It was impossible to isolate single goals for agency activities, and interaction effects among activities made considering the budget for any activity without regard to the others questionable. The amount of paperwork was significantly increased under ZBB and there were very few changes in budget outcomes as a result of it. Reagan abandoned it immediately upon taking office, but he kept one feature of ZBB, the multiple budget formats. Now the emphasis would shift to cost cutting, and the relevant spending categories were, appropriately, the reduction budget, the maintenance budget, and the agency request budget.

Cutback Budgeting

President Ronald Reagan had an answer to the economic woes of the 1970s: government is not the solution; government is the problem. Reduce the size of government, and you reduce the size of the problem. Reagan's committee on reorganization, the Grace Commission, reflected the president's diagnosis. It was filled with examples of government inefficiency, and unfavorable comparisons of government operations with the private sector. Critics would note that many of the examples were wrong or misleading,[39] and most of the recommendations it made in a series of reports spanning two years were never implemented. The Grace Commission's effort was not necessarily a failure, however, as it helped cement the idea that government is wasteful and inefficient in public opinion and legitimated Reagan's position that a weaker public sector would strengthen the private sector.

Under cutback budgeting, the role of the budget office changed again. It did not revert from a programmatic focus back to the institutional "no" to new expenditures, but was changed to active targeting of potential cost savings. As Behn described, cutback budgeting involved examining the base budget for potential cuts, putting programs and their advocates in competition with each other for existing resources.[40] The process of separating mandatory spending (i.e., transfer payments to individuals) from discretionary spending (i.e., spending for programs or services) and targeting cuts to the latter was complicated by the difficulty of holding together a political coalition to implement the cuts once they were identified.

> It is mathematically difficult to discover a set of budgetary savings, all of which are necessarily small, that add up to the deficit total. And, since any

individual budget cut contributes so little to eliminating the deficit, there is an obvious argument against including it in the package. Since the cut will not (by itself) make a significant dent in the deficit, why impose the pain that the cut will create?[41]

Cutback budgeting is no different today when states or localities grapple with deficits. Previously cooperative relations become uncooperative as programs are threatened. Budget analysts make recommendations for cuts that political actors are often unwilling to carry through. The modern legacy of the cutback budgeting era is the practice of backward budgeting. The government determines how much revenue it is able or willing to raise, and makes program funding decisions based on those resources. This is fundamentally different from deciding what level of programs and services are necessary and appropriate to meet needs and raising the revenue necessary to provide them. Another legacy that endures from this period is the idea that government programs are generally ineffective and inefficient. This powerful idea can be seen in the assumptions underlying the next reform stage.

Performance Budgeting, the Sequel

President Bill Clinton's budget reform efforts were predicated on the same set of assumptions that Reagan offered—that government was too big, unwieldy, rule-bound, and process driven. This time the federal government looked to a practice that was growing among states and local governments called performance measurement. Most public sector professional organizations were already advocating performance measurement before a popular book called *Reinventing Government* captured the administration's imagination.[42] It promised that "idle" government employees could be put to work and the "bloat" cut from government when the federal government was transformed into a responsive, results-driven organization. The message reinforced stereotype, and was appealing both as a diagnosis and prescription. Vice President Al Gore's National Performance Review (NPR) reflected these same themes, asserting that government needed to act more like a business—taking chances, focusing on customers, and eliminating cumbersome administrative routines.[43] Previous presidential commissions focused on how to make the bureaucracy stronger (Brownlow Committee), or more effective (Hoover Commission), or more efficient (Johnson's Price Commission), or more aligned with executive priorities (Nixon's Ash Commission), or more accountable (Carter's Reorganization Commission), or less wasteful (Reagan's Grace Commission). Wilson asserted that the NPR's goal was to make government more "likable" in an era when public confidence in the federal gov-

ernment was low.[44] The NPR's record of changing program or policy outcomes is modest, and it was plagued by implementation problems described
more fully later. Still, the NPR called for a link between service accomplishments and program funding, and clearly had a budget component though it
was intended to be a system reform and not just a budget reform.[45] The link
was more explicit in states that adopted performance budgeting, and the record
of their experience is more fully documented. Many local governments, especially larger ones, adopted performance measurement systems and incorporated them into their budget process. In the next section we examine the
record to see what, if anything, changed as a result.

The Record on Performance Budgeting

Federal Government

The record on performance budgeting is difficult to assess because the implementation of performance budgeting has been shackled by some unrealistic
assumptions: (1) that meaningful and appropriate measures, especially outcome measures, are readily available, (2) that managers have the expertise to
develop and run performance systems, and (3) that the process will result in
higher quality services at lower costs. This last assumption was especially
evident from the federal experience with performance measurement. The
NPR was built around the assumption that savings from the elimination of
poorly performing programs would permit the expansion of successful programs, apparently without regard to legal or political imperatives that created the poorly performing programs in the first place. Federal performance
objectives were high on rhetoric and low on specifics, making assessment of
the system difficult.[46]

The goals of the NPR were ambitious: reduce the size of the federal
workforce, reduce the cost of programs and services to taxpayers while improving their quality and efficiency, decentralize decision making to give front-
line workers more authority, and generally change the culture of the federal
government to be more flexible and responsive.[47] Some of the objectives are
obviously contradictory; quality improvements are difficult with decreased
funding and fewer personnel. These contradictions have been thoroughly ex-
plored elsewhere,[48] but one deserves special attention because it goes to matters of line-employee support for performance-based reforms. The first goal
of the NPR was downsizing; federal reformers asked employees to cooperate
in a venture that, if successful, might cost them their jobs.[49] It is amazing that
the federal experience has any success stories, considering the implementation obstacles and contradictions. The success stories in federal agencies tend

to have the same theme: strong leaders helped change organizational culture to a performance focus because they convinced their workers that the change was necessary and appropriate; the Government Performance Results Act (GPRA) may have been the impetus, but leadership was the most important factor. We return to the leadership factor later in the chapter.

State Government

States began to experiment with the idea of performance budgeting after the Hoover Commission's report in 1949. Maryland was first, and several states assembled their own "Hoover Commissions" to consider the reform.[50] At last count, forty-seven out of fifty states have some sort of performance budgeting requirement, some through legislative initiative and others through administrative initiative.[51] That record and the scholarly attention given to the results provide the most complete record to examine. However, the record is not sufficient to establish that performance budgeting changed state budgetary outcomes. States suffered from the same obstacles to implementation that plagued the federal performance reform initiative. At best, we might conclude that states have gradually adopted performance measurement into their budget processes as time, resources, and data availability permitted.

Still, some generalizations are possible and important. The first is that states did not abandon their line-item budgets. They added performance measures to their traditional format to create what is widely known as a "hybrid budget." Fourteen states indicated that they use performance information for budgetary decision making,[52] thirty-seven require program-level performance measures, and twenty-three require each agency to submit them as part of their budget request.[53] We may fairly conclude that most states are reporting performance information at the program level and about half the states submit their performance data with their budget request, rather than later when the budget document is assembled. However, only about a third of states collecting and reporting data are actually doing what we have defined as performance budgeting—using performance information in the budget deliberations process.

Even if states do not use performance data for budgetary decisions, they may still be using performance standards to motivate their employees and managers. Seven states offer incentives for good performance (California, Florida, Georgia, Illinois, Louisiana, Mississippi, and Texas).[54] Some are directed at managers (increased budget, more managerial flexibility in personnel and budgetary matters) while others are directed at employees (bonuses, public commendations). Two states specify disincentives for poor performance, Florida and Texas. Florida reduces managerial flexibility and requires more reporting while Texas's disincentives range from reduced funding to transfer of the program to another entity.[55] Neither Florida nor Texas has used disincentives for performance to date; the record on the other states' use of positive incentives is unclear. A multistate survey also concluded that the threat of a relationship between poor performance and reduced funding may be implied, but is seldom carried through.[56]

Multistate and single-state studies have not converged on a set of problems or prospects for performance budgeting programs. A 1995 study painted an optimistic picture of the prospect for real change as a result of performance initiatives in five states.[57] Single-state case studies in Georgia, Missouri, and Florida reached different conclusions. In fifteen executive departments in Missouri, performance results had not demonstrated an impact on the budget office's spending recommendation nor on staffing recommendations.[58] Georgia's experience, ongoing since 1977, demonstrated that a requirement to use performance data in the budget process did not create its own capacity; that appropriate and reliable measures did not "just happen" after they were mandated.[59] Florida encountered serious problems with the implementation of its Government Performance and Accountability Act that were not unlike the federal experience. A recent review of the Florida experience identifies some challenges for the future of performance budgeting, including how to incorporate performance information in legislative appropriation decisions and how to approach administrative sanctions for agencies that fail to meet performance standards.[60]

State budget officers report that the mandate to performance budgeting often comes without adequate time, personnel, financial resources, executive and legislative leadership and commitment, and interest in performance information at all levels of state government.[61] A survey of state budget officers suggested a limited link between performance information and budgetary allocations. Sixty-three percent of responding state budget officers said that performance indicators were important for making budget allocations; 37 percent said they were not. Twenty-five percent said that performance funding was a success in their state; 64 percent said it was not. Yet, 86 percent of responding state budget officers predicted that performance funding would be expanded in their state.[62]

Although most indicators point toward increased collection and reporting of performance measures in states, one study reported that the use of performance information in budget requests declined from 1990 to 1995, perhaps because state budget officers were dissatisfied with the accuracy of the information and preferred no performance justification to a suspect one.[63] As Caiden pointed out, "Even relevant, accurate and timely data will serve no purpose unless they are actually used."[64] Another way to consider Caiden's remark is that collecting and reporting performance data may be necessary but not sufficient to expand organizational capacity. The potential to improve capacity through innovation depends on the willingness of the organization to use performance information for decision making.

Local Government

The record on local government is not as clear because issues of size and response rate influence findings. According to a 1998 International City/County Management Association (ICMA) survey of cities with populations 25,000 and above, about 30 percent of cities with populations greater than 25,000 and less than 50,000 reported using performance measures. About half of cities with populations between 50,000 and 75,000 reported using performance measures, and over 75 percent of cities with populations over 75,000 reported using performance measures. About 40 percent of respondents that used performance measures reported "meaningful" use of performance data for decision making, as opposed to simply collecting and reporting performance data.[65]

When smaller jurisdictions were added to the database, the use of performance measures dropped precipitously. The larger sample revealed that 62 percent of responding municipalities reported that they did not use performance measures.[66] That figure was clearly driven by cities in the population category between 5,000 and 49,999, where the nonuse of performance measures was 68 percent.[67] We decided to explore the relationship between city size and the use of performance measures a little further in a 2002 survey of municipal members of the Government Finance Officers Association. Our findings were similar to those of the ICMA study with regard to smaller cities. Stratifying for size in the survey,[68] we found that 81 percent of municipalities answered "no" or "no, not in any systematic way" to the question "Has your organization formally adopted a performance measurement system?" We think this may be a bit more reflective of the nationwide average because most cities are smaller and they are represented in proportion here. However, there is no such thing as the "average" city; comparisons between cities at the low and high ends of the population scale are typically worthless. But because we need some way of understanding the extent to which municipalities may have an underlying capacity for performance budgeting based on adoption of a performance measurement program, a summary based on small-medium-large categories is preferable to a single percentage (see Table 2.1).

Roughly 16 percent of small municipalities (2,500–9,999) have adopted a performance measurement system. Approximately 20 percent of medium-

Table 2.1

Distribution of Municipal Survey Responses to "Has Your Organization Adopted a Performance Measurement System?"

Size of responding municipality	No	No, not in any systematic way	Yes, but only for for certain departments or programs	Yes, but there is no written require-ment	Yes, it is written policy for all de-partments	Row total (row %)
2,500–9,999	88	77	8	14	9	196
	(44.9%)	(39.3%)	(4.1%)	(7.1%)	(4.6%)	(100%)
10,000–49,999	48	47	7	10	6	118
	(40.7%)	(39.8%)	(5.9%)	(8.5%)	(5.1%)	(100%)
50,000 and	8	6	3	7	0	24
above	(33.8%)	(25.0%)	(12.5%)	(29.2%)	(0%)	(100%)
Column total	144	130	18	31	15	338
	(42.6%)	(38.5%)	(5.3%)	(9.2%)	(4.4%)	(100%)

sized municipalities (10,000–49,999) have adopted a performance measurement system, either for all departments or certain departments. By contrast, approximately 42 pecent of larger municipalities have adopted performance measurement, though the small sample size (N = 24) in that category leaves us reluctant to generalize. We conclude that there may be a capacity gap for performance budgeting based on size, a topic we explore more fully in chapter 8.

Finally, a recent survey of performance measurement practices in counties with populations over 50,000 offers some insight on the extent of adoption, as well as the types of functions most likely to be measured and the extent to which those counties were using the preferred types of performance measures, outcome and quality measures.[69] Berman and Wang found that a little over a third (33.6 percent) of counties use performance measures of some type, but their use of them varies considerably by function and type. Defining use of performance measures in at least 75 percent of functions as "high use," Berman and Wang concluded that about 7 percent of all counties could be characterized that way.[70] Of those counties using performance measures, most are measuring workloads and activities, just as their municipal counterparts do. However, Berman and Wang estimated that effectiveness or outcome measures are applied to 45–50 percent of county functions and that quality measures are applied to 35–45 percent of county functions, again in the counties that use performance measures.[71] These counties are more likely to have the capacity for a performance measurement program, and hence a performance budgeting program. Although there are multiple capabilities associated with capacity (Berman and Wang identify six), they can be summarized as having competent staff to collect and analyze performance data and having the support of elected officials and top managers for a performance program.

The Leadership Factor

There are several unifying themes running through the experience with performance management and performance budgeting at all three levels of government. The first is that it, like other reforms, has a strong rhetorical component compared to its action agenda. The idea of government programs being held accountable for results is appealing, even if no one can define accountability or results. One criticism of performance-based reforms is the omission of consequences for lack of performance. We will not join those critics because we know that performance is not easy to capture with numbers and that many elements of performance are outside a manager's control. Another criticism is the lack of any rewards for good performance. The manager may be in a position of encouraging employees to meet new performance challenges without offering them any resources for the program or for their paycheck if they succeed. Under these circumstances, one wonders why performance reforms have any record of success at all.

If there is a common thread binding success stories in states and local governments, it is leadership. There are a variety of ways to describe leadership; one is a set of four competencies: management of attention (ability to focus employees on a shared vision for the organization), management of meaning (ability of a manager to communicate his/her vision to the organization), management of trust (reliability or consistency of a manager's actions), and management of self (the manager's ability to compensate for his/her weaknesses by applying his/her strengths).[72] These competencies are necessary to bring about a change in organizational culture, another hard concept to define. For simplicity's sake, we adopt a simple and elegant definition of organizational culture as being "to an organization what personality is to an individual."[73] In a study of performance reform in four federal agencies, Hennessey found that the critical factor for success was changing organizational culture, and that no one of these four competencies was more important than others in affecting that change.[74] Good leaders encouraged employees to make changes in processes that needed improvement. Successful leadership recognized the obstacles to those kinds of changes and took action to eliminate the obstacles, facilitating the change.[75] Changing the organizational culture to emphasize performance requires more than encouragement and vision on the part of leaders; it requires recognition of the obstacles to change (e.g., rules, resources, incentives) and action to eliminate them.

Reviewing the Record

With benefit of a historical backdrop and the experience of government at all levels with performance budgeting, we are now ready to answer the questions we posed at the beginning of the chapter.

1. Is performance budgeting democratic; that is, can it accommodate public preferences for programs and activities while keeping a performance focus?

   Yes, because performance budgeting does not supplant values, it only adds facts.

2. Are there some credible results to review from a fair test of performance budgeting?

   Yes, some good case studies are emerging, especially at the state level. But there is not enough evidence of the demonstrated use of performance data in budgetary decision making to draw a reliable set of conclusions.

3. Is performance budgeting another in a series of budget reforms, representing current leadership priorities?

   No, we have learned that every budget reform leaves footprints for future reformers. Performance budgeting is leaving deep footprints.

4. Is performance budgeting a way to look reformed without changing budget outcomes?

   It can be, and it has been, especially when a state or local government is coping with a fiscal or political crisis. However, the availability of performance information during the budget preparation process creates capacity to change budget outcomes.

Is Performance Budgeting a Theory?

We conclude with a larger, almost philosophical issue in public budgeting—that of whether anything we have just described from the turn of the century forward amounts to a theory of budgeting. In 1940, V.O. Key lamented the lack of a budgetary theory in an article that still haunts the field today. Key said politics appeared to be part of any descriptive theory we might use to explain budgeting if we believed our political system reflected the "general will" and if we were committed to serving that will.[76] In other words, we were not making progress toward getting the politics out of budgeting and never would so long as we remained sensitive to public preferences for programs and services. Verne Lewis's 1952 response reflected the administrative environment of the time. The problem, Lewis asserted, is not that we of reform dictates (with performance measures, program evaluations, and cost-benefit analyses), but the traditional budget format is our touchstone over time. Nothing that followed the New York Bureau of Municipal Research's line-item budget was as important to the profession as identification of cost, and nothing remains as useful in what we think of as accountability, either in the financial or political sense.

The line-item format supports an incremental process. We look at what our governments do against the backdrop of what they did last budget year. The line-item budget facilitates that examination, and the American political system rests on it, because this is how we have defined both accountability and responsiveness. As a nation, we have shown a remarkable ability to renegotiate the role of government in society, or at least the role of government in solving certain social problems, over the past century. Budgets reflect that renegotiation. It would be a mistake to say our profession has somehow failed to embrace reform because the line-item budget dominates budget practice, or that the persistence of incrementalism in public budgeting demonstrates bureaucratic resistance to real reform. It also would be a mistake to judge reform efforts by looking for changes in budgetary outcomes. Wildavsky contended that an attempt to reform the budget process without altering the political system that produced it is doomed to failure.[85] In other words, it is up to elected officials to redirect resources when appropriate, the budget process cannot do it for them and it certainly cannot do it without them.

Performance budgeting is not a theory of budgeting or of politics. It is not even a change in the two foundation practices; performance budgeting fits nicely within the line-item format and is consistent with the incremental approach. Each of the major efforts at budget reform, including performance budgeting, has given us new ideas and new techniques, and we have incorporated them into our budget processes. We use marginal analysis, program evaluation, performance measures, and cost-benefit analysis to inform a budget process that culminates in a document that meets the public's demand on elected officials for accountability. We make adjustments to the budget, through bargaining and negotiation, consistent with public preferences, visible because of the traditional format. Perhaps the next reform will further enhance our deliberations during the budget process, but if history predicts the future, it probably will not change the format of the document or the way the political system deals with it.

Conclusion

Proceeding from the idea that government is "broken"[86] and that science offers the means to repair it, performance budgeting took its place with PPBS, lack theory but we lack facts. "It can be shown, I think, that the problem ir government, so far as it exists, arises out of a lack of firm numbers rathe than out of the lack of a method."[77] It was in this era of confidence in ratio nality and science to bring about optimal decisions that Charles Lindblom' 1959 essay appeared.

Lindblom argued that what Key sought (a theory) and what Lewis foun (better facts) were prescriptive, not descriptive. Policy, Lindblom said, i made at the margins, but not through the application of marginal utility theor It is a system of successive limited comparisons among finite numbers (alternatives.[78]

> It may be worth emphasizing that theory is sometimes of extremely limite helpfulness in policy-making for at least two rather different reasons. It greedy for facts; it can be constructed only through a great collection observations. And it is typically insufficiently precise for application to policy process that moves through small changes.[79]

Lindblom asserted that we do not need more theory or more facts to ma better decisions. We need to understand what we really do and seek ways do it more strategically. He would make this case even more clearly in later essay on "muddling through," where he argued that describing what actually do and trying to improve offers public administrators both intell tual honesty and a path to improve outcomes.[80]

Aaron Wildavsky advanced Lindblom's argument by pointing out t bargaining and negotiation, not the application of science, determines put policy. Moreover, he asserted, the former is consistent with democracy wl the latter is not.[81] In a 1964 budgeting text that still is relevant to mod public budgeting, Wildavsky described the theory of incremental budget based on this same concept. In practice, agencies receive small incre over their base budget (defined as what they got last year). The practic incremental budgeting promotes stability and cooperative relations am budget actors; it is both descriptive and prescriptive.[82] Incrementalism is meable to the political system, which translates public preferences into po outcomes. Other scholars would question both the descriptive and norma value of the incremental model,[83] but it would remain the dominant p digm in budgeting theory throughout the rest of the century.

Wildavsky concluded with a caution that all students of budgeting shi consider before they get too caught up in the zeal for reform: "Surely, not asking too much to suggest that a lot of reform be preceded by a l knowledge."[84] Here is what we know: a century of budget reform prodi two constants, the traditional, line-item budget format and an increme budgeting process. We may decorate the line-item budget as the latest v

MBO, and ZBB in the genre of reforms that would improve decisions by rationally produced data systems.[87] Like the previous reforms, performance budgeting was built on assumptions about the ability of a change in process to change outcomes, without understanding the mechanism by which that would be accomplished in a political system. Our persistent confidence that changing the budget process will positively affect policy outcomes is remarkable, especially since history shows otherwise.[88]

Fifteen years after it emerged, performance budgeting is still growing in states and local governments. It still challenges managers to continually improve their service delivery processes, which managers embrace as evidence of their commitment to professional standards and public service. And it gives elected officials a way to justify local government expenditures, reassuring the public that their services are evaluated by the same efficiency and effectiveness criteria used for decision making in the private sector.

Yet the support for performance budgeting rests on how much government people want and what they want it to do. Our leaders at the federal, state, and local levels have used the appetite for reform to refocus the priorities of government action. But to what end? Can we eliminate popular programs that do not work and redirect our resources to unpopular programs with a high degree of effectiveness? If we adopt that standard, are we not operating in a closed budget system, and threatening exactly the kind of public support on which all public policy rests?

Despite significant obstacles, federal, state, and local government seized performance measurement as a way to both improve the quality of services and perhaps reduce service costs. This carried two important messages to the public, which remained skeptical about government efficiency and resistant to taxation. First, it suggested that professionals were in charge of service delivery and were making decisions based on efficiency criteria. Second, it suggested that budget officers were scrutinizing each expenditure to maximize the benefit to the taxpayer. More than anything else, just as in the Progressive era, this reform seemed to take the politics out of budgeting and hold governments to the same efficiency-based criteria that the private sector uses to determine how to allocate its resources. It was reform and justification for expenditures, all at once. And just as in the early days of public administration, it promised to develop a science of administration practiced by professionals.

— Chapter 3 —

Budget Process for State
and Local Government

The process used in state and local government to prepare and adopt the annual operating budget generally is guided by the budget calendar, beginning with the distribution of budget guidelines by the budget officer and ending with the adoption of a balanced budget by the elected officials. Budget officers often refer to the six months prior to the new fiscal year as the "budget season." It is a critical period of time when program managers, agency and department heads, chief administrators, and elected officials must bargain, negotiate, and compromise to produce a balanced budget under the demands of state and local law and under the constraints of limited resources.

The National Advisory Council on State and Local Budgeting defines the budget process as more than just budget preparation for producing a legal document that appropriates the necessary funds for service delivery. Its definition of the budget process identifies three budget stages: development, implementation, and evaluation of service provision. It also describes the budget as a policy plan that contains political, managerial, planning, communication, and financial dimensions.[1] "Budget season" corresponds to the developmental and decision-making stage of the budget process. After the budget is adopted, the next stage is implementation, where the budget is entered by line item into the financial management system and budget responsibility is assigned over those accounts. Evaluation is the final stage of the process, where the budget is monitored throughout the remainder of the fiscal year for both financial (budget to actual expenditures) and operational (delivery of services) compliance. Although the development stage always precedes the implementation and the evaluation stage, it would be wrong to characterize the budget process as orderly and predictable. Rather, it is a dynamic and ongoing process, where changes in revenue estimates or spending needs force reconsideration of previous decisions. The budget is constantly being updated and reconsidered to accommodate past, current, and future financial and service performance information.

It is hard to describe a typical budget process for state and local government because, while the overall process is similar, the details vary considerably. These differences arise from variations in legal requirements, administrative philosophy, organizational capacity, and demands of elected officials. An example of a legal variation in state government is a balanced budget requirement. Currently, forty-four of the fifty states require their governors, either statutorily or constitutionally, to submit a balanced budget to their legislatures for approval.[2] The remaining six states do not. An example of variation in administrative philosophy comes from states or local governments that have a centralized versus a decentralized budget process. In some governments, the budget office controls budget preparation without much input from agencies and departments. In a decentralized budget process, agency and departmental requests are the starting point for the annual budget. Variation in capacity is often related to size of local governments, and to the number and expertise of budget support staff. Larger governments have the resources to support a staff that can manage both financial and operational accountability while smaller ones tend to focus on financial compliance. Some state budget offices have a strong policy orientation and expect their staff to make budget recommendations based on service performance and policy priorities, while other state budget offices have a control orientation and expect their staff to find ways to control cost. Finally, the demands elected officials make on the budget process are often related to how involved they are in the budget process and whether the elected officials can agree on goals, strategies, and mandates to form public policy. Regardless of these differences across governments, we maintain that a general understanding of the budget process is necessary to conceptualize performance budgeting—especially during the budget's preparation or developmental stage when allocation decisions are supported with performance information.

This chapter presents an overview of the developmental phase of the budget process in state and local government, using the line-item format for producing a balanced operating budget as the foundation for explanation. The process begins with constructing a chart of accounts and ends with elected officials adopting a balanced budget where estimated revenues equal appropriations. We defined a balanced budget as the condition where the budget ordinance is unequivocally in balance, permitting neither a deficit (expenditures exceeding revenues) nor a surplus (revenues exceeding expenditures).[3] This definition does not preclude states from making a contribution to their rainy day funds or local governments from designating money for their contingency funds. We present budget calendars for two jurisdictions, the state of West Virginia and the village of Sauk Village, Illinois, to illustrate the developmental phase used by states and localities to produce a balanced budget. We conclude the first section with a discussion on budget implementation and evaluation in states and local governments.

We present budget processes for the state of Washington, the county of Fairfax, Virginia, and the city of Hickory, North Carolina, in the next section. These three governments were chosen for their successful performance management systems and to illustrate how they expanded their budget processes to accommodate performance information and created the environment for performance budgeting. Just as we described in chapter 1, these governments aligned service priorities and service spending, expanded budget deliberations to include performance information, motivated managers to focus on goals and objectives, and enhanced the accountability of service delivery within agencies, departments, and programs. While we present only three examples in this chapter, many governments are enjoying the advantages of performance budgeting, some in well-documented, formal systems and some with nothing more elaborate than a solid performance measurement system and a commitment to use performance information in their budget deliberations.

In the final section, we explore some misconceptions about performance budgeting that have limited its use in state and local government, explaining some notable performance budgeting efforts that have been judged unsuccessful. We reiterate that performance budgeting is not a new or different budgeting format; it builds on program and line-item budgeting. Nor is it a new approach to budget presentation where performance measures are added to the budget document to make it look more professional. While this may be important from a presentational standpoint and to make the government eligible for a presentation award, performance budgeting requires data to enter the budget preparation process well before the final document is prepared. Performance is not the only relevant factor in budget preparation. Political mandates, fiscal constraints, and prior year budget decisions also play important roles in allocation decisions. A commitment to performance budgeting requires only that performance is part of the deliberation process for making allocation decisions, along with the political, fiscal, and legal demands present in every state and local government budgeting process.

Overview of Budget Process

Budgeting begins with constructing or updating the chart of accounts. The chart of accounts is the classification framework for budgeting, recording, and reporting the financial transactions in state and local government. This step is rarely discussed in budgeting textbooks or shown on government budget calendars. It is an informal component of budgeting handled between the budget director and the comptroller, but it establishes the foundation for program budgeting. Program managers must collaborate with budget staff to determine how financial activities are tracked for their programs, and how the inputs (dollars) are translated to outputs and outcomes for service delivery. These decisions become the lines in the line-item budget for the program or service. Once established, they become the basis for tracking revenues and expenditures, and reporting of financial information.

The next step is to establish a detailed budget calendar for guiding the budget preparation process, including the specific dates by which certain activities must be accomplished. An example is the initial revenue forecast, which must be completed in time to make preliminary funding decisions and updated periodically as actual data become available. Once the proposed budget is drafted, it is presented to the elected officials for their review, feedback, and approval. The proposed budget is more than just a discussion draft, and the approach the budget office takes to crafting the proposal affects the approach that elected officials take to deliberating it. Administrators often "frame the question" or set the stage for the amount of emphasis elected officials place on performance information. When performance information accompanies the budget request in the proposed budget, elected officials may assume that it is relevant to their deliberations. The administrative focus also impacts budget implementation and evaluation.

Chart of Accounts

The chart of accounts provides a classification system for recording the financial activities of an organization. The chart of accounts in state and local government begins with fund accounting, identifying the types of funds used to budget, record, and report the financial activities associated with service delivery. All state and local governments have a general fund, which falls under the category of governmental funds as shown in Table 3.1. There is only one general fund for each organization, accounting for all the financial resources of the reporting entity except those required to be accounted for in other funds.

Property tax is the major general fund revenue source at the local level. Municipalities often account for the activities of public safety (police and fire) and public works in the general fund. Common activities accounted for in the general fund at the county level include law enforcement (sheriff), social services, public works, and judicial services. Sales and income taxes are the major general fund revenues for most states. States use the general fund to account for a wide variety of activities, including general administration, human services, law enforcement, and public education.

The other governmental fund types are special revenue, capital project, debt service, and permanent funds. Special revenue funds are used to account for collection and expenditure of resources earmarked by state or local

Table 3.1

Overview of Funds

A. Governmental funds—focus primarily on the sources, uses, and balances of current financial resources that often have a budgetary orientation. The governmental fund category includes four types of funds.
   (1) General fund—accounts for all financial resources except those required to be accounted for in another fund.
   (2) Special revenue funds—accounts for proceeds or specific revenue sources that are restricted to expenditure for specific purposes.
   (3) Capital projects funds—account for financial resources to be used for the acquisition or construction of capital assets.
   (4) Debt service funds—account for funds accumulated for the payment of general long-term debt, including principal and interest.
   (5) Permanent funds—account for resources that are legally restricted to the extent that only earnings, and not principal, may be used for purposes that support the general government.

B. Proprietary funds—focus on the determination of operating income, changes in net assets, financial position, and cash flows. There are two types of proprietary funds.
   (1) Enterprise funds—used to account for activities for which a fee is charged to external users for goods and services.
   (2) Internal service funds—used to account for activities that provide goods and services to other funds, departments, or agencies on a cost-reimbursement basis.

C. Fiduciary funds—focus on net assets and changes in net assets from assets held in trustee or agency capacity for others and therefore cannot be used to support the general government. There are four types of fiduciary funds.
   (1) Pension funds—used to report on resources that are required to be held in trust for the members and beneficiaries as defined by the benefit plan.
   (2) Investment trust funds—used to report the external portion of investment pools reported by the sponsoring government.
   (3) Private-purpose trust funds—used to report all other trust arrangements under which principal and income benefit individuals, private organizations, or other governments.
   (4) Agency funds—used to report resources held by the reporting government in a purely custodial capacity.

Sources: Jerome B. McKinney, *Effective Financial Management in Public and Non-profit Agencies* (Westport, CT: Quorum Books, 1995); and Governmental Accounting Standards Board, *Basic Financial Statements and Management's Discussion and Analysis for State and Local Government* (Norwalk, CT: Author, 1999).

law for specific purposes. An example at the state level is a gasoline tax imposed for highway maintenance and repair. Capital project funds are used to account for financial resources dedicated for the acquisition or construction of capital assets. A common use of a capital project fund is to record the proceeds of general obligation bonds and to record the expenditures for the construction of a new facility. Debt service funds are used to account for the accumulation of financial resources for amortizing the principal and interest payments of general long-term debt. The final governmental fund type is permanent funds, formerly known as "nonexpendable trust funds" before the passage of Statement No. 34 by the Governmental Accounting Standards Board.[4] These funds account for financial resources where the principal (the amount originally designated for the activity) cannot legally be spent, but the interest earnings are available for the purposes of general government. A cemetery fund is an example of a permanent fund where only the interest earnings from the corpus (sorry, we could not resist) can be used for the perpetual care of the cemetery.

Proprietary funds, as shown in Table 3.1, are commonly used in state and local government to account for service provision that is financed with specific fees as opposed to general tax revenue. There are two main types of proprietary funds, enterprise and internal service funds. Enterprise funds are used to account for activities for which fees are imposed on external customers. Municipalities occasionally account for residential refuse collection in an enterprise fund, charging each customer a collection fee. The financial activities associated with parking garages and toll bridges also are typically accounted for in enterprise funds. Internal service funds, on the other hand, account for activities for which fees are imposed on internal customers. State print shops are commonly accounted for in internal service funds; print shops provide services to other state agencies on a cost-reimbursement basis. Flexible budgets are often adopted for proprietary funds; they are guides for managerial control as opposed to fixed budgets for regular governmental funds.[5]

The final category of funds in Table 3.1 is fiduciary funds, including pension, investment trust, private-purpose trust, and agency funds. These fund types are not directly involved in the annual budget preparation process insofar as they are primarily used to account for financial resources that do not provide tangible services to the general public. For example, pension funds are established for the retirement of government employees and operate under the criteria contained within pension plans approved by state or local law.[6] Another example of a fiduciary fund is agency funds. Counties use agency funds for recording and disbursing property tax collections for cities and townships within their jurisdictions. This arrangement is often governed by an intergovernmental agreement between the county and the municipalities, which includes the administrative fee cities and townships pay for tax collection and disbursement.

The level of detail in which financial activities are budgeted and tracked is determined after the fund structure of the organization is established and the services that are accounted for within each fund type are identified. Figure

---

Box 3.1

Basis of Budgeting

State and local governments differ on how they prepare their annual operating budgets. Some organizations budget their governmental funds on the cash basis, recognizing revenues and expenditures when the cash is actually received or disbursed. Other organizations budget their governmental funds on the modified accrual basis, recognizing revenues in the accounting period in which they become available and measurable and expenditures in the accounting period in which the liability is incurred. It is common practice for most governments—regardless of the basis for preparing the budget—to maintain their accounts on the cash basis during the fiscal year for budgetary control and for interim budgetary reporting and then make the necessary adjustments to modified accrual at fiscal year end for the annual financial statements and for compliance with generally accepted accounting principles (GAAP).

Source: Robert J. Freeman and Craig D. Shoulders, *Governmental and Nonprofit Accounting*, 5th ed. (Upper Saddle River, NJ: Prentice -Hall, 1996).

3.1 presents an account structure used for building a chart of accounts and for budgeting and recording financial activities within the general fund. Building a chart of accounts for revenues is not as complicated as building a chart of accounts on the expenditure side of the general ledger. The first two digits of the ten-digit account code located in Figure 3.1 represent the fund type, with 10 representing the general fund in this example. The next four digits are zero for revenue accounts in that revenues are not designated in the general fund by department or program, even though certain service delivery programs may be responsible for charging fees for their services. In other words, revenues in the general fund are not earmarked for specific expenditures.

The final four digits of the account code for general fund revenues represent two levels of funding sources. The first two digits (32) represent the funding type. Examples include taxes, fees, and intergovernmental and interest income. The final two digits (36) represent the specific funding source. The detail at which revenues are tracked depends on the needs of the organization. Revenues are typically recorded by revenue type and by revenue source, providing the organization with the necessary information for accurately forecasting them during the budgetary process and for accurately reporting them

Figure 3.1   **Account Structure for the General Fund**

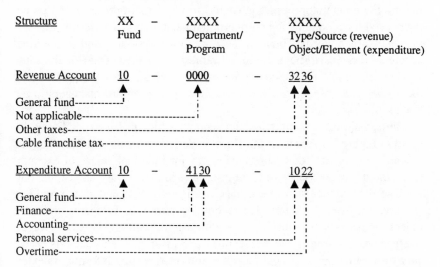

in the annual financial statements at fiscal year end. It should be noted that revenue sources are reported by type (interest income) as opposed to source (180-day certificate of deposit with Hometown Bank) in the annual financial statements. However, the external auditors must have access to the detail to ensure that the revenues reported at the aggregate level are materially accurate.

The account structure for expenditures, just as with revenues, begins with the fund type. Again, the number 10 in Figure 3.1 represents the general fund. Unlike revenues, however, the next four digits of the account structure represent the department (41) and the program (30) for which the expenditure is realized. It matters how the chart of accounts is structured around agencies, departments, divisions, and programs within state and local government because the structure is going to dictate the level of responsibility in how financial resources are managed during the fiscal year. It also sets the stage for performance budgeting since financial resources represent the major input for service delivery in state and local government. We argue that the chart of accounts should be structured around programs rather than units, so that they represent a group of activities, operations, or functions used to accomplish a group of related goals and objectives.[7]

The recommendation to structure the chart of accounts around programs is not new for state and local government budgeting. In fact, program budgeting is one of the oldest and most durable budgetary reforms used in developing budget requests.[8] Program budgeting is the preferred method for one major reason. It ensures that the chart of accounts and the annual budget process is structured around programs that represent actual service delivery, linking the annual appropriation (input) to the actual processes and procedures used for producing the outputs and the outcomes of governmental services. In other words, financial accountability (budget) and operational accountability (performance) simply represent different sides of the same service delivery coin. Program budgeting, as a result, is designed to compare these two so as to increase the responsibility of program managers in the budget process.

The remaining two digits on the account structure for expenditures located in Figure 3.1 represent the object code (10) and element (22). For this example, the object code represents the major functional areas of expenditures, including personnel, operating supplies and materials, and capital outlay. The element represents the actual classification of expenditures, providing the necessary detail required for accounting purposes. Elements under the object code of personnel include expenditure items such as salaries and wages, overtime pay, retirement, social security, and insurance. This detail is necessary for internal management purposes and for reporting information externally. An internal management example is the ability to track overtime pay for employees and for the management functions of planning and staffing. An external reporting example is the detail needed to comply with the requirements of the Internal Revenue Service, ensuring that employees receive accurate W-2s for completing their annual tax returns.

The practice of cost accounting has gained more attention in the public sector in recent years, increasing the importance of how organizations frame their charts of accounts. Cost accounting identifies the total cost (direct, indirect, and capital) of resources sacrificed for service provision, supporting the utility of performance budgeting. There are two ways for a government to implement cost accounting. One is to develop a stand-alone cost accounting system, which must be reconciled with the existing financial management system on a regular basis to ensure accuracy. Organizations that take this approach typically use a double-entry bookkeeping system.[9] An advantage of this approach is the flexibility to identify the costs of service functions separately and collectively, including the ability to implement activity-based costing. The disadvantage of this approach is the time and resources required for maintaining two separate systems.

An alternative approach to cost accounting is program-based costing.[10] The first step in this methodology is to structure the chart of accounts around programs, which results in a program budget format. This allows organizations to track the bulk of direct program costs on an ongoing basis with the financial management system. The organization can then calculate the total cost of each program by recasting the expenditure data for support services

from the financial management system across programs with a standard indirect cost methodology and depreciate the program's capital assets.

Budget Calendar

The budget calendar is the timeline for producing a balanced budget in state
and local government. Administrators are encouraged to construct detailed
budget calendars, identifying a timeline for all the activities that must be
accomplished during the budget year. Administrators also are encouraged to
effectively manage the budget calendar, ensuring that elected officials receive a proposed budget for consideration well before the start of the new
fiscal year. Most governments follow similar budget calendars and use similar steps to manage their overall budget cycles, though there are numerous
differences in cycle details. Some organizations even adopt biennial budgets. Twenty-three states currently use biennial budget cycles, including two
that use a combination of biennial and annual budgeting.[11] While biennial
budgeting is less common at the local level, the Government Finance Officers Association promotes it as a way to emphasize program evaluation and
monitoring, to improve long-term planning, and to reduce the staff time spent
on budget development.[12]

Village of Sauk Village

Figure 3.2 is the budget calendar for the village of Sauk Village, Illinois. Its
budget process begins in September with a citizen survey, which is five months
into the new fiscal year (May 1–April 30). The annual survey is a questionnaire mailed to a random sample of village residents for their opinions on the
quality of village services. Local governments vary greatly in the amount of
citizen input in their budget processes, ranging from public hearings required
by law to focus groups on defining goals and objectives of service delivery.
The use of a citizen survey by the village of Sauk Village is not unique in
local government. Surveys are a popular way for governments to gather input from citizens; however, the use of an annual survey to begin each budget
preparation cycle is far less common.[13]

   The next step as shown in Figure 3.2 is the preparation of financial forecast models for revenues, expenditures, and fund balances for a four-year
period. These forecasts produce the necessary information for guiding budget preparation for the new fiscal year. This planning exercise is critical in
state and local government because the previous year's actual results and the
current year's base budget have such a large impact on the preparation of
future budgets. Specifically, planning information in the form of financial

Figure 3.2   **Budget Calendar for Village of Sauk Village**

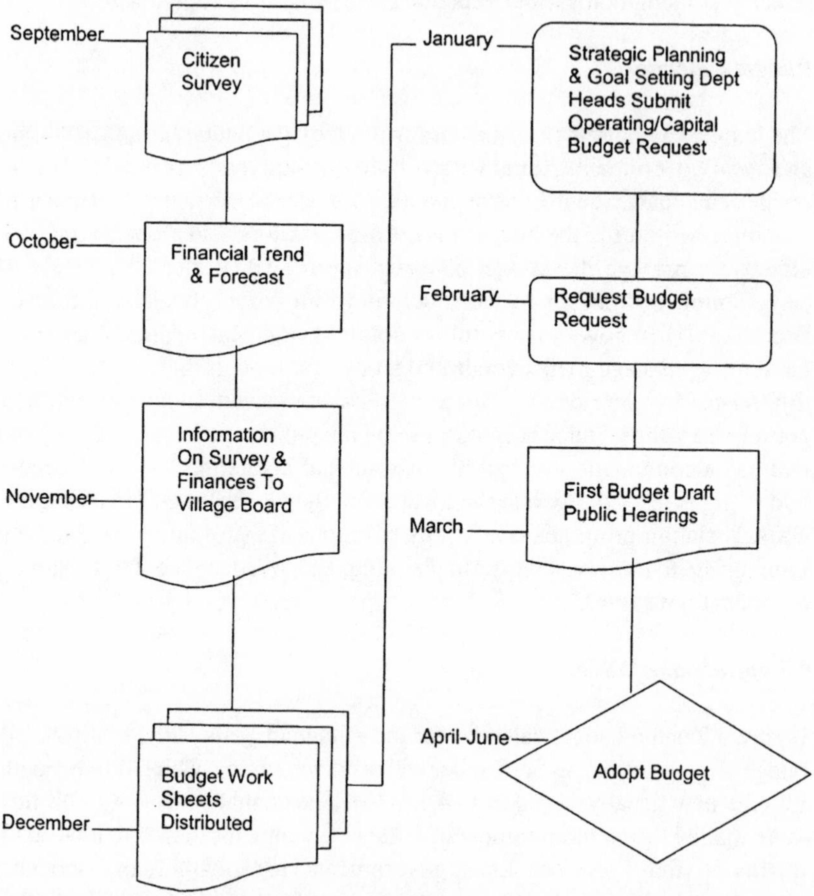

Source: Annual Budget, Village of Sauk Village, Illinois, May 1, 2002 to April 30, 2003.

forecasts helps local governments avoid budget strategies that may cause problems in future budget years. Although actual changes in allocation may remain modest from one year to the next, Sauk Village's budgeting process is not strictly incremental.

Results from the financial forecast models, the citizen survey, and the status of prior year goals are due in November, and are presented to council members and department heads. The deadline allows the organization to set the stage for the overall budget preparation process based on planning and analysis. It also provides critical direction to department heads and program managers when preparing their budgets and to budget officers when estimating revenues and planning for the amount of fund balance or cash reserves, which generally must equal or exceed a certain percentage of total general fund expenditures.

The operating and capital budget worksheets are distributed to department heads in December as the first step in departmental budget preparation. Local governments often place budget worksheets in a packet of information that includes a cover memo from the chief executive and budget guidelines for the new fiscal year. The cover memo is designed to outline the budget "drivers" of the organization, which are derived from the citizen survey, the village board, and the fiscal limitations identified from the financial forecasts. A typical financial limitation is the amount of cost-of-living or merit increases expected for employees in the coming fiscal year.

Budget guidelines are normally prepared by the finance or budget department, detailing the information required for completing the budget worksheets, ranging from the inflationary adjustments for certain expenditure line items to the overall spending target for that department. The worksheets contain the line-item expenditure accounts generated from the chart of accounts. Table 3.2 provides a sample worksheet of expenditure line items for emergency communications, a program within the police department. These expenditure line items are grouped by the three major expenditure categories of personnel, operating, and capital outlay.

The program information located in Table 3.2 is combined with the other programs in police services to create a departmental total. This total becomes the initial budget request for police services and is forwarded to the finance or budget office. The departmental totals from all functional areas are then combined for an overall total for the general fund. The general fund total request is compared to the total revenue estimate for the general fund. The result is normally a deficit, as department heads ask for more than expected revenues can support. However, the deficit will be eliminated as the budget cycle progresses, through reductions in departmental requests and perhaps by revised revenue estimates.

January is a busy budget month in Sauk Village, as shown on the budget calendar in Figure 3.2. A strategic planning session is held with the village board, the village manager, and the finance officer to identify goals and strategies for the forthcoming fiscal year. The budget worksheets from the department heads and completed revenue estimates also are due in January. These revenue estimates are for only the forthcoming fiscal year, and are based on last fiscal year's actual results and on current fiscal year's year-to-date results. The village manager, finance officer, and department heads review the estimated revenues and budgetary requests in the month of February,

Table 3.2

Budget Worksheet for Emergency Communications

Account	Personnel	Amount	Explanation
10–5054–10–10	Salaries and wages	$350,000	Based on 3 percent merit
10–5054–10–11	Temporary	20,000	Prior year amount
10–5054–10–12	Overtime	25,000	Prior year amount
10–5054–10–20	FICA/Social Security	35,000	Per budget guidelines
10–5054–10–21	Insurance	10,000	Per budget guidelines
10–5054–10–30	Retirement	21,000	Per budget guidelines
10–5054–10–40	Other benefits	15,500	Per budget guidelines

Account	Operating	Amount	Explanation
10–5054–20–10	Office supplies	$11,000	Inflationary adjustment
10–5054–20–11	Computer supplies	9,000	Inflationary adjustment
10–5054–20–20	Uniforms	12,500	Per rental agreement
10–5054–20–30	Telephone	15,000	Per contract
10–5054–20–31	Printing	2,500	Prior year amount
10–5054–20–40	Training	5,000	Prior year amount
10–5054–20–50	Contractual services	20,000	Per contract
10–5054–20–60	Rent	75,000	Per lease agreement

Account	Capital	Amount	Explanation
10–5054–30–10	Equipment	$5,000	Computer replacement
10–5054–30–20	Furniture	10,000	New console
10–5054–30–30	Vehicles	25,000	Per replacement schedule

reconciling them with the financial situation of the organization and the goals established in the strategic planning session. In Sauk Village, these budget workshops are where the operating deficit that normally occurs in the first round of revenue estimates and budgetary requests is eliminated. The goal is to balance the proposed budget so that it can be presented to the village board in March.

One aspect of budgeting that deserves more attention—especially at the local level—is forecasting revenues. Budget requests from departments and programs seem to dominate budget preparation given the time and individuals involved in the process. But decisions about budget requests are predicated on revenue expectations. Good revenue estimates facilitate good budget decisions. Poor revenue estimates may cause the government to unnecessarily limit services or cause dreaded mid-year cutbacks. Table 3.3 contains a worksheet used in local government for estimating revenues. It shows the account, the revenue source, the estimated amount, and the basis for estimation. Property taxes represent the major revenue source in this example. The basis for estimation in each property tax category is assessed value of taxable property, millage or tax rate, and historical collection rate. Property taxes

Table 3.3

Revenue Worksheet for Local Government

Account	Revenue source	Estimated amount	Basis for estimation
10–0000–10–10	Property taxes—residential	$4,350,000	Based on assessed value, millage rate, and historical collection rate
10–0000–10–11	Property taxes—commercial	7,220,000	Based on assessed value, millage rate, and historical collection rate
10–0000–10–12	Property taxes—mobile homes	15,000	Based on assessed value, millage rate, and historical collection rate
10–0000–10–13	Prior year taxes—real	235,000	Based on collection history as percentage of total outstanding
10–0000–20–10	Property taxes—personal	910,000	Based on assessed value, millage rate, and historical collection rate
10–0000–20–11	Prior year taxes—personal	21,000	Based on collection history as percentage of total outstanding
10–0000–30–10	Local option sales tax	815,500	Based on projection derived from regression analysis
10–0000–40–10	Franchise fee—cable	374,000	Based on franchise agreement
10–0000–40–11	Franchise fee—power	1,790,000	Based on franchise agreement
10–0000–40–12	Franchise fee—phone	65,000	Based on franchise agreement
10–0000–50–10	Permits—building	446,000	Based on trend analysis
10–0000–50–11	Permits—plumbing	42,000	Based on trend analysis
10–0000–50–12	Permits—electrical	93,000	Based on trend analysis
10–0000–70–10	Interest earnings	55,000	Based on expert analysis from comptroller's office

tend to be less volatile than other revenue sources, allowing budget officers to make very accurate forecasts.

The local option sales tax, on the other hand, is very volatile compared to property taxes and is impacted by a range of variables, including the local, state, and national economies. Regression analysis may be used as the basis of sales tax estimation as shown in Table 3.3, with historical sales tax collections representing the dependent variable (y) and time (fiscal year) representing the independent variable (x). This allows the forecaster to estimate the slope of the collection trend line based on historical data, providing an initial estimate for sales tax collection the following fiscal year. Other common forecasting techniques are incremental adjustments, expert analysis, and moving averages.

The remaining revenue forecasts are built on more specific information. Franchise agreements are used to estimate franchise fees, and trend analysis is used for estimating fees from permits. The organization's comptroller estimates the revenue source of interest earnings, using estimated funds for investment, prior year collections, and financial forecasts of interest rates. Good revenue forecast practices require that each revenue source be estimated separately and tracked during the fiscal year for budget to actual variances, allowing governments to make expenditure adjustments if needed based on actual revenue receipts.

Adoption is the final step in the budget process as shown in Figure 3.2. The village board adopts the proposed budget in April. The typical adoption process in local government is the passage of a budget ordinance by the elected officials, normally after two public hearings where citizens and interest groups have an opportunity to comment on the budget recommendation. Budget adoption by ordinance means the budget is public policy made by law. One could argue that adopting a budget by resolution rather than ordinance is more appropriate in that the budget recommendation is an administratively driven process and that it is in effect for only one fiscal year. Regardless, Sauk Village's budget is now ready for implementation and evaluation.

State of West Virginia

The budget process for the state of West Virginia is shown in Figure 3.3. The state's fiscal year begins on July 1 and ends on June 30. The Secretary of Administration is responsible for developing the budget guidelines used by the spending units when submitting their budget requests that are due by law on September 1 for the forthcoming fiscal year. These guidelines establish the base budget for each department, bureau, commission, and division, defining the base budget as the amount of funds received by each unit in the current fiscal year's budget. The agencies are permitted to move funds between programs within their discretion, allowing agency heads to increase the amount of resources for high priority programs without an increase in their total agency budgets. Any budget request that exceeds the base budget must be submitted on a separate improvement package with the necessary justification for approval. The Secretary of Administration issues the budget guidelines in July, beginning the budget preparation process.[14]

After the agencies submit their budget worksheets by September 1, the Secretary of Administration reviews the budget requests and the budget office schedules budget hearings in September and October. These hearings allow the agency heads to present their budget requests to the Department of Administration and convey additional information about their budget priorities to the Governor's Office. The goal is to produce a balanced budget by December, after all budget requests are reviewed and official revenue estimates are completed. The governor has the sole responsibility to establish revenue estimates in the state of West Virginia under the authority of the state's constitution.

The major revenue sources for the state of West Virginia are personal income tax and consumer sales and use tax; they comprise approximately 70 percent of total general fund revenue. As we noted before, revenues from the income tax and the sales tax are vulnerable to the national and state economies. Therefore, states typically use more sophisticated forecasting techniques than local governments. For example, one survey reported that approximately 75 percent and 48 percent of local governments used judgment decisions and trend analysis, respectively, as their primary forecasting techniques.[15] On the other hand, a state survey reported that 68 percent of states used econometric modeling as a key forecasting technique.[16] The reality is that the types of revenue sources states typically rely on force them to use more advanced revenue forecasting techniques.

After the governor presents the proposed budget to the legislature in January, it is forwarded to the finance committees in the House of Delegates and the Senate for their review. Additional budget hearings between the two finance committees and the state agencies are held in January, February, and March to review the funding levels for each agency contained within the proposed budget. Budget bills are then passed by the House and Senate and are referred to the Budget Conference Committee, comprised of members of both the House and Senate, to reconcile the differences between the two bills for final approval by the respective legislative bodies. The legislature is legally required to pass a balanced budget. However, the budget bill passed by the legislature is then subject to veto by the governor. The legislature has the power to override the governor's veto with a two-thirds vote by both the

Figure 3.3   **Budget Calendar for State of West Virginia**

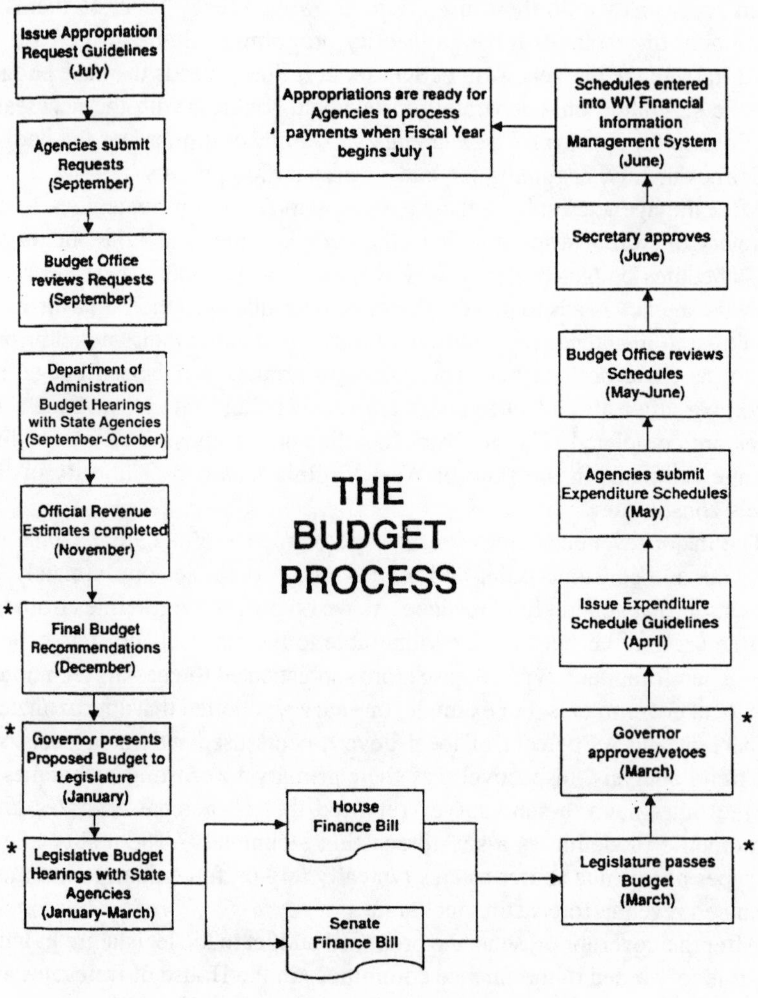

```
Issue Appropriation
Request Guidelines
     (July)
        │
        ▼
 Agencies submit
    Requests
  (September)
        │
        ▼
 Budget Office
reviews Requests
 (September)
        │
        ▼
 Department of
 Administration
 Budget Hearings
with State Agencies
(September-October)
        │
        ▼
 Official Revenue
Estimates completed
  (November)
        │
*       ▼
 Final Budget
Recommendations
  (December)
        │
*       ▼
Governor presents
Proposed Budget to
  Legislature
   (January)
        │
*       ▼
Legislative Budget
Hearings with State
   Agencies
(January-March)
```

THE
BUDGET
PROCESS

```
Appropriations are ready for
  Agencies to process
payments when Fiscal Year
   begins July 1

Schedules entered
into WV Financial
   Information
Management System
     (June)

Secretary approves
     (June)

Budget Office reviews
   Schedules
  (May-June)

Agencies submit
Expenditure Schedules
     (May)

Issue Expenditure
Schedule Guidelines
     (April)

   Governor            *
approves/vetoes
   (March)

House
Finance Bill

Senate
Finance Bill

Legislature passes     *
    Budget
   (March)
```

Source: State of West Virginia Executive Budget, FY 2003, Volume 1.

House and Senate. Once signed by the governor, the budget bill becomes the budget act for the following fiscal year.

After the budget act is passed, several additional steps must be completed before the beginning of the new fiscal year. The budget office issues expenditure schedule guidelines in April to obtain feedback from state agencies on how funds will be used during the following fiscal year. Expenditure guidelines help to reconcile spending patterns with cash flow. Insofar as the personal income tax is collected annually during the second half of the fiscal year, major purchases by state agencies must be timed with cash availability. Agencies submit their expenditure schedules in May, giving the budget office the months of May and June for review. The Secretary of Administration approves all guidelines in June so that the schedules can be entered into the West Virginia financial information management system. The budget calendar is designed to allow state agencies to begin submitting payment requests on July 1, the beginning of the new fiscal year.

West Virginia's budget preparation process is typical, though we must caution that there are numerous details contained within each step of the budgetary process that are not shown on the budget calendar. Each state has its own brand of budgetary politics, strongly influencing whether deadlines are met and even whether responsibilities are fulfilled. Still, states generally engage in the following: (1) issue budget guidelines for budget submissions by state agencies; (2) forecast revenues to determine the availability of financial resources; (3) receive budget requests from state agencies based on a combination of their current year budgets, revenue forecasts, priorities of service delivery, and their ability to communicate with the governor's office and the legislature; (4) balance a budget where estimated revenues plus fund balance equal appropriations; and (5) approve that budget in the form of state law.

Implementation and Evaluation

The difficulty with discussing budget implementation and evaluation is that the two overlap in many respects. One could argue that implementing and evaluating the budget occur simultaneously throughout the fiscal year. For this discussion, implementation refers to the entering of the approved budget by line-item in the financial management system and the assignment of budgetary responsibility over those line-items throughout the fiscal year. Evaluation refers to the ongoing analytical work required to submit budget requests in the developmental phase of budgeting, to monitor budget variances according to budgetary policy, and to track the services being provided with regard to output, outcome, and efficiency. Note that evaluation also overlaps with the developmental phase. Rubin calls this "real-time budgeting" where one phase of the budget process is constantly adjusting to changes in the external environment, including changes in another phase of the budget process.[17] As we said in the introduction to this chapter, the reality is that budgeting in state and local government is a dynamic process—it cannot be neatly separated into independent work processes. Actual revenue receipts significantly less than forecasted, for example, require immediate action in the implementation phase, and an adjustment in the development phase for the following fiscal year.

Implementation

The budget document will commonly report only aggregate expenditures by the selected organizational classification system (e.g., program or unit). A typical budget might list major expenditure areas of personnel, operating, and capital for each program or unit. But underneath this aggregate presentation are all the individual line-items derived from the chart of accounts. The major expenditure category of "operating" has a multitude of line-item accounts, including materials and supplies, telephone and postage, insurance, printing, equipment repair, travel and training, contractual services, and professional services. At the beginning of the new fiscal year, the approved budget at this level of detail is entered in the financial management system, which is how expenditures will be tracked through the payroll (personnel) and accounts payable (operating and capital) processes.

Budget implementation also involves identifying the responsibilities for monitoring the budget, the procedure for budget transfers, and the process for making major capital expenditures. While these components of implementation take on aspects of the evaluation phase of budgeting, they should be resolved during implementation so that financial accountability is clear throughout the fiscal year. Budget responsibility normally follows the government's organizational chart. The chief executive is responsible for ensuring that funds remain within their approved budget. Department heads are responsible for ensuring that departmental expenditures remain within departmental budgets, and each program manager is responsible for his or her program budget. The division and assignment of responsibility ensures that each line-item in the chart of accounts is being monitored and ensures that aggregate budgets are being monitored as well.

It is common for budgetary policy to provide for a certain level of flexibility, allowing department heads to cover a budget overrun in one program with budget savings from another program; this is called "reprogramming." Department heads are generally given authority to redirect resources so long as their decisions about where to redirect them are consistent with the goals and priorities established during the budget process. One could argue that a constant flow of budget transfers reflects the inability of an organization to accurately budget for its service provisions. On the other hand, department heads must have some budget flexibility because they are ultimately responsible for the outputs and outcomes of service delivery.

There are exceptions to manager flexibility. It is common to allow program managers to request budget transfers (from one line-item to another) *within* the major expenditure categories of personnel, operating, and capital. For example, funds designated for supplies can be spent for training. However, budgetary policy often prevents budget transfers *between* these major expenditure categories without the approval from the department head or the chief executive. Funds designated for supplies cannot be used to hire a new analyst. This policy is intended to prevent program managers, for example, from using lapsed salaries from unfilled positions or postponed capital expenditures to cover operating expenditures.

The process of managing capital outlay accounts is one area of budget implementation often overlooked in the budgeting literature. Once the budget is loaded into the financial management system, it does not necessarily mean that cash is available for program managers to purchase all of their capital equipment approved in the adopted budget. This requires open communication between the budget office, the programs, and the accounting office to ensure that cash flow is able to support capital outlay. It is common for localities to postpone major capital expenditures until after property taxes are collected, when they have the cash to buy a new backhoe or snowplow. But sometimes replacing the snowplow is unexpected, and tax collections do not provide enough revenue for this expenditure regardless of the cash-flow cycle.

This is why an adequate fund balance in state and local government is so important. The fund balance is created by the accumulation of cash in governmental funds that occurs from revenues exceeding expenditures in prior fiscal years. States often designate a portion of the fund balance as "rainy day" funds. Local governments call them contingency funds. Both names are descriptive as they permit normal spending when revenues decline unexpectedly or expenditures increase because of unforeseen events.

States dependent on the income and sales taxes often find it difficult to meet their revenue projections when the national economy takes a downturn. To save money in the middle of a budget year, they may postpone certain capital spending. They cannot, however, postpone payroll. They dip into their rainy day funds to pay for what is necessary while hoping to recover the amount in future fiscal years. If there is not enough money in the rainy day fund to cover their budget needs, they might have to borrow. States facing a fiscal crisis will often take out short-term loans in the form of tax anticipation notes, especially if they cannot otherwise make payroll. Of course, the interest payments only add to the list of financial woes that they must address as they look for long-term solutions to their fiscal problems.

Local governments maintain contingency funds to help them cope with these same types of problems. It should be noted that bond rating agencies place a premium on healthy fund balances, giving governments flexibility in

---

Box 3.2

Analysis of Social Services for Budget Preparation

The FY 2003 performance indicators for this program show an increasing trend in the demand for residential services as indicated by workload. The program has performed well to meet planned goals to extend and maintain an effective length of stay for all services.

The agency indicates that approximately six beds at Country Oaks that have been supported by the state of Illinois will be freed up for use in Iowa. Illinois is requiring that they provide this residential program in the state and they are working to accomplish this request. The agency believes that there is sufficient need for the beds on the Iowa side and that there will be no problem in filling them. This would allow a reduction in the waiting time for admission.

Scott County is involved in funding the Detox Services, shown as acute care in this program. Indicators for this program remain relatively stable, with a slight increase in the length of stay. They indicate that they are still able to meet the service need in the community with this program.

The agency is requesting a 3 percent inflationary increase in the Scott County contribution for this program. Funding is recommended at the requested level of $239,052.

---

meeting current obligations until the necessary adjustments can be made. Bond rating agencies are especially interested in the government's capacity to meet its principal and interest payments on long-term debt regardless of the particular circumstances it faces.

Evaluation

Ongoing evaluation is critical to well-managed programs. It is the link between financial and performance data and is the key to performance budgeting. Evaluation in regard to program evaluation and performance auditing is discussed in chapter 7. This discussion is directed toward the general oversight of programs based on a variety of indicators that provide assurance that reasonable levels of effectiveness and efficiency are being maintained. This sort of evaluation begins during the developmental phase of budgeting, supporting budgetary requests with goals, objectives, and performance measures of service delivery. Box 3.2 contains an analysis located in the FY 2002–2003 adopted operating budget for Scott County, Iowa.

The evaluation in Box 3.2 demonstrates that Scott County's Detox Program is tracking workload trends and measuring its goal to extend and maintain an effective length of stay for all chemically dependent service users. This analysis is supplemented with the program mission statement, program objectives, and a mix of demand, workload, productivity, and effectiveness measures. Although budget documents commonly contain budget highlights for departments and programs, Scott County is one of the few jurisdictions that actually places its analytical work directly in the budget document.

Tracking and evaluating *budget* variances during the fiscal year is common in state and local government. Financial management systems typically produce monthly reports that contain the budgeted amount by line-item, actual expenditures and encumbrances by line-item, and the budget variance, or the difference between the budgeted amount and the remaining amount available for expenditure. An "encumbrance" is a commitment for a service that has not been performed or a good that has not been delivered. When the service is performed or the good is delivered, the encumbrance then becomes an actual expenditure. So the variance report shows how much is budgeted for that account, how much has been spent or is committed to be spent, and the difference (variance). The budget variance report is used by program managers to monitor accounts and as the basis for budget transfers when needed.

Tracking and evaluating *performance* variances during the fiscal year is not as common. It requires the collection of performance data on a monthly or quarterly basis, which often creates time and effort issues. However, the advantage of tracking performance variances during the fiscal year allows program managers to make service delivery changes before the fiscal year ends. Some organizations—like the state of Washington and the county of Fairfax, Virginia, track performance variances throughout the fiscal year, approaching budget preparation and budget evaluation as ongoing processes. Washington and Fairfax are discussed in the following section on expanding the budget preparation process to realize the benefits of performance budgeting.

Expanding the Budget Process

One of the best approaches to incorporating performance into budget preparation is to require program managers to submit performance information along with their annual budget requests, including performance data to justify new programs and expand or eliminate existing programs. The classic example of justifying a request for a new staff position is, "We are busy." That may be true, but it tells decision makers nothing about how existing resources are deployed and what is being accomplished as a result. If an additional position is needed to support an increase in demand for service provision provided by a particular program, then the program manager is expected to support this need with output and outcome data. This allows the allocation decision to be based, in part, on the level of service being provided and on some notion of effectiveness. If the manager makes a convincing case and the request is denied, performance budgeting still worked, as the decision was made with performance as a part of the deliberation process. Sometimes other factors, such as declines in revenue forecasts, make the most persuasive performance-based arguments moot.

State and local governments are making progress in expanding their budget processes to include performance data. This section presents three organizations that have been successful in expanding their budget preparation processes to include performance data: the state of Washington, the county of Fairfax, Virginia, and the city of Hickory, North Carolina. Again, we define performance budgeting as emphasizing performance management in the annual budget preparation process. In other words, performance becomes at least a part of budget deliberations, understanding that other factors such as political mandates, fiscal constraints, and prior year appropriations impact the budget preparation process as well.

Washington State

Washington enacts a biennial budget, beginning on July 1 of each odd-numbered fiscal year. Its budget cannot be characterized by any single budget model, as it contains elements of program, target, line-item, and performance budgeting. This budget description is critical to the success of performance budgeting. Public officials in Washington understand that a stand-alone performance budget is not a realistic model. They focus on a budget preparation process that considers changes in services and performance through revisions of the current year expenditure base. The state is committed to making allocations decisions based on the availability of resources, the level of services being provided, and the performance of those services regarding efficiency and effectiveness.[18]

The budget calendar for Washington's biennial budget process is shown in Figure 3.4. It begins with agency strategic planning, a process they describe as "action planning," which requires agencies and programs to update their strategic goals on an annual basis and to reconcile them with the organization-wide strategic plan. Strategic goals represent specific strategies by programs to expand their service capacity consistent with organization-wide goals or the mission of the program itself. Agencies and programs also have

Figure 3.4   **Budget Process for State of Washington**

WASHINGTON STATE 2003–2005 BUDGET

Biennial Budget Process

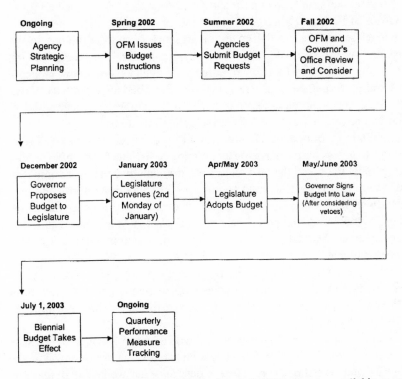

Source: A description of Washington State's budget process; available at www. ofm.wa.gov.

service delivery goals that are consistent with the program's mission statement but are not necessarily linked to organization-wide goals.

For example, a state's mission statement may be silent on the issue of speeding on interstate highways, and the public safety division's mission statement may not specifically address speeding either. But we can be sure that the state troopers have service delivery goals for speed enforcement and accident reduction, monitoring them with performance indicators. If the state-wide goals included vehicular safety, the service delivery goals also could reflect strategic goals. Whether they are relevant to decisions above the program level depends on the alignment of service delivery goals and organization-wide goals. We return to this idea and expand on it in chapters 4 and 5.

The second step on the Washington budget calendar is for the Office of Financial Management to issue budget instructions, including a cover memo from the director. Appendix A contains a copy of the cover memo for the 2003–2005 operating budget. The first due date for agency 2003–2005 operating budget submittals (budget requests) is August 5. This schedule gives the Office of Financial Management and the Governor's Office four months for budget review before the governor presents a proposed budget to the legislature as shown in step 5 of the budget calendar. The state's Budget, Accounting, and Reporting Act requires state agencies to submit strategic plans and performance measures along with their budget submittals in August. State law requires that performance information accompany budget requests, ensuring its availability for budget deliberations.

Washington's Budget, Accounting, and Reporting Act also requires state agencies to assess performance on an ongoing basis. The Office of Financial Management has taken the lead on this requirement by creating a computerized system for agencies to enter and update the following information on a quarterly basis: mission statements, goal statements, performance measures, and estimated and actual performance levels. Agencies also are required to submit quarterly variance reports, providing information on the differences between budgeted and actual expenditures. As a result, Washington adheres to a performance budgeting process for budget development and to a performance budgeting process during budget implementation and evaluation. In other words, Washington tracks financial and performance variances throughout the fiscal year.

The final steps on the budget calendar involve budget adoption by the state legislature. Again, a critical step in budget preparation that is not shown on the budget calendar is estimating revenues to determine the availability of financial resources. The Economic and Revenue Forecast Council conducts the revenue estimates for the state of Washington. This body is composed of representatives from both the legislative and executive branches of government and adopts an official forecast for general fund revenues on a quarterly basis. The primary revenue source for the state's general fund is retail sales and use tax.

Fairfax County, Virginia

The budget process for Fairfax County is shown in Figure 3.5. The purpose of the budget is to: (1) convert long-range plans and policies into service delivery; (2) serve as the primary vehicle to communicate these plans to the citizenry; (3) approve the appropriations necessary for service delivery; and

(4) outline the financial resources needed for service delivery, including the rate of taxation for the coming fiscal year. The tax rate is extremely important because property taxes represent the primary revenue source for the county. The county enacts an annual budget each fiscal year beginning on July 1. However, the current year budget plays a large part in the budget adoption process for the next fiscal year. It establishes the base for the new budget, which is common for state and local government budgeting and also provides the information for carryover reviews, allowing remaining budget balances to be considered in the new budget process as shown in Figure 3.5.[19]

Agencies submit their budget requests to the Department of Management and Budget in September for the new fiscal year. The budget requests are presented in two parts: the baseline request and the addendum. The addendum contains requests for program expansions beyond the budget development criteria (budget guidelines) issued by the Department of Management and Budget. Review of the budget submission occurs in the months of September, October, and November as shown on the budget calendar. Fairfax County's commitment to performance budgeting is evident in the review process. The Department of Management and Budget is responsible for making budget recommendations to the county executive based on an expenditure analysis and an evaluation of goals, objectives, and performance measures by agency. An agency narrative is then constructed based on this dual analysis of both financial and performance data and included in the budget package forwarded to the chief executive. Performance budgeting is a natural extension of Fairfax County's performance measurement program.

Another key component in the budget preparation process in Fairfax County is the senior management meetings and the county executive meetings that occur in December and January. These meetings are designed to discuss the budget issues and priorities for the new fiscal year and beyond. Performance plays a major role in these meetings given that the budget packages used during these discussions are based on financial and performance data. It is up to county leaders to decide what response is appropriate based on the performance of agencies and programs. At a minimum, Fairfax County ensures that the necessary performance information is available. Once the executive budget is finalized, it is forwarded to the county's board of supervisors for adoption. Public hearings are used as the forum for citizen input in the budget process.

City of Hickory, North Carolina

The city of Hickory has been successful in creating a performance budget by developing a comprehensive performance management approach to service delivery. The city manager and the department heads are committed to mak-

Figure 3.5   **Budget Process for Fairfax County, Virginia**

BUDGET PROCESS

THE BUDGET CYCLE

The budget has several major purposes. It converts the County's long-range plans and policies into services and programs; serves as a vehicle to communicate these plans to the public; details the costs of County services and programs; and, outlines the revenues (taxes and fees) that support the County's services, including the rate of taxation for the coming fiscal year. Once the budget has been adopted by the Board of Supervisors, it becomes a work plan of objectives to be accomplished during the next fiscal year.

The annual Fairfax County budgetary process is an ongoing cyclical process simultaneously looking at two fiscal years (current and future). The budget year officially starts on July 1; however, the budget process itself is a continuum which involves both the current year budget and the next fiscal year's budget. Changes to the current year budget are made at the Third Quarter and Carryover Reviews. The Carryover Review both closes out the current year and revises the expenditure level for the subsequent year. These changes must be approved by the Board of Supervisors. During the fiscal year, quarterly reviews of revenue and expenditures are undertaken by the Department of Management and Budget, and any necessary adjustments are made to the budget. On the basis of these reviews, the Board of Supervisors revises appropriations. Public hearings are held prior to Board action when potential appropriation increases are greater than $500,000.

Citizen involvement and understanding of the budget are a key part of the review process. Public hearings on the County Executive's FY 2003 Advertised Budget Plan and the FY 2003–FY 2007 Capital Improvement Program (CIP) were held on April 8, 9 and 10, 2002.

The mark-up of the FY 2003 budget occurred on Monday, April 22, 2002, and the Board of Supervisors formally adopted the FY 2003 Budget Plan on Monday, April 29, 2002.

July

The End-of-Year Closeout
The end-of-year closeout finalizes actual expenditures for all agencies, and when necessary, the fiscal plan is adjusted to reconcile the actual expenditure amounts. Such adjustments are accomplished through reallocations or supplemental appropriations.

Carryover Review
Carryover represents the analysis of balances remaining from the prior year and provision for the appropriation of funds to cover the prior year's legal obligations (encumbered items) in the new fiscal year without loss of continuity in processing payments. Carryover extends the previous year funding for the purchase of specific items previously approved in the budget process, but for which procurement could not be obtained for various reasons. Funding for those items carried over can be expended without a second full-scale justification and approval procedure.

Source: Department of Management and Budget; see www.fairfaxcounty.gov.dmb.

BUDGET PROCESS

THE BUDGET CYCLE

September

Budget Submissions
Agencies submit their budget requests for the upcoming fiscal year to the Department of Management and Budget in two parts: the baseline request and the addendum, which includes program expansions and other requests beyond the budget development criteria.

Board of Supervisors' Action on the Carryover Review
Carryover revisions represent the first formal revision to the current year Adopted Budget. After public hearings to allow County citizens to voice their opinions on potential Carryover adjustments, the Board of Supervisors takes action on the Carryover Review as submitted by the County Executive.

September through November

Review of Budget Submissions
The Department of Management and Budget reviews each agency's budget submission and provides recommendations to the County Executive. These recommendations consist of expenditure analyses and evaluations of agency goals, objectives, and performance measures. This review culminates in an agency narrative, which is included in a package forwarded to the County Executive for review and decision, and ultimately published in the Advertised Budget Plan.

December through Early January

Department of Management and Budget
The Department of Management and Budget finalizes recommendations on upcoming fiscal year requirements. These recommendations are forwarded to the County Executive, the Deputy County Executives, the Chief Financial Officer and the Chief Information Officer.

Senior Management Meetings
The County Executive meets with the Senior Management Team to discuss budget issues and priorities for the upcoming year and beyond.

County Executive Meetings
The County Executive, Deputy County Executives, Chief Financial Officer, Chief Information Officer and Department of Management and Budget staff meet to discuss budget recommendations.

BUDGET PROCESS

THE BUDGET CYCLE

February

The County Executive releases the upcoming year's Advertised Budget Plan, which summarizes estimated revenues, expenditures, transfers, agency goals, objectives and performance data. In addition, sections are included to show major budgetary/financial policies and guidelines used in the fiscal management of the County.

March through April

Third Quarter Review
In mid-March, Department of Management and Budget conducts the Third Quarter Review on the current year Revised Budget Plan including a line item analysis of expenditure requirements. The Department of Management and Budget's recommendations are forwarded to the County Executive for review and adjustment. The package is then forwarded to the Board of Supervisors for action.

Public Hearings
Public hearings are held on the upcoming year's Advertised Budget Plan, the Capital Improvement Program and the Third Quarter Review providing a forum for County citizens to voice their opinions.

Board of Supervisors' Action on the Third Quarter Review and the Advertised Budget Plan
After public hearings, the Board of Supervisors approves the Third Quarter Review. Included are revisions to current year revenue estimates, which are used as the basis for final adjustments to the next fiscal year's budget. Following the public hearings on the Advertised Budget Plan, the Board of Supervisors conducts a mark-up session in which adjustments to the Advertised Budget Plan are made.

Board of Supervisors' Action on the Adopted Budget Plan and Tax Rate
Following the mark-up session, the Board of Supervisors adopts the budget and establishes the tax rates for the upcoming year.

June

Adopted Budget Plan Distributed
Copies of the Adopted Budget Plan are distributed to all County agencies and made available at County libraries and at the Publications Center in the Government Center. The budget is also published on the Department of Management and Budget's website: http://www.fairfaxcounty.gov/dmb.

ing performance the primary focal point for the basic functions of management, including planning, organizing, staffing, budgeting, and evaluation. This approach is important to performance budgeting in two fundamental ways. First, it raises the level of professionalism, promoting open discussion of the successes and failures of service delivery. Second, it allows performance to enter budget deliberations beyond discussing a handful of performance measures associated with various dimensions of service delivery. In other words, performance is discussed in connection with organization-wide and programmatic goals, in comparison to historical, current, and projected outputs and outcomes, and with evaluation of programmatic services in regard to economy, efficiency, and effectiveness.

Hickory's budget development calendar is shown in Figure 3.6. It begins in the month of October with personnel and risk projections, two major expenditure areas in state and local government. Risk expenditures are often projected in the following five categories: property, workers' compensation, general liability, law enforcement liability, and public officials' liability. The budget manuals (guidelines) are distributed to department heads in November in preparation for the budget kick-off meeting. During the meeting, the city manager provides an overview of the budget development process and then distributes performance measurement diskettes. A potential benefit of distributing the performance measurement diskettes at the kick-off meeting as opposed to their distribution with the budget manuals is that it allows the manager to place special emphasis on performance management. It also allows performance from an organization-wide perspective to set the stage for budget preparation, a critical planning process in state and local government.

Several key components of the budget preparation process in Hickory occur in December. The costs associated with master plans and neighborhood plans are projected, the resources required to amortize current debt are determined, transfers and contingencies are calculated based on financial policy, and new position requests and reclassifications are reviewed by the human resources department according to the city's personnel ordinance. These budget adjustments provide the city manager with the necessary information to engage in meaningful conversation with department heads as they negotiate their budgets in January. Departments must enter their initial budget requests in the financial management system by January 11; however, budget adjustments continue during the remainder of the process.

The performance measurement diskettes are officially due in the budget office by March 8, as shown in Figure 3.6. However, performance information is relevant throughout each stage of the process. For example, performance drives the discussion during budget negotiation meetings between the city manager and department heads. Performance also is a major part of the annual council-staff workshop held in early March. This session is used to review the goals and strategies from an organization-wide perspective and to build consensus around the desired levels of service for all city programs. Therefore, staff members must be prepared to present historical and current levels of performance in addition to future targets. The final months of the budget calendar contain the public notice, the first and second readings for adopting the budget ordinance, and the notification of the approved tax rate.

Misconceptions About Performance Budgeting Programs

The premise of performance budgeting is not new. As discussed in chapter 2, it actually dates back to the early 1940s as a resource allocation methodology. However, the prospects of performance budgeting have been limited because it has traditionally been promoted as a stand-alone budgeting technique. Table 3.4 shows an example of performance budgeting for police patrol, using output measures and unit costs as the foundation for requesting a $24,000 increase in the proposed FY 1997–98 budget. Decision makers have the information they need to make sound business decisions regarding planning, staffing, and budgeting from the standpoint of performance management. This information does not make the decision for them. Performance data supplement the kinds of analysis that the line-item budget invites (focus on cost control, comparison of previous year's expenditures to current request), not to replace it.

Performance budgeting, therefore, is not some new budget format that takes the place of basic line-item budgeting. Line-item budgeting cannot be replaced. The chart of accounts forms the basis of the line-item budget, which is the basis for external reporting and auditing. Furthermore, line-item revenue and expenditure accounts must be reviewed in detail in order to accurately estimate revenues and to determine needed resources for service delivery. For example, budgeting on an aggregate basis or by unit cost as shown in Table 3.4 would not reveal that a source of a unit cost increase was a major cost increase in specific health insurance accounts, though that information is essential for responsible budget decision making. The line-item format does not prevent the police department from examining unit cost after the initial budget is prepared, but it is required to determine the base and isolate the source of cost changes. The line-item budget is no impediment to performance budgeting either. Performance budgeting expands line-item budgeting to include performance data. The state of Washington describes its budgeting process as a traditional line-item approach supplemented by elements of program, target, and performance budgeting. Had Washington tried to replace its line-item budget with a performance budget, we predict it would already have been abandoned as unworkable.

Figure 3.6   **Budget Process for the City of Hickory, North Carolina**

Budget Development Calendar

• **October 31**	Personnel expenditures projected by Human Resources
• **October 31**	Worker's Comp., Property and Liability insurance projected by Risk Management
• **November 20**	FY02-03 Budget Manuals distributed to departments
• **November 30**	Budget Kick-off Meeting in Council Chambers: Budget Development Process Overview. Performance Measurement Diskettes Distributed.
• **December 3**	Master Plan and Neighborhood Plan Costs are projected by the Executive Assistant over Development
• **December 3**	Debt projected by Finance (existing debt only)
• **December 3**	City Council Financial Policy expenditures (transfers and contingency) projected by Budget Office
• **December 3**	New position requests and reclassification requests due to Human Resources (per Personnel Ordinance)
• **December 3**	External appropriation request letters sent out
• **January 2 – 25**	Departments may request to meet with the City Manager to make additional budget requests or to negotiate budgets
• **January 11**	Departments to have entered FY02-03 operational budget requests into H.T.E. Requests to balance to your department's initial budget allocation.
	Departments to have entered FY02-03 capital budget requests into H.T.E.
• **January 18**	Projected revenues entered into H.T.E. by Budget Office
• **January 31**	External Appropriation requests due
• **January 31**	Fleet Management to review and make recommendations on new capital equipment requests
• **January 31**	City Engineer to review and make recommendations on capital construction requests
• **January 31**	Information Services Director to review and make recommendations on technology requests.

Source: Hickory, North Carolina, FY 2002–2003 Annual Operating Budget.

Budget Development Calendar

- **February 4**   Fee Schedule sent to departments for FY02-03 changes

- **February 15**   Board & Commission work plans due

- **February 19**   City Council Meeting:
                      External appropriation requests presented

- **February 22**   5-year CIP to be entered into H.T.E. by departments

- **February 27**   Departments to return FY02-03 Fee Schedule changes to
                      Budget Office

- **March 5**   City Council Meeting:
                      Board & Commission work plans presented

- **March 8**   Performance Measurement diskettes due to Budget Office
                      from departments

- **March 8**   City Manager's Recommended Budget balanced

- **April 16**   City Council Meeting:
                      Present City Manager's Recommended Budget
                      Call for public hearing on Recommended Budget

- **April 17**   Publish notice of public hearing and make a copy available
                      to news media in the County

- **May 7**   City Council Meeting:
                      Public Hearing on Recommended Budget
                      FY02-03 Budget approved on 1st reading

- **May 21**   City Council Meeting:
                      FY02-03 Budget adopted on 2nd reading

- **May 22**   Notification of tax rate sent to Tax Administrators in Burke,
                      Caldwell and Catawba Counties

- **May 22**   Notify organizations who requested appropriation of City
                      funds of funding status

- **July 1**   New fiscal year begins

Another misconception is that, somehow, placing performance measures in budget documents amounts to performance budgeting. Performance measures certainly enhance the professional look of budget documents, especially when the measures reflect program outputs and outcomes. Moreover, the budget document is an excellent venue for this kind of communication with citizens about resources and results. Reporting some measures of performance also might advance the government's case for the distinguished budget presenta-

Table 3.4

City of Bright, Sample Performance Budget

Fund: General   Department: Police   Activity: Patrolling

Function
The Patrol Division of the Police Department provides prevention, suppression, and detection of criminal activity and traffic law enforcement to residents of the city of Bright.

Program Comments
The Patrol Division responds directly to calls for service received at its headquarters and through the emergency number 911. This program proposes twenty full-time patrol officers and two sergeants. An increase of $24,000 is requested in this FY 1997–98 proposed budget.

Performance Measurement

Activity	Actual FY 1995–1996	Budget FY 1996–1997	Proposed FY 1997–1998
Patrolling residential areas (hours)	9,825	10,927	11,308
Patrolling business areas (hours)	10,570	10,925	12,215

Work Description

Activity	Actual FY 1995–1996	Budget FY 1996–1997	Proposed FY 1997–1998
Patrolling residential areas (hours)			
Unit: hours	9,825	10,927	11,308
Unit: cost	$13.571	$13.651	$13.885
Total cost	$133,335	$149,164	$157,012
Patrolling business areas (hours)			
Unit: hours	10,570	10,925	12,215
Unit: cost	$13.726	$13.866	$13.707
Total cost	$145,084	$151,486	$167,431

Source: Adapted from Jerome B. McKinney, *Effective Financial Management in Public and Nonprofit Agencies* (Westport, CT: Quorum Books, 1995).

tion award from the Government Finance Officers Association, an organization that has a genuine commitment to performance management. However, placing a set of performance measures on the program's budget page does not constitute performance budgeting. As Washington, Fairfax County, and the city of Hickory demonstrated, performance budgeting is defined by the use of performance data throughout the budget preparation process and by the commitment of decision makers to consider performance data when making resource allocation decisions.

A final misconception about performance budgeting is that it represents the sole methodology for making allocation decisions. Factors like prior year appropriations, current and projected fiscal constraints, and political mandates from elected officials are just as important to the budget preparation process as performance information. Performance budgeting is not a substitute for the necessary leadership it takes to prepare the annual operating budget. It is the expansion of the annual budget process to include elements of performance management, allowing state and local leaders to understand the performance impact of service delivery even when political and financial considerations dominate allocation decisions.

Conclusion

Performance budgeting combines operational and financial accountability. The failure of the Planning-Programming-Budgeting System (PPBS) described in chapter 2 illustrates the result of separating and budgeting systems. As summarized by experts on the subject, "the PPB[S] or program budget concentrates on the goal and impact aspects of the process, the performance budget on the throughput (activities and outputs), and the line-item or object budget on the goods and services furnished. It seems, then, what is needed is not a program structure budget that replaces existing budget formats, but one that supplements them by providing information on goal direction and impact."[20] That is just what we have described.

The following chapters on planning, performance measurement, benchmarking, and evaluation also cannot be approached as separate processes. The information derived from them informs the budget preparation process. As we describe in the final chapter, organizations must have the managerial capacity to deploy the tools of planning, performance measurement, benchmarking and evaluation if they truly embrace a performance-based approach to budgeting and service delivery.

We present performance budgeting as an extension of the line-item budgeting process in this chapter, not as a stand-alone process that replaces basic budgeting techniques. A government considering adopting a performance budgeting system needs to plan for it and confront issues of how it will integrate with the existing budget process. Ideally, some major changes early in the adoption process will decrease the amount of maintenance work required once the system is implemented. The following steps describe how that plan could proceed:

1. Create a program chart (similar to an organizational chart) for the organization.
2. Structure the chart of accounts to coincide with the programs. This

provides for program budgeting and sets the stage for a program-based approach to cost accounting.

3. Create missions, goals, objectives, and performance measures for programs of service delivery.

4. Use the annual budget process to collect budget requests and updated performance measures with expanded budget guidelines.

5. Focus on performance during budget workshops with senior managers and with elected officials, ensuring that performance is considered during the allocation process.

6. Manage the performance budgeting process over time, drawing upon the budget process, the performance measurement system, the financial management system, and the cost accounting system on a regular basis.

We stated in chapter 1 that performance budgeting begins with performance management in agencies, departments, and programs. Performance budgeting becomes reality when managers use performance as a basis for making managerial decisions during one of the major functions of management, the budget preparation process. A performance approach provides continuity of purpose for the daily management of service delivery and for the annual operating budget cycle in state and local government.

Appendix A

Cover Memorandum for Budget Instructions

STATE OF WASHINGTON

OFFICE OF FINANCIAL MANAGEMENT

Insurance Building, PO Box 43113 ● Olympia, Washington 98504-3113 ● (360) 902-0555

May 6, 2002

TO: Agency Directors
             Budget Officers

FROM: Marty Brown
             Director

SUBJECT: **2003–2005 Operating Budget Instructions**

The magnitude of last year's budget shortfall and the related impacts on future biennia called for a different approach to developing the upcoming biennial budget. Last fall, we asked agencies to reprioritize their services and look for ways to restructure and refocus government to fit within available means. Under great pressure and time constraints, agencies identified cuts to valuable, but lower priority programs, in order to preserve essential state services.

We are not finished with this task. Early forecasts for next biennium indicate that the state will once again face a significant gap between resources and service demands. Recognizing this challenge, the 2003–2005 budget instructions reflect Governor Locke's intent to build a budget that concentrates on core government functions. This means we are asking for more information about agencies' base level services, not just about the incremental changes that are being proposed.

Specifically, we need more detail about what services are delivered, who benefits, how much these services cost, and—most importantly—what results you expect to achieve. The budget instructions also call on you to prioritize your activities as higher, medium and lower priority, with at least one-third of the total agency expenditures in the lower priority category. This information is critical to our understanding of your agency's business. It also will serve as the means to analyze statewide functions and priorities. In the end, we think this approach will allow us to do a better job in arriving at budget decisions, and in explaining those decisions to the citizens of this state.

Budget pressures will put us all at risk of cuts in our maintenance level budgets. We ask that you be prepared to work with OFM analysts to identify cost-saving policy changes and lower-priority activities that can be cut or reshaped. It is also important to understand that the need to refocus services applies to all of state government—not just general fund activities.

Agency Directors
Budget Officers
May 6, 2002
Page 2

As you prepare new budget requests, work with the principles we outlined last fall:

- Define your most important, central missions
- Minimize impact on quality of life
- Maintain the social service safety net
- Maintain performance standards

In these instructions, you also will find the expectation that agencies pursue recognized financial management principles as part of their budget development strategy. OFM budget analysts will be talking to agencies about the application of best management practices, risk management strategies, and use of the state enterprise-wide view for information technology solutions. These strategies can help the state avoid significant costs, and OFM will ensure that agencies achieve all they can from these approaches before entertaining requests to maintain existing funding.

These are extraordinary times for Washington. Citizens across the state are coping with economic conditions that require them to rethink family budgets. The state should do no less. Our challenge is to match state governments highest priorities with available resources. In doing so, we not only meet our obligation to balance the budget, but also build a new foundation for state government that better serves the interests of its taxpayers now, and in years to come. Thank you for your help.

Source: www.ofm.wa.gov.

— Chapter 4 —

Planning for Performance

Planning is one of the basic functions of management; good managers always prepare for the future. Strategic planning is one of the most common forms of planning in public organizations, involving the creation of long-term goals, the adoption of courses of action, and the allocation of resources necessary to accomplish goals.[1] Planning typically occurs at one of two levels in state and local government. The first is the organization-wide level (the entire state or local government) to create broad goals for the organization. The second is the programmatic level (air quality monitoring, curbside garbage pickup) to create specific goals and objectives for service delivery. Planning at both levels provides the direction for the future by building on the past and is fundamental to the success of performance budgeting.

Research has demonstrated that strategic planning has been used in state and local government for productivity improvement and for policy and program direction.[2] This same research suggests that strategic planning can even be described as a successful management tool in the public sector, but hedges that future research is needed on the contextual uses of strategic planning for determining its impact on organizational culture, capacity, outcomes, and fiscal stress. This conclusion is extremely important to the connection between planning and performance budgeting. It is one thing for us to check the box on a national survey that we are engaged in strategic planning in our organizations, it is another to actually use the information derived from a strategic planning process to manage the daily activities of service delivery and to make resource allocation decisions during the budget preparation process. Another issue that complicates the effectiveness of strategic planning is the often-blurred relationship between the two levels of planning (organizational goals vs. programmatic goals) that states and local governments undertake.

The Planning-Programming-Budgeting System (PPBS) developed in the Defense Department, is an excellent example of how planning failed to support service delivery in any meaningful way for non-Defense agencies.[3] The problem was that non-Defense agencies were not supported with an overall strategic plan, so they relied on program memoranda for budget justification. By doing so, they substituted programmatic goals for organizational goals, and the link between the planning and budgeting reform that PPBS offered was broken.[4] We can learn from the failure of PPBS that effective planning must occur at both the organization-wide and programmatic levels, and there must be a relationship between the two if managers are expected to move beyond budget justification based on what they are currently doing to what they should be doing in response to organizational goals.

The Government Finance Officers Association (GFOA) endorses the work of the National Advisory Council on State and Local Budgeting (NACSLB) as a way to promote planning in state and local government.[5] The GFOA specifically included the following characteristics of the budget process in its recommended practice to adopt the NACLSB framework for improved state and local government budgeting:

1. Incorporate a long-term perspective;
2. Establish linkages to broad organizational goals;
3. Focus budget decisions on results and outcomes;
4. Involve and promote effective communication with stakeholders; and
5. Provide incentives to government management and employees.[6]

These characteristics attempt to overcome the problems inherent in the PPBS by starting with a budget process that is focused on a long-term perspective. This requires establishing organizational goals related to community, to priorities, to challenges, and to opportunities, and establishing programmatic goals based on types of services offered and factors that could affect their provision in the future.[7] It also requires that programs create both strategic goals and service delivery goals to effectively link planning at the programmatic level to broad organizational goals as provided in the second characteristic. Strategic goals are short-term goals to expand the capacity of programs and to help realize organizational goals, which often change when new elected officials and senior administrators enter the organization. Service delivery goals are long-term goals created from the program's mission statement and are supported with at least one quantifiable objective and one performance measure (see chapter 5 for more information on strategic goals and service delivery goals at the programmatic level).

The GFOA encourages organizations to focus their budget decisions on the results and outcomes of governmental programs, requiring performance measurement systems for tracking the performance of service delivery. Effective communication with stakeholders and incentives to managers and line employees are then used to make performance efforts relevant to the organizational culture. In essence, these characteristics help states and local governments overcome the tendency to use strategic planning as a means to look professional while they continue to do what they are already doing.[8]

Figure 4.1   **Town Council-Strategic Goals**

I. Traffic Management and Circulation

Address issues of community concern in areas of traffic management, enforcement, and circulation—including speeding, running of red lights, pedestrian safety, driver courtesy, cut through traffic, and other safety and traffic-flow concerns.

II. Retail Development

Identify a strategy for recruiting a department/variety store to locate within the town's corporate limits.

III. Upgrading Substandard Housing

Step up and consolidate enforcement of private property building maintenance, yard maintenance, control of trash and debris, occupancy restrictions, and other relevant issues that impact the quality of housing in neighborhoods throughout the town.

IV. Open Space Acquisition and Preservation

Implement a strategy including a financial plan that identifies and pursues acquisition and preservation of open space throughout the town consistent with the comprehensive plan.

V. Town Border Issues

Complimentary to the recent boundary adjustment agreement that impacted the southern boundary of the town and in accord with the Comprehensive Plan, work to ensure a seamless border between the town and the unincorporated county that will result in compatible land uses and the efficient provisions of public water and sewer services.

Source: Town of Blacksburg, Virginia, *FY 2000–2001 Adopted Operating Budget.*

Figure 4.1 presents a partial list of organization-wide goals in the FY 2000–2001 annual operating budget for the town of Blacksburg, Virginia. These goals address common issues faced by municipalities, including traffic management, retail development, substandard housing, and open space. Each goal is then supported with broad strategies for accomplishment, reconciling with the long-term perspective promoted by the GFOA. For example, upgrading standard housing includes enforcement of private property building maintenance and control of trash and debris.

The town of Blacksburg's budget document also contains accomplishments-to-date and strategic goals by programmatic unit. Their strategic goals link to the organization-wide goals, reconciling with the GFOA's recommended practice. What is missing, however, are service delivery goals, quantifiable objectives, and performance measures by programmatic unit, which would allow budget decisions to be made in part on the results and outcomes of service delivery. This means that additional planning work is needed to completely satisfy the practices supported by the NACSLB and the GFOA. Although planning at both levels is strongly preferred, the absence of one should not prevent the other from occurring. For example, if the organization does not have a strategic plan, this should not prevent planning at the programmatic level for creating mission statements, service delivery goals, quantifiable objectives, and performance measures (planning at the programmatic level is presented in the following chapter on performance measurement).

This chapter describes how strategic planning can be used to move beyond simply documenting what a government is doing to documenting progress toward what the government wants to be doing, including how organizations are using planning in their performance budgeting programs. It begins by discussing the basic steps to strategic planning. Examples of how organizations have produced meaningful and useful strategic plans to enhance the budgetary process are presented from the state of Oregon, the county of Dakota, Minnesota, and the city of Scottsdale, Arizona. This discussion also includes how these plans link overall organizational goals to the daily management functions of service delivery. This section of the chapter concludes with a revised process for strategic planning.

The second section of the chapter is dedicated to the balanced scorecard approach to planning, providing a methodology to link planning efforts at all levels of the organization to the performance budgeting program. To be frank, the limited research on the balanced scorecard tends to take the form of promotion as opposed to description, due in part to the limited number of public organizations that have adopted the technique.[9] The balanced scorecard transforms organizational goals derived from strategic planning into an action plan divided into four quadrants: financial accountability, internal business processes, innovation and learning, and customers. Agencies, departments, and programs use this action plan for reconciling their strategic goals and service delivery goals with the overall direction of the organization. Performance measurement systems are then used to track organizational and programmatic progress over time. The premise is this: program improvements across the organization accumulate into overall improvement at the organization-wide level, allowing the organization to move in the direction identified in the strategic plan by building on the interrelated connections of strategy, action, budgeting, and performance. Another reason that we chose to present the balanced scorecard approach in this chapter on planning is that managers make decisions, either formally or informally, on multiple organizational dimensions as opposed to a single dimension.

The final section of this chapter offers a discussion on citizen perception and satisfaction, expanding on the customer perspective of the balanced scorecard approach to managing service delivery. It includes common problems faced by state and local government officials when they try to gauge the perception of citizens toward public services, including whether citizen survey results reconcile with internal administrative outcome measures of service delivery. Two case studies are used to expand the discussion of citizen surveys, one from Auburn, Alabama, and another from St. Charles, Illinois. Citizen perception and satisfaction are presented in this chapter because of their relationship with the balanced scorecard and because of their growing importance among public organizations for augmenting strategic planning processes and for promoting the use of external outcome data with performance budgeting.

Strategic Planning

A strategic planning process can start with a one-day retreat for elected officials, or a comprehensive forum for elected officials, citizens, administrators, and other interested parties. Some planning efforts are organized and directed on an informal basis while others are planned in detail and guided by professional facilitators. The growing literature on governance suggests that comprehensive, community-based planning is an effective approach for incorporating citizen input into the strategic plan. Other research has demonstrated that there is a correlation between employee participation in the strategic planning process and job satisfaction.[10] However, employees should be included in the process for reasons beyond job satisfaction. The employees who actually deliver the services are the most familiar with the policies and procedures surrounding service delivery. They have an in-depth understanding of the internal environment of operation that an executive does not. They also understand the financial condition of the program because change often requires additional resources for implementation.

What we know about strategic planning is that a large number of public organizations embrace it as a management tool and that they follow some standard approach as presented in Table 4.1. The process begins with initiating and agreeing on a strategic planning process and ends with an organizational vision for the future. What we do not know about strategic planning is why some organizations embrace it while others do not, how the general process is tailored to fit the individual needs of the organization, and how the plan is used once the process is completed. Therefore, the general process presented in Table 4.1 should be approached with an understanding that strategic planning can look very different based on the individual needs of each organization. Another factor that complicates the situation is the role of organizational and managerial capacity, which directly impacts the breadth

Table 4.1

An Effective Strategic Planning Approach

Step 1   Initiating and agreeing on a strategic planning process
Step 2   Identifying organizational mandates
Step 3   Clarifying organizational mission and values
Step 4   Assessing the external environment: opportunities and threats
Step 5   Assessing the internal environment: strengths and weaknesses
Step 6   Identifying the strategic issues facing an organization
Step 7   Formulating strategies to manage the issues
Step 8   Establishing an effective organizational vision for the future

Source: John M. Bryson, *Strategic Planning for Public and Nonprofit Organizations* (San Francisco, CA: Jossey-Bass, 1988).

and depth of the strategic plan and the likelihood of it becoming a meaningful part of the organizational culture. This requires leadership from both elected officials and from administrators.

Many organizations report that hiring a skilled facilitator was an important factor in a successful strategic planning process, especially when the individuals involved in the process have varied interests.[11] Elected officials may have one vision for the government, while employees and line managers view the whole organization through the prism of their program or service. Interest groups almost certainly have narrow concerns, and community activists typically have issue or geographic biases. An outside facilitator is extremely useful in establishing the ground rules of the process, assisting with identifying the stakeholders of the process and why they should or should not be included, and tailoring the general process of strategic planning to fit the individual needs of the organization. Facilitators are also beneficial in building consensus around the purpose of producing a strategic plan, how it will be used, and the organizational vision that emanates from the process.

State of Oregon

The two strategic planning processes conducted by the state of Oregon highlight the fact that each planning process has unique characteristics even when they are undertaken by the same organization. Oregon has received national recognition for its efforts in the areas of strategic planning and benchmarking. The first plan—*Oregon Shines: An Economic Strategy for the Pacific Century (Oregon Shines I)*—was put together by 150 business and community leaders under the direction of the governor and was released in 1989. Here is a brief description of the process:

The planning process they adopted included some regional meetings but was driven primarily by a series of committees that worked on detailed recommendations in designated problem areas. The plan they created described three strategic initiatives: (1) a superior workforce, (2) an attractive quality of life, and (3) an international frame of mind. In the following year the state legislature adopted several of the plan's recommendations. . . . The state legislature also created the Oregon Progress Board to monitor benchmarks to determine if the state was moving toward the *Oregon Shines I* vision.[12]

The process used by the state to produce its first strategic plan was a top-down approach, producing detailed recommendations. The advantage of the top-down approach was that the legislature was motivated to act on many of the specific concerns presented in the plan. However, the legislature did not stop there. It also created the Oregon Progress Board to measure the benchmarks or performance targets established in the plan to monitor progress toward the state's three strategic initiatives. Oregon's process raises some important questions about the relationship between strategic planning and performance budgeting. (Does a top-down approach to strategic planning engender support from elected officials who have the most influence over the budget process? Should the creation of benchmarks or performance targets include state program managers who understand service delivery, or elected officials, or performance "experts," or some combination of the three? Did Oregon's process result in planning at the organization-wide level and at the programmatic level all at once?) The answers to these questions would probably vary among the actors involved in *Oregon Shines I* and among the advocates of planning in general. Regardless, it represents a major planning initiative for state government and provides a framework for making allocation decisions based on some notion of performance.

The governor of the state of Oregon formed a forty-six-member Oregon Shines Task Force in 1996 to update the original plan. The process used for the second iteration of the state's strategic plan differed in several ways, including the following: (1) significant university involvement, (2) analysis of benchmarks established in *Oregon Shines I*, (3) a bottom-up approach, and (4) broad recommendations rather than specific tactics.[13] Table 4.2 contains an overview of a goal presented in *Oregon Shines II*.

One of the major differences between Oregon's two reports is that the first contained hundreds of specific and detailed recommendations. The second report took a broader approach. Two advantages to the broader approach are that it allows for an evolving action plan for implementation and that it is based on the individual planning activities of state agencies. For example, an

Table 4.2

Oregon's Strategic Plan

	Goal 2: Safe, caring, and engaged community
Finding	In spite of Oregon's economic turnaround, government social service agencies and nonprofit organizations have seen an increasing number of more complex cases in the 1990s. Poverty and criminal behavior have not declined. Changes in American society are placing a variety of stresses on families.
Solution	Oregon must address the root causes of social problems through local, targeted projects with shared responsibility for improved outcomes.
Values	Family life is at the top of our list of personal values, while civic affairs are near the bottom.
Vision	Oregon will be a place where all families and individuals can prosper.
Objectives	• All aspects of society will encourage responsible parenting and adult mentoring of children. • Oregon will be a leader in developing state and local partnerships that address the root causes of social problems. • Oregon will prevent crime by emphasizing cost-effective prevention programs that avoid future incarceration costs. • Oregon will be a leader in reducing personal abuse and protecting vulnerable individuals. • More Oregonians will be healthy and self-sufficient. • More Oregonians will actively participate in strengthening their communities.
Key benchmarks	• High school dropout rate • Eighth grade use of alcohol, illicit drugs, and cigarettes • Incomes below 100 percent of federal poverty level • Overall reported crimes • Reported child abuse • Oregonians without health insurance • Volunteerism

Source: Oregon Progress Board and governor's Oregon Shines Task Force, *Oregon's Strategic Plan* (A Report to the People of Oregon, January 21, 1997).

objective listed in Table 4.2 is that Oregon will be a leader in developing state and local partnerships that address the root causes of social problems, followed by benchmarks on high school dropout rates and eighth grade use of alcohol, illicit drugs, and cigarettes. State agencies that work in these areas are now responsible for identifying strategic goals to specifically address this overall state strategy. Performance measures are used to track progress toward quantifiable objectives and used for justifying new budget requests (performance budgeting). The key benchmarks at the state level are monitored over time to determine if the goals and objectives of state agencies are having an impact on reaching the objectives contained within the strategic plan.

Dakota County, Minnesota

The Board of Commissioners of Dakota County, Minnesota, undertook a planning initiative in 1997 to create a mission statement and organizational goals for the county. The mission of Dakota County government is *to provide efficient, effective, responsive government dedicated to contributing to a vital economy, safe communities, healthy families, and a quality physical environment.*[14] A retreat for county commissioners and senior county managers was used as the forum for the planning process.[15] The process did not include interest group or direct citizen input, which may or may not be a limitation of the process, depending on one's perspective. Some would say that planning based primarily on the direction of elected officials results in a representative strategic plan similar to representative democracy. Others would say that the priorities of elected officials, and particularly their time horizons, may not fully represent the interests of service providers or service recipients.

The strategic plan produced by Dakota County was not based on a specific timeframe but was left open for deliberation by future county boards. In February 2001, the Board of Commissioners reconfirmed its commitment to the mission of the county and issued a report on the progress being made with regard to organizational goals. This technique is certainly efficient in that it does not require another planning process. The effectiveness of this technique can be questioned given the lack of involvement from stakeholders beyond elected officials. Table 4.3 contains information taken from the report issued in 2001.

The organization-wide goals are used as the starting point for the annual budget process in Dakota County, providing the background for resource allocation. Departments are then required to support their proposed budgets with outcome measures. However, there is no link between the information derived from departments and the overall goals of the organization. The Office of Planning, Evaluation, and Development is working on this connection and is identifying ways to use performance measures for making more decisions during the budget preparation process. One approach has been to conduct program evaluations for making recommendations on service delivery improvement, using the strategic plan as the basis for selecting programs for review.

Table 4.3

Dakota County's Planning and Progress Report

Mission	The Board of Commissioners made it the mission of Dakota County government to provide efficient, effective, responsive government dedicated to contributing to a vital economy, safe communities, healthy families, and a quality physical environment.
Measuring success	The Dakota County Board of Commissioners has defined a series of measures of success in achieving its vision for the future of Dakota County and for measuring how well county government is achieving its mission.
Social goals	Success in providing safe, healthy, vital communities is measured by the following social indicators: • Thriving children • Safe communities • Healthy communities • Fully informed and involved communities
Tracking progress	Dakota County is a safe place to work and live.
Measures	• Part I and Part II crime rate, state and county • Part I and Part II arrest rate in Dakota County • Residents who feel safe walking after dark

Source: Dakota County, *Dakota County Indicators 2001: Measuring Progress* (Dakota County, MN: Author, 2001).

Scottsdale, Arizona

One of the most effective ways to link strategic planning with the budgetary process was developed by the city of Scottsdale, Arizona, in 1994. What is unique about this process is that, unlike a one-time planning process, it is ongoing, flexible, and responsive. The advantages of this approach are that the strategies of the organization are updated at least annually, that the strategies drive the budget process, and that the strategies are linked to a performance measurement system. A possible disadvantage is the absence of a long-term strategic plan and the lack of consistency over an extended period of time. On the other hand, budget preparation occurs annually and performance data are available to support a performance budget. Figure 4.2 illustrates the strategic budget process used by the city of Scottsdale.

The process begins with stakeholder input, which requires feedback from citizens, elected officials, and staff members. A point of interest in this step

Figure 4.2   **City of Scottsdale Strategic Budget Process**

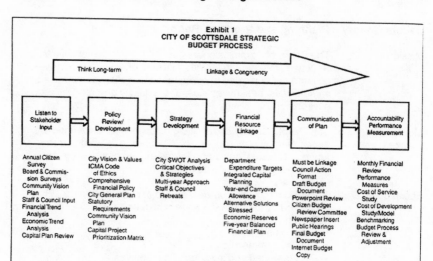

Source: Craig Clifford, "Linking Strategic Planning and Budgeting in Scottsdale, Arizona," *Government Finance Review* 14 (August 1998): 9–14.

is the introduction of economic and financial trend analysis. Trend analysis allows key decision makers to evaluate stakeholder input in the context of financial capacity by analyzing both the external (citizen) and internal (employees) environments. Policy review and development occurs in the second step of the process, which includes the statutory requirements of the organization. A common argument against a planning process is that statutory requirements dictate the services that must be provided by public organizations, so that any planning effort amounts to decision making at the margins. On the other hand, there is more than a little difference between how and whether to provide a service. Planning efforts should acknowledge the former (the city will always field a police force) and concentrate on the latter (what methods of policing are consistent with the city's mission and provide good service to citizens).

The final step in the process is accountability with performance measurement, including the evaluation process that is often omitted in many strategic planning processes. Scottsdale's process is one of the most comprehensive for linking strategy directly to resource allocation, providing the foundation for performance budgeting. Another notable aspect of Scottsdale's process is that strengths and weaknesses of the strategic budgeting process are identified to continually improve upon the program's success.[16]

Looking Forward

The strategic planning examples presented for Oregon, Dakota County, and Scottsdale illustrate what we know and don't know about strategic planning in state and local government. All three governments used their strategic planning processes to produce a document, but the similarities don't extend much farther. Each process had different formats, different participants, different results and different benefits for the government. When researchers try to understand how governments use strategic planning, their methods are limited to case studies and surveys. Case studies provide the detail necessary to understand how the government used the process and what it accomplished, but the results are often not generalizable to other governments. Surveys can provide useful estimates of how many governments use strategic planning and what characteristics they share, but they cannot capture the kind of information that most practitioners want—what worked, what did not, and why. We need more research on strategic planning now that the process has become widely used, but we have a few guidelines that seem to be applicable to every process. Hatry identified some characteristics of effective strategic plans:

1. Identify the specific outcomes sought, the associated indicators against which progress will be measured, and the latest available data on the current values for each of these indicators (to provide a baseline for later determining feasible out-year targets and for subsequently measuring progress). It is surprising how seldom this information is included in strategic plans.
2. Posit the future environment within which the service is expected to operate, including likely problems and obstacles.
3. Identify alternative ways to achieve the desired outcomes, including any needed changes in legislation and policies.
4. Estimate each alternative's cost, feasibility, and potential effect on the outcomes—in the future environment.
5. Select a recommended alternative along with the outcome indicators.
6. Link all these elements to the annual [action] plan and forthcoming budgets.[17]

A successful strategic planning process is tailored to the individual needs of the organization. However, we think a combination of the process in Table 4.1 with Hatry's elements for meaningful strategic planning is a good approach. We review it in seven steps:

Step 1. *Initiating and Agreeing on Process.* How you start often influences where you end up. The chief administrator is usually responsible for initiating and building consensus for conducting a strategic plan, but other top officials such as governors, mayors, and senior managers are important partners in planning. The governor took the lead in the initial and follow-up process for the state of Oregon. If there is no consensus for the process, or if there is no willingness to change direction based on the results of the plan, the effort will be wasted. Once the consensus to plan is achieved, consensus on how the process will be conducted is the next hurdle. This includes identifying the stakeholders involved, the timeframe needed for completion, the goal of the strategic plan and how it will be used, who will facilitate the process, how decisions will be made, and what use will be made of the results. For example, the city of Scottsdale used its planning process primarily for driving the annual budget process for performance budgeting.

Step 2. *Mission and Values.* This step asks what purpose the organization serves. Organizational missions in the public sector normally contain vague language about providing the highest quality of services with the most efficient and effective means possible. Values often include statements of professionalism, customer service, equity, and teamwork. Mission and values have two fundamental roles in public organizations. First, they guide the organization in how services are provided. Second, they determine where the organization is headed (mission) and suggest the ground rules (values) on how to get there. The mission of Dakota County is to "provide efficient, effective, and responsive government and to be a premier county in which to live and work." The values of the city of Scottsdale are "plan and innovate for the future; listen, communicate, and take action; respect the individual; collaborate as a team; learn and grow continuously; focus on quality customer service; be accountable and act with integrity; and show caring and compassion for others."

Step 3. *SWOT.* This step forces an organization to identify its strengths (S), weaknesses (W), opportunities (O), and threats (T). It reconciles with steps 4 and 5 in Table 4.1 and with the element proposed by Hatry where organizations examine the future environment within which they will operate. The state of Oregon expanded their process for the second round of strategic planning after university faculty participants identified the major forces of change in the state over the next several years. The city of Scottsdale put SWOT in the strategy development phase of its strategic budget process. This approach often increases the amount of time needed for conducting a strategic plan depending on how comprehensive the organization is with the SWOT process. A SWOT process can be beneficial to an organization as a stand-alone exercise, as well as in conjunction with a strategic plan.

Step 4. *Organizational Mandates.* Most public organizations are required by law to provide certain services. Identifying organizational mandates provides the foundation for the strategic plan. Mandates may be imposed by statute, ordinance, administrative rule, or legal ruling. They may be limited to identifying required services, or setting standards of service quality, or perhaps even describing how certain services must be provided. The strategic planning process in Table 4.1 identifies organizational mandates in Step 2 of the process. We recommend identifying organizational mandates in Step 4 to minimize their impact on mission and values and on the SWOT process. In other words, we believe mandates should be considered in the planning process, but the planning process should not be structured around mandates. Scottsdale places statutory requirements in the policy review/development stage of its strategic planning process.

Step 5. *Identifying Outcomes.* This step contains the goals, strategies, performance measures, and benchmarks (performance targets) of the process at the organization-wide level. Oregon, Dakota County, and Scottsdale have all emphasized this step, as is shown by their processes and outcomes. However, Hatry suggests that few public organizations move beyond the goals portion of this step.[18] What is needed is an evaluation of the current performance of the organization, benchmarks or performance targets for improvement, and potential strategies for improvement. This takes planning to a new level for many public organizations.

Step 6. *Alternatives and Strategies.* This step is an extension of Step 5, identifying alternatives and strategies for accomplishment based on the desired outcomes. A major consideration in this step is cost feasibility. Dakota County uses outcomes from its strategic plan as the first step in the annual budget process, so cost feasibility is always a concern. Scottsdale uses the financial resource linkage phase of its process to analyze alternative solutions, an approach similar to Dakota County. Oregon provided detailed recommendations in its first planning process. It provided only goals, objectives, measures, and benchmarks in its second strategic plan, using a separate process for identifying alternatives, strategies, and financial resources for accomplishment.

Step 7. *Strategic Plan.* The final step is to produce the strategic plan, but the end of the process is just the beginning of the real work, linking the information in the strategic plan to the annual (action) plan and to forthcoming budgets. Scottsdale's process is designed specifically for this link. It plans for performance budgeting. However, there is another reason for using an action plan. It sets the stage for bottom-up performance budgeting as well.

An annual (action) plan offers a connection between the strategic plan at the organization-wide level and the plans that support agency and departmental budgets. The reason that this connection is often blurred in state and local government is that the two are approached with different time horizons by different actors, who often have different goals. Strategic planning is focused on long-term goals, and strategies of the organization, which are often determined by elected officials based on factors external to the organization, are broad and far-reaching, and remain constant over time. Program planning, especially as related to the annual budget process, is focused on short-term strategic goals, which are often determined by program managers, specific in nature, constantly changing, and significantly impacted by internal factors. An action plan provides an intermediate planning process for linking long-term and short-term perspectives.

There are a number of approaches to action planning; we like the balanced scorecard. The GFOA defines the balanced scorecard as a management improvement system and framework that utilizes financial and nonfinancial information for enhancing organizational goals, objectives, performance measurement, and operational strategies by assessing organizational performance across four dimensions: financial accountability, internal business processes, innovation and learning, and customers.[19] The following section describes the balanced scorecard, then uses Charlotte, North Carolina, as an illustration of how, with an annual action plan based on the balanced scorecard, a public organization can make the connection between organization-wide and programmatic planning.[20]

Balanced Scorecard

Senior managers in state and local government operate in a complex and demanding environment. On one side, elected officials are engaged in policy making, strategic planning, and resource allocation. They are pushing senior managers, both formally and informally, to adopt their mandates for moving the organization in the direction they want and believe best serves their constituents. On the other side, program managers are pulling on senior managers for additional resources, for assistance with direction and control, and for handling daily problems of service delivery. The senior manager cannot make good decisions if he/she limits his/her attention to the push or pull factions. He or she needs a way to understand how a decision on one dimension of the organization impacts other dimensions of the organization, that is, a system for placing multiple dimensions into a manageable context.

Kaplan and Norton introduced the balanced scorecard approach in 1992 as a method to avoid an information overload on senior managers by identifying the four dimensions shown in Figure 4.3.[21] Although the balanced scorecard was created for the private sector, it provides public organizations with a methodology for placing the different levels of planning into the four major areas of management.

Figure 4.3 **The Balanced Scorecard: Linking Strategy and Performance**

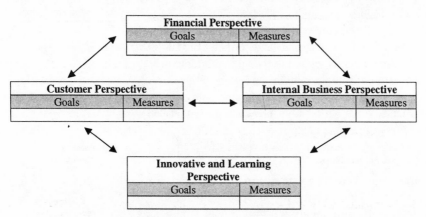

Source: Robert S. Kaplan and David P. Norton, "The Balanced Scorecard—Measures That Drive Performance," *Harvard Business Review* (January–February 1992): 71–79.

The strength of the balanced scorecard lies in the connections between the four major quadrants of service delivery, requiring a multiple dimension approach to strategy formulation. For example, an internal process like emergency 911 response to calls from citizens could be improved with an investment of resources in communication technology and personnel. However, there are other organizational issues to consider. Will this investment impact the financial condition of the organization? Will other internal processes be impacted by this investment of resources? Will customers (citizens) recognize this investment in the quality of their service? Will employees need training to manage the new technology? The answers to these questions link organization-wide strategy to daily management of service delivery. It also sets the stage for performance budgeting, allowing organizational and programmatic outcomes to drive budget deliberations.

Figure 4.4 provides an overview of the strategy development cycle used by the city of Charlotte. It begins with an annual retreat used to create new strategy, to review and change existing strategy, and to review and validate existing strategy, reconciling with the strategic planning process at the organization-wide level. More work invested in the planning process at this stage allows an organization to create priorities that will last over an extended period of time. This holds true for the performance measurement process as well. The more effort invested in creating good performance measures, the less likely they will have to be changed or adjusted from one reporting period to another. The second step in the process converts strategy into an action plan. The four quadrants of the scorecard are updated along with

Figure 4.4   **City of Charlotte's Annual Planning Cycle**

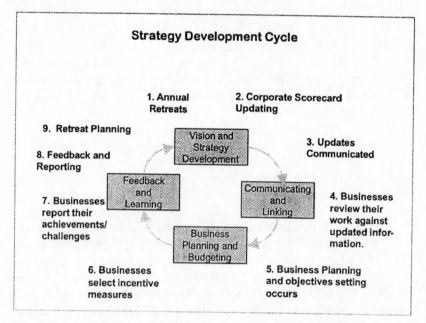

Source: City of Charlotte, North Carolina, *Year-End FY 2001 Corporate Performance Report.*

strategies, measures, targets, and achievements contained within each. This phase of the process is called *vision and strategy development.*

After the scorecard is updated and communicated to the stakeholders in Step 3, businesses (departments and programs) reconcile their goals, objectives, strategies, measures, and processes against the new, updated, and existing overall direction of the organization in Steps 4 and 5. This phase of the process is known as *communicating and linking*, which includes where planning at both the organization-wide and programmatic levels is connected. The next phase of the process is *business planning and budgeting*, moving from Step 5 to Step 6 where programs select incentive measures of achievement. The budget has to accommodate both the strategies for program improvement and the incentives for achievement. Incentives may come in a variety of forms, from greater training opportunities, increased resources for program activities, or individual salary incentives. Charlotte directly rewards employee performance based on program performance, giving its employees annual bonuses if performance goals are met.

The last phase of the process is *feedback and learning*, including achievement reporting and retreat planning. The information derived from this phase creates an annual baseline to track organizational performance from the four quadrants of the balanced scorecard, which is determined by the performance of individual departments and programs. This baseline is then used for retreat planning, which drives strategy change and validates the process from the stakeholder perspective. The process is then repeated the following fiscal year as information is constantly collected and reported from departments and programs.

Financial Quadrant

The first quadrant of the balanced scorecard approach is the financial perspective, the cornerstone of accountability for state and local government. It contains budgetary implications from a policy perspective, financial implications from a controlling and reporting perspective, management implications from a decision-making perspective, and planning implications from a fiscal stability perspective.

Figure 4.5 shows the four major strategic areas of the financial perspective for Charlotte, including secure funding/service partners, maximize benefit/cost, grow tax base, and maintain AAA bond rating. The strategy behind the secure funding/service partners is to extend city resources and diversify the revenue portfolio by partnering with businesses, nonprofit organizations, and community members for programs and service provision and by maximizing revenues from federal, state, and other local agencies. The measure for the strategy is property tax revenue as a percentage of total city revenues. The target is to maintain property tax revenue as a percentage of total city revenues at 20 percent or below. The city reported that property tax revenue comprised 16.2 percent of total city revenues in FY 2002, a decrease from 18.5 percent in FY 2001.

Figure 4.5 also highlights some other activities that helped the city realize its overall target of maintaining property tax revenue as a percentage of total city revenues at 20 percent or below. As you can see, Charlotte was awarded several major grants, is negotiating a regional wastewater treatment plant and collection system, and has a public/private revenue ratio of approximately 1:8. Figure 4.5 includes a graph constructed by the Community Relations Committee to highlight its efforts over the past three years. This information is used not only to report the success of the city, it is used as a planning tool in preparation of the annual retreats to update the overall goals of the organization.

Financial accountability, however, does not stop with the four strategic goals established by the city of Charlotte. One major area of financial accountability is budget compliance by departments and by funds, requiring that program managers remain within their annual budgets so that the city

Figure 4.5   City of Charlotte's Balanced Scorecard—Financial Quadrant

Secure Funding/ Service Partners	Maximize Benefit Cost	Grow Tax Base	Maintain AAA Rating

Highlights:

- The City was awarded two grants totaling $400,000 for the Charlotte-Mecklenburg Development Corporation's efforts to develop an inner-city business park on Wilkinson Boulevard. The City also helped secure a $750,000 grant to the Workforce Development Board to determine the best process for implementing the Workforce Investment Act locally.

- Operating agreements and governance documents are being developed with Union County and the Water and Sewer Authority of Cabarrus County to construct and operate a regional wastewater treatment plant and collection system. This is an example of regional cooperation to develop additional treatment capacity for underdeveloped areas in the drainage basin.

- Neighborhood Development leverages public money with private money, typically consisting of bank loans and owner equity. Using $3.5 million of public money, $28.9 million of private investment funding was leveraged in FY2001. The public/private investment ratio was 1:8.24, just exceeding the target ratio of 1:8. The public money was derived from the HouseCharlotte program, CWAC Equity Loan program, and other housing loan programs.

- Several City business units worked with Mecklenburg County and the U. S. Environmental Protection Agency to obtain a $100,000 grant for a regional environmental demonstration project. This project has enabled the City and County to use federal resources to help improve regional understanding, communication, and governance of environmental issues.

- The Community Relations Committee obtained a total of $315,143 in federal, state, and private grant revenue for its Dispute Settlement Program, enforcement of the Fair Housing Ordinances, and support of community awards programs. This total is a 222% increase from FY2000 and significantly exceeds the FY2001 target of $119,293.

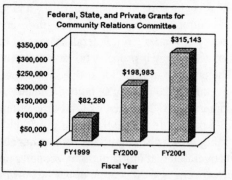

Source: City of Charlotte, North Carolina, *Year-End FY 2001 Corporate Performance Report.*

stays within its budget at the general fund level (e.g., general fund). Another major area of financial accountability is fiscal stability, or tracking the performance of the organization's financial operations from the annual financial statements. This is an excellent way to supplement the financial quadrant of the balanced scorecard. The city of Charlotte uses its bond rating as a proxy for fiscal stability insofar as rating agencies use an organization's financial operating results as a major factor for establishing bond ratings for

Table 4.4

Factors That Drive Bond Rating Changes

Credit factor	Potential rating change drivers
Economy	• Significant development in the local tax base driving continued growth in total property values • Increased or decreased diversification of local economic base • Loss of key industry or employer with no workout plan
Finances	• Expected augmentation or loss of financial flexibility • Expectation that significant growth or decline of reserves will continue
Debt	• Significant increase in debt obligations without correlating development to offset tax-base leveraging • Utilization of debt structure not appropriately matched to asset's useful life
Administration/ management strategies	• Implementation of new strategies that are expected to augment or to detract from operating flexibility • Change in political environment that affects ability to react to unanticipated events

Source: Linda Hird Lipnick, Yaffa Rattner, and Linda Ebrahim, *The Determinants of Credit Quality* (New York: Moody's Investors Service, 1999).

public organizations. Table 4.4 presents factors that impact an organization's bond rating.

It is interesting to note that the factors located in Table 4.4 go well beyond the financial operating results of the organization as reported by the augmentation or loss of financial flexibility and the significant growth or decline of reserves. Bond ratings are influenced by the administrative capacity and management strategies of the organization. Rating agencies predict whether the implementation of new strategies will enhance or detract from operating flexibility. For example, public organizations often look for economic development opportunities as a means to diversify the local economic base.

Another approach to supplement the financial quadrant of the balanced scorecard is to track and analyze financial trends internally, using a methodology like the ten-point test located in Table 4.5. Similar to the balanced scorecard approach, this test transforms a large amount of financial data into a manageable format that allows senior managers to communicate the financial condition of the organization to the elected officials and to the citizens.[22] The data needed to calculate the ratios in Table 4.5 are taken from the annual financial statements produced by state and local governments. This is why it is extremely important for public organizations to receive a favorable (or

Table 4.5

Ten Key Ratios of Financial Condition

Ratio	Explanation	Interpretation
Total revenues / Population	Total revenues is the total revenues for all governmental funds.	A low ratio suggests a greater ability to acquire additional revenue.
Total general fund revenues from own sources / Total general fund revenues	Total general fund revenues from own sources is the difference between total general fund revenues and amounts classified in the general fund as intergovernmental revenues.	A high ratio suggests the city is not reliant on external governmental organizations.
General fund sources from other funds / Total general fund sources	General fund sources from other funds is general fund operating transfers in. Total general fund sources is the total of general fund revenues and operating transfers in.	A low ratio suggests the city does not have to rely on operating transfers to finance general government operations in the general fund.
Operating expenditures / Total expenditures	Operating expenditures is the total expenditures for the general, special revenue, and debt service funds. Total expenditures is the total expenditures for all governmental funds.	A low ratio suggests the city experienced a positive interperiod equity.
Total revenues / Total expenditures	Total revenues is the total revenues for all governmental funds. Total expenditures is the total expenditures for all governmental funds.	A high ratio suggests the city experienced a positive interperiod equity.
Unreserved general fund balance / Total general fund revenues	Unreserved general fund balance is the total of both unreserved designated and unreserved undesignated fund balance for the general fund.	A high ratio suggests the presence of resources that can be used to overcome a temporary shortfall in revenues.

Total general fund cash and investments / Total general fund liabilities	The components are self-explanatory.	A high ratio suggests sufficient cash with which to pay short-term obligations.
Total general fund liabilities / Total general fund revenues	The components are self-explanatory.	A low ratio suggests short-term obligations can be easily serviced by the normal flow of annual revenues.
Direct long-term debt / Population	Direct debt is general obligation debt to be repaid from property tax revenues.	A low ratio suggests the city has the ability to repay its general long-term debt.
Debt service / Total revenues	Debt service is the total expenditures in the debt service fund. Total revenues is the total revenues of all governmental funds.	A low ratio suggests the city is able to pay its debt service requirements when due.

Source: Ken W. Brown, "The 10-Point Test of Financial Condition: Toward an Easy-to-Use Assessment Tool for Smaller Cities," *Government Finance Review* 9 (December 1993): 21–26.

"unqualified") auditor opinion from their annual financial audits—the financial data are fundamental to financial accountability and fiscal stability (see chapter 7 for information on the financial audit process).

One of the most common performance financial ratios used in state and local government is fund balance as a percentage of expenditures for the general fund. However, the ratio shown in Table 4.5 is unreserved general fund balance as a percentage of total general fund revenues, and preferable in that it recognizes that the fund balance includes encumbrances, and that revenues, not expenditures, determine organizational flexibility. The ten-point test also contains ratios on debt, including direct long-term debt per capita and debt service as a percentage of total revenues. This information helps organizations take a proactive approach to upgrading their bond ratings and provides them with better trend information as they contemplate debt financing.

Financial condition assessments augment financial forecasting, estimating revenues and expenditures over an extended period of time to reconcile with the strategic plan. One locality that uses financial forecasting as part of its budget process is Johnson County, Kansas.[23] The county uses multiyear budget projections to provide an advance warning of potential fiscal problems, determining if policy adjustments are needed to offset future problems. Even a comprehensive approach like the balanced scorecard must be supplemented with other sources of information to make sound managerial decisions, including financial assessments and financial forecasting. Information derived from analyzing the historical and future financial condition of the organization also is directly linked with performance budgeting, and permits sound resource allocation decisions based on the financial performance of the organization.

Internal Business Quadrant

The second quadrant of the balanced scorecard is the internal business perspective, the perspective of the program manager as he/she adjusts the primary process of service delivery. Line managers' goals, objectives, and strategies for programs and service delivery fall into this quadrant. This area also contains the organization's performance measurement system for tracking the performance of service delivery with output, outcome, and efficiency indicators. A large percentage of a manager's time is invested in performance monitoring, because it is a daily management function of public organizations, even if there is no formal performance management system. The internal business perspective contains a direct link to the other three perspectives. Its link to the financial perspective comes from the annual budget process,

Figure 4.6 **City of Charlotte's Balanced Scorecard—Internal Business Quadrant**

| Streamline Customer Interactions | Promote Community-Based Problem Solving | Improve Productivity | Increase Positive Contacts | Increase Infrastructure Capacity |

Highlights:

- Business Support Services had a target of maintaining the City's vehicle fleet to ensure availability of an average of 91% of vehicles at all times. This target was met as the fleet availability was an average of 96%. Select results included a 97% availability of Police vehicles (target of 95%) and a 98% availability of light duty vehicles (target of 95%).

- Charlotte-Mecklenburg Utilities participated in two evaluation programs to review the business unit's service delivery and internal operations. The first program was a self-audit sponsored by the U.S. Environmental Protection Agency, while the second was a program sponsored by the American Water Works Association that involved "peer review" by other municipalities. While the findings were positive overall, key findings from these programs will help Utilities improve its operations and work environment.

- The City's Procurement Services Division developed a procurement card program that reduced the cost of certain transactions by $50 compared to the cost of the same transaction made by a purchase order. This program helped reduce procurement transaction costs by $32,316 on over 600 transactions.

- Neighborhood Development worked with an outside consultant to analyze its Small Business Loan Program and assess whether process improvements were necessary. This analysis indicated that the City's administration of this program is comparable to those in cities of similar size and that the appropriate processes were in place for this program.

- Finance automated the loan escrow recalculation process for housing rehabilitation, small business, and other City-sponsored loan programs. This automation significantly reduces the manual preparation time spent by staff processing these loans.

Source: City of Charlotte, North Carolina, *Year-End FY 2001 Corporate Performance Report.*

which must include tracking and reporting of resource consumption and should include performance information. Its link to the customer perspective is the satisfaction that the citizen receives from services that programs provide. Its link to the innovation and learning perspective focuses on individuals who provide services in public organizations.

Figure 4.6 shows the four major strategic areas of the internal process perspective for Charlotte: streamline customer interactions, promote community-based problem solving, improve productivity, increase positive contacts, and increase infrastructure capacity. The strategy behind *improve productivity* is to serve a growing population while lowering the portion of the general fund budget that supports functions other than public safety. Charlotte's measure is nonpublic safety general fund support costs as a percentage of the actual operating budget. Although the city did not specifically report a performance target, it did report that the nonpublic safety general fund support costs decreased from 15.8 percent in the FY 2000 operating budget to 15.6 percent in the FY 2001 operating budget. The measure is a good proxy measure for productivity and process improvement for activities, functions, and processes associated with general fund support activities like financial administration, human resources, purchasing, fleet management, and risk management. The city uses other measures to track productivity and process improvement within public safety departments.

Figure 4.6 shows individual highlights of activities that helped Charlotte decrease the percentage of nonpublic safety general fund support costs. They include fleet availability, implementing recommendations from two program evaluations, procurement card implementation, and automation of loan escrow calculations. Program evaluations and performance auditing are excellent ways for organizations to identify methods to increase productivity (we cover both in chapter 7). The city of Charlotte also analyzes its processes periodically to support the overall strategy of productivity improvement.

Although chapter 5 on performance measurement addresses internal business processes in more detail, the General Accounting Office's description of management controls offers an excellent summary overview for this section of the balanced scorecard.[24] Management controls include the plan of the program, methods, and procedures adopted to ensure that goals are attained within a designated timeframe. They also include organizing, directing, and controlling program activities and functions, including the systems for measuring, reporting, and monitoring program performance. In other words, management controls as described by the General Accounting Office are the essence of performance budgeting.

Innovation and Learning Quadrant

The third quadrant of the balanced scorecard is innovation and learning, a component of management often overlooked in planning processes. This perspective involves the most important resource in state and local government, the employees of the organization. Innovation and learning involves hiring qualified individuals, providing them continuous training and skill development, including them in the planning process, promoting continuing education, planning for career advancement, and creating a positive work environment.

Figure 4.7 shows the three major strategic areas of the innovation and learning perspective for the city of Charlotte: enhance information management, close skill gaps, and achieve positive employee climate. The strategies for this overall area are the use of technology to enhance information gather-

Figure 4.7   **City of Charlotte's Balanced Scorecard—Innovation and Learning Quadrant**

| Enhance Information Management | Close Skills Gap | Achieve Positive Employee Climate |

Highlights:

- Pre- and post-test evaluations were completed to assess the outcomes of the City's leadership development programs. The evaluations indicated a 7% increase in achievement of specific leadership objectives in the Trailblazers minority leadership program and an 11% increase in the objectives achievement in the Insights women in leadership program.

- The City's success in training supervisors in legal compliance and grievance claims was indicated by the lack of any City payments for Equal Employment Opportunity Commission claims in FY2001.

- Solid Waste Services' aggressive mandatory safety training program led to an 8.4% reduction in the number of vehicular accidents from FY2000 to FY2001. This was the second consecutive year the number of vehicular accidents has decreased.

- FY2001 attendance in citywide computer training classes declined by 40% from FY2000. This decrease is to be expected due to the City's concentrated effort regarding computer training for employees in previous years and a 33% increase in the number of participants taking business unit-specific computer training. Continued development of training plans in business units will help encourage further development opportunities overall.

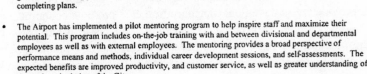

Participants in Business Unit-Specific Computer Training
FY2000: 78
FY2001: 133

- 11 of 14 (79%) Key Business Units reported the completion of training plans, below the target of 100% of business units. However, the remaining business units were still developing training plans and anticipate completion in FY2002. The target of achieving 80% of the goals in the training plans was achieved, as 90% of the goals were achieved in the 11 business units completing plans.

- The Airport has implemented a pilot mentoring program to help inspire staff and maximize their potential. This program includes on-the-job training with and between divisional and departmental employees as well as with external employees. The mentoring provides a broad perspective of performance means and methods, individual career development sessions, and self-assessments. The expected benefits are improved productivity, and customer service, as well as greater understanding of the goals and mission of the City.

Source: City of Charlotte, North Carolina, *Year-End FY 2001 Corporate Performance Report.*

ing and analysis in order to improve processes and service delivery (enhance information management), increase availability of skills in leadership, customer service, problem solving and technology (close skills gap), and strengthen work-life environment so that employees are motivated, productive, and fairly compensated (achieve positive employee climate).

The highlights section in Figure 4.7 indicates how the city of Charlotte is making progress toward its strategy of *closing skills gaps* among employees. Examples include how supervisors have been trained in legal compliance and grievance claims and how key business units are completing their training plans. One approach to building employee skills is to begin with high-impact hiring, a methodology for recruiting and hiring employees derived from performance-based management.[25] However, once employees are hired and become a part of the organization, skills development must be ongoing so the employee and the government can keep pace with the constantly changing environment.

The Customer Quadrant

Customer service means something different in the private sector than it does in the public sector. Kaplan and Norton noted that monitoring voluntary feedback on performance is not enough information for the private sector company that is focused on customer satisfaction.[26] Governments have long depended on the citizen complaint to assess the level of satisfaction with their service delivery, though we know that a variety of factors may determine the citizen's propensity to initiate contact with government, and only a small number of those factors may involve a demonstrable change or diminution of the quality of service received. Like business, government must solicit performance information from those citizens who do not initiate contact because their impressions are likely to reveal more about the overall performance of that service than is revealed by any tallying of self-initiated complaints.

Figure 4.8 shows the seven major strategic areas of the customer perspective for the city of Charlotte: reduce crime, increase perception of safety, strengthen neighborhoods, enhance service delivery, maintain competitive tax rate, provide safe, convenient transportation, and promote economic opportunity. Their strategy for *enhance service delivery* is to meet customer expectations by improving internal processes and using best practices. The measure for this strategy is service delivery ratings by citizens as reported in the biennial citywide phone survey. The target is to be rated excellent or good in overall service delivery by at least 75 percent of citizens surveyed. In the most recent survey conducted in FY 1999, 68 percent of respondents rated the city excellent or good in overall service delivery.

It is interesting to note that, in addition to its biennial telephone survey, the city of Charlotte uses a variety of administrative measures to track progress toward the overall strategy of enhance service delivery as shown by the highlights in Figure 4.8. These indicators also take the form of outcome measures, including response time to water leaks and response time to fire emergencies. Two questions arising from the customer quadrant of the bal-

Figure 4.8 **City of Charlotte's Balanced Scorecard—Customer Quadrant**

| Reduce Crime | Increase Perception of Safety | Strengthen Neighborhoods | Enhance Service Delivery | Maintain Competitive Tax Rate | Provide Safe, Convenient Transportation | Promote Economic Opportunity |

Highlights:

- Utilities reduced the response time to water leaks to two weeks, a reduction of approximately 80% from the 9.48 weeks in FY2000. This is also nearly a 90% reduction from the FY1999 response time of 16 weeks. An additional rapid response crew has contributed to this substantial reduction.

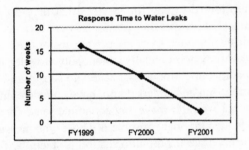

- The "Water Smart" public education campaign by Charlotte-Mecklenburg Utilities was successful in maintaining adequate service levels through conservation, as evidenced by only a 0.13% increase in average usage compared with a 4.5% increase in new accounts.

- Utilities also met its target of reducing the number of sewer overflows per 1,000 miles of pipe from 262 in FY2000 to 200 in FY2001.

- The Fire Department responded to 82% of all emergencies within six minutes, exceeding its target of 80%. An additional goal was to maintain an average response time within 3% of the five-year average. 32 of the department's 44 first-response engine and ladder companies stayed within this 3% target. The longer response times in the other 12 companies were due to several ongoing factors, including speed humps, road construction, and reassignment of ladder trucks.

Fire Average Response Time				
FY1997	FY1998	FY1999	FY2000	FY2001
4:19	4:14	4:13	4:21	4:23

Source: City of Charlotte, North Carolina, *Year-End FY 2001 Corporate Performance Report.*

anced scorecard that are still debated in the public administration literature are how citizens arrive at their evaluations of service satisfaction and whether citizen perceptions reconcile with administrative performance measures. The remainder of this chapter is dedicated to exploring these issues. If states and local governments are going to take customer satisfaction seriously and use survey instruments to gauge satisfaction of service delivery, they need to understand the dimensions of citizen satisfaction and how it may or may not reflect service improvement as indicated by performance measures.

Citizen Perception and Service Satisfaction

Application of the private sector definition of customer satisfaction to government requires some assumptions about the transaction that are almost always violated in the public sector. The most basic of these assumptions is that the transaction is voluntary. Perhaps nothing explains the emotional reaction citizens have to taxes more than the fact that they are legally coercible. Citizens are forced to pay for services that they do not consume or expect to consume. Other times they pay for services that others receive while purchasing their own service from the private sector (i.e., private schools). Because their government is typically a monopoly provider, they do not have choices among competing products or access to substitutes.

Second, most citizen/consumers do not have complete information about public services, nor would it make any economic sense for them to acquire it. This is the bounded rationality problem. Those who measure citizen satisfaction try to compensate for the information problem by filtering out citizens who have not had direct experience with the service. But this is itself problematic. If the service is used by most residents, like residential garbage collection, then a random sampling process should produce a representative sample of service users to poll for their opinion. However, if the service is used by a small percentage of residents (or at their own initiation, as in the case of a traffic ticket), the distribution of service users is not random and the sample of service users may not be representative. Service satisfaction information from services that are not widely used may not be reliable.

The "co-production" problem also can be illustrated by police services. Residents of some neighborhoods may actively assist police in crime prevention while residents of other neighborhoods may not call police when they see a crime, or may do so anonymously, and refuse to talk to officers when they respond. Elaine Sharp posited a model of citizen satisfaction with police service that incorporated the co-production problem, identifying the factors associated with satisfaction as fear of crime and alienation from the provider.[27] The co-production problem is usually viewed from the citizen's decision process—why some citizens "get involved" and others do not—but can be seen from the provider's point of view. If managers believe that citizens' perceptions have meaning for their delivery decisions, they may choose strategies that may not have a positive effect on performance criteria but have real consequences for outcomes. The examples of team policing and community-based law enforcement come to mind.

Finally, there is the problem of public sector product comparability. If a citizen believes that residents of another neighborhood are receiving a higher level of service at the same tax price, that calculus may affect his/her service satisfaction, even though it may not be strictly relevant to the service quality. Typically, an individual determines satisfaction based on the relationship between service expectation and service experience. When products are homogeneous and price is relatively constant this is the appropriate calculus. The neighborhood disparity perception is an example of nonhomogeneous products. If a citizen living in the city limits believes that county residents are receiving a comparable service bundle without paying city taxes, the price variation problem arises. Citizen satisfaction may have a collective dimension, but also may be based on the comparison of the quality of services received by others for the same tax price. Individual satisfaction is predicated on information that "(a) either all were treated equally, or (b) that if people were treated differently, they were treated equitably and fairly according to criteria that I or those who represent me accepted for valid reasons."[28]

We turn now from citizens' perceptions to explore managerial reluctance to use citizen satisfaction as a performance measure. If any measure could capture accountability to citizens for outcomes, surely this is it. Excellent handbooks for citizen surveying for service performance have been widely available for decades, so technical limitations are not an issue.[29] But managers remain reluctant to use the results of the citizen survey for decision making because there is a lack of consensus on the reliability of citizen satisfaction survey results as indicators of government performance, which makes this topic interesting. The private sector does not question the reliability of customer evaluations of product quality, because they understand that satisfaction with the product is not dependent on how much the consumer knows about its manufacturing process, the manufacturer, the distributor, or any other aspect of the product other than its consumption value to the user. Governments, which should be even more focused on the intangible aspects of citizen satisfaction with service quality because they rely on citizens' confidence and goodwill for their legitimacy, have often demanded proof that citizens' impressions of service quality reflect quantifiable aspects of service delivery. In other words, governments demand evidence that the citizens are properly informed as a condition for paying attention to satisfaction data.

"Hard" and "Soft" Measures of Service Performance

The first issue to surmount is the relationship between "hard" indicators of service quality (quantitative performance measures) and "soft" indicators (citizen satisfaction). In general, managers want to judge the validity of the latter by the former. Cases studies do offer evidence that citizens can produce evaluations that approximate some objective standard of service quality. There is evidence that citizens' perceptions and experiences affect their evaluation of municipal services; that a change in some objective measure (like service quantity) can affect citizen subjective perceptions of service effectiveness.[30] For example, citizen perception of police response time corresponded with actual response time as measured by the agency (one of the more reliable measures of service quality).[31] A comparison of city employees' evaluation of street conditions with citizen evaluations indicated that citizens could make accurate evaluations, especially when the multiple, specific dimensions of the services were presented to citizens.[32]

Demographic Characteristics

There also is a body of work that suggests that citizens' attitudes are affected by a set of factors that are not service related. Race and income may influence the evaluation of service quality.[33] Specifically, African Americans and Hispanics may rate urban services consistently lower than Anglo residents rate them. Additionally, neighborhood characteristics may lead citizens to evaluate services differently.[34] One problem with this line of thinking is that the service performance measure is often calculated in the aggregate while citizen satisfaction may be disaggregated into regions or neighborhoods. Unless service performance data are collected and analyzed at the neighborhood level for comparison, one cannot dismiss the possibility that service disparities may exist across neighborhoods and that citizen surveys capture that disparity in ways aggregate performance measures do not.

Source of Error in Citizen Surveys

There are two general types of errors citizens might make in evaluating service delivery. First, there are errors of attribution. A citizen may believe that a government is providing a service that it is not providing, or may believe a government is not providing a service when it is. Attribution error can occur in fragmented urban governments where services may be provided by a number of general purpose governments, special district, or private contractors.[35] A recent survey in the Detroit metropolitan area found that citizens frequently attribute service delivery to their city or township, even when another jurisdiction or a private contractor provides the service.[36] However, it is not apparent that the failure to identify the provider of a service leaves the citizen incapable of evaluating the quality of the service provided, so this is the lesser of the two sources of error.

The second type of error a citizen might make is assessment error. Here the citizen evaluates the quality of services in a way that contradicts some objective indicator of service quality, such as a performance measure. Some contend that this type of error is possible even when the respondent has had recent, personal contact with the service being evaluated. Many scholars of survey research believe that assessment error is the norm when the citizen's evaluation of service quality has not been informed by personal contact. They recommend that only those citizens with recent, direct contact with the service producer answer questions about service performance. In fact, most of the handbooks on citizen surveying offered by professional organizations take that position resulting in the filtering we described earlier.

Another comparison between the public and private sector may be helpful here. The private sector surveys both users and nonusers of their product, but along different dimensions. Users are asked to evaluate their experience with the purchase, the consumption, and maybe even the support after purchase (think of the automobile dealership that calls customers to ask them about their buying experience). But the private sector also surveys nonusers to determine their expectation of satisfaction if they were to purchase the product (think of the marketer who asks the respondent to respond to words about a car or car company). In the same way, governments can ask nonusers to evaluate their satisfaction with police services even if they have not directly or recently had an encounter with the police. In fact, the expectation of satisfaction with police services by the 90 percent of citizens who have not had direct contact is likely to tell the manager much more about police service performance than a satisfaction question from the 10 percent who have had personal contact, especially if that contact was self-initiated (e.g., a speeding ticket). That position is not established, though it is undeniably important that citizens have knowledge of, or be able to visualize the service they are evaluating.[37]

Is the likelihood of assessment error in citizen evaluation serious enough to call into question the use of surveying techniques for managerial decision making? Some say yes, especially when the questions about service quality are nonspecific and tied to personal experience. "Responses to vague satisfaction or evaluation questions probably reflect at best some unknown mixture of different aspects of service provision."[38] A study of police service in an Alabama city led one author to conclude that there is no link between actual quantity and quality of service provided and citizen perceptions of service quantity and quality.[39] "The general tendency [is] to attribute differences between citizen perceptions and agency record measures to erroneous perceptions on the part of citizens."[40] But it would be presumptuous to assume that the survey question itself was not a contributor to a revealed disparity between performance measures and citizen perceptions. Surveys typically ask recent users of a service to rate their satisfaction on a five-point Likert scale from very dissatisfied to very satisfied. What does this tell us, especially when we know that the likelihood of the citizen's having a personal interaction with the service provider was not random and that the interaction had multiple dimensions? For example, if a respondent called police to her home to resolve a domestic dispute and the officers were polite and helpful but declined the respondent's request to make an arrest, would that respondent be satisfied or not? For services such as police services that have multiple dimensions, the survey instrument should attempt to measure at multiple levels.

Kaplan and Norton illustrated the point in the private sector in their discussion of Metro Bank's identification of the key elements of its relationship with its customers. Metro Bank included the knowledge level of service representatives, the ability of representatives to recognize service needs, the convenience of access to service, and the congruence of the service provider's response time to the customer's perceived sense of urgency.[41] The police department could likewise break down the elements of a service response and permit the respondents to assess their satisfaction with say, the professionalism and demeanor of the officer, and the extent to which the outcome of the contact was resolved in a way that satisfied the citizen. The issue of the reliability of citizens' assessment of service quality may abate if as much attention is given to the composition of citizen survey questions as is given to the composition of outcome measures. We would never construct a performance outcome measure as "ratio of arrests per citizen contact." Why would we construct a measure of satisfaction as "level of satisfaction per contact with police department"?

In Defense of Citizen-Based Performance Measures

Contrary to the expectations of those who believe citizens dislike and distrust government, citizens give their local governments generally high marks for service delivery.[42] It is not so much that citizens distrust government, but that many administrators do not trust citizens to render fair or accurate judgments about government. A recent study revealed that administrators in Atlanta municipal government believed that citizens would rate city services much lower than they actually did.[43] The wise use of citizen surveys to inform aspects of service delivery that cannot be revealed through quantitative measures requires some careful thinking about what to ask (specific dimensions from actual users, expectations of satisfaction from citizens who have not used the service), and who to ask (a random sample of citizens, stratified by neighborhood). It is perfectly fine to interview a sample of citizens after a contact with a service provider to identify certain aspects of their experience that is of interest to managers, but as a supplement to and not a substitute for, a citywide or countywide general survey. The following two case studies illustrate the potential value of citizen surveys.

Auburn, Alabama

When government is willing, citizen perceptions can inform priorities. In Auburn, Alabama, citizen satisfaction results influence funding patterns for city government. A university community of about 45,000 near the Georgia border, Auburn began surveying citizens in 1986 as a way to help city council determine budget priorities.[44] In addition to the service satisfaction questions common to most citizen surveys, Auburn's survey includes a section asking respondents whether the city should spend more, less, or the same amount on a set of services. The survey is updated each year with a set of policy questions that gauge citizen attitudes about matters facing city council in the upcoming year. Survey results are presented to city council each year as part of the budget process and are available for council's use as they deliberate the budget. All nine Auburn city council members reported that survey results influenced their budgetary decisions and priorities.[45]

Auburn's decision to incorporate a citizen survey into the budget process is unusual. Many localities survey their citizens to assess satisfaction with services, and some include policy questions to help leaders understand community attitudes about certain issues. However, relatively few local governments actually view citizen survey results as an outcome measure of service performance. Many, probably most, view the citizen survey as an outreach tool to demonstrate to citizens that their government cares what they think about service quality. The act of soliciting citizen communication with government may itself positively prejudice results. A comprehensive model of satisfaction factors suggested that the more a citizen is invested in her community and feels efficacious toward local government, the greater her satisfaction with services, regardless of individual and neighborhood characteristics.[46] To the extent that the survey is an outreach exercise, a response bias concern may arise in that citizens who believe their voice counts to government are more likely to choose to participate.

St. Charles, Illinois

Located forty-five miles west of Chicago, St. Charles is adapting to its new role as a fast-growing suburban community. With change in population, and changing service demands from it, St. Charles adopted a balanced scorecard approach to performance measurement to help them transition to a

Table 4.6

Sources of Performance Data by Perspective

Perspective	Indicator
Financial	Financial trends report
	Financial policies versus actual
Customer	Citizen survey
	Business retention survey
	Town meetings
	City Hall house calls
	Site visits
	Focus groups
Growth and learning	Employee input survey
	Internal customer survey
	Listen and learn
Internal business processes	Process improvement program
	Incident follow-up cards

Source: Larry Mulholland and Patrick Muetz, "A Balanced Scorecard Approach to Performance Measurement," *Government Finance Review* 18 (April 2002): 12–16.

new identity while retaining aspects of their old identity as a small town. A strategic planning process helped them to determine their vision, which drives their annual business plan. The business plan consists of goals, objectives, strategies, and performance targets for each department. A citizen survey is specifically used with the customer quadrant of the balanced scorecard as shown in Table 4.6.

Some types of activities that St. Charles calls surveying are actually outreach, such as town meetings, "house calls," site visits, and focus groups. These nonrandom processes can be very helpful in identifying localized or particular problems with service quality. However, the citizen survey and the business retention survey are critical in identifying patterns of satisfaction and dissatisfaction in service provision that managers would not know from citizen-initiated contacts with government. While citizen and business surveying can be undertaken outside the balanced scorecard model, it is easy to see how the focus on stakeholders (citizens and businesses) drove the need for performance information, which drove managerial decisions about service delivery.

Conclusion

Is strategic planning necessary for an organization to undertake performance budgeting? The short answer is no. Most services provided by state and local government are mandated by law and must be provided with or without a strategic plan. Managers could build a performance measurement system based on the mission, goals, and objectives of core service areas and link the information derived from the system to the annual budget process for resource justification. This results in performance budgeting without the need for strategic planning. However, there are some major limitations to this approach to performance budgeting that strategic planning can overcome.

Strategic planning ensures that organizations adopt a long-term perspective for identifying goals and objectives at the organization-wide level. These goals and objectives may include traditional and nontraditional service provisions. For example, one goal may address street infrastructure, a core function for state and local government. Other goals may address the privatization of certain services, investment of public dollars in economic development activities, and the creation of new programs to prevent social problems. The state of Oregon went one step further by creating a strategic plan for where it wanted to be in five years, and established benchmarks to measure progress toward getting there. Without the strategic planning effort, the state agencies in Oregon would have been left to create their own individual plans. Their plans might have been forward-looking and ambitious, or they might have been justifications for decisions they had already made about services and validations for familiar ways of providing them.

Strategic planning allows program managers to expand their goals and objectives of service delivery to include strategic goals that reconcile with the organization-wide strategic plan. This allows managers to base budget allocation requests not only on service performance but also on the extent to which those services support the overall strategy of the organization. This approach overcomes the primary reason that the PPBS failed at the federal level. Federal agencies justified their planning and budgeting activities based on internal direction as opposed to organization-wide direction. This disconnect between organization-wide planning and programmatic planning is very common in state and local government. We presented three governments— the state of Oregon, Dakota County, Minnesota, and Scottsdale, Arizona— that reconciled both levels of planning. Strategic plans provide the framework for placing performance budgeting into context based on a long-term perspective.

We offered a managerial approach that links organization-wide planning and programmatic planning, the balanced scorecard. The balanced scorecard integrates four quadrants for a comprehensive management strategy: financial, internal business, innovation and learning, and customer. The balanced scorecard approach also sets the stage for performance budgeting, building on the notion that performance budgeting involves more than tracking the outputs and outcomes of service delivery. Organizations must track dimensions of financial performance, must promote an innovative and learning environment for employees who impact the performance of service delivery, and must manage internal business processes of service delivery. The fourth dimension of the balanced scorecard, the customer perspective, requires states and local governments to acknowledge the importance of citizen perception of service quality and satisfaction with service delivery.

When government is willing, citizens can inform priorities, just as customers inform business priorities in the private sector. The only downside to customer feedback is that the act of soliciting citizen communication with government may itself positively prejudice results. A comprehensive model of satisfaction factors suggests that the more a citizen is invested in his/her community and feels efficacious toward local government, the greater her satisfaction with services, regardless of individual and neighborhood characteristics.[47] This is a very pleasant problem to have. As the two cases demonstrate, the results of a carefully crafted citizen survey can be an important part of a performance budgeting program. Auburn made the link directly to their budget process. St. Charles adopted the balanced scorecard approach, linking all four quadrants to their decisions about how to allocate resources in a comprehensive performance-based management model.

— Chapter 5 —

Performance Measurement

All too often, performance measurement begins with a memo from the budget office to program managers to the effect that they should turn in their performance measures by a certain date so that the statistics can be added to the budget document before it goes to the printer. Managers then develop a set of criteria for the performance measures that ultimately determines their usefulness. The first may be that whatever is reported should reflect well on the program's current performance. The manager may conclude that it would be unwise to show need for productivity improvement when success is unlikely to be rewarded but failure might be punished. The second decision is that the measure reported should already be available so as to minimize the time, effort, and cost associated with compliance. The manager may reasonably assume that what the program is currently doing is what it should be doing and offers indicators to reinforce that assumption. Finally, managers often check with managers of similar programs in other jurisdictions to see what they reported for performance measures. As odd as it sounds, a manager may be reassured by the knowledge that he/she is about to make a "safe" choice—that is, a choice that someone else has made. This is the process by which ideas, good and bad, are diffused in the public sector.

However, this is not the way to begin a successful performance measurement program. There is, indeed, something to be said for this approach in that it provides positive feedback on some aspects of current service delivery with minimal cost and effort. But convenience statistics are a poor basis for the managerial decision-making process and an even poorer platform for deliberating funding decisions—the goal of performance budgeting. Playing it safe with the numbers may fulfill the manager's obligation to report something positive about his or her program in the budget document, but it probably will not buttress the manager's case for an expansion or reallocation of resources. Because performance budgeting requires decision makers to consider performance information with budget requests, we must find some way to make the connection between what gets measured and how the measures are used.

The "why" question of performance measurement has been covered in detail by academicians, practitioners, elected officials, and professional organizations. If one were to summarize all the reasons for measuring performance in state and local government, operational accountability for service delivery would be the consensus response. Insofar as we, as public administration professionals, no longer argue against performance measurement, we can move on to the question of how to construct good measures. Fortunately, there are a number of fine guides to constructing performance measures that are suitable for students and practitioners, for example, David N. Ammons's *Municipal Benchmarks* and Harry P. Hatry's *Performance Measurement*.[1] Professional organizations like the Government Finance Officers Association also provide resources for constructing good measures (see chapter 8 for a partial list of professional organizations that support the performance agenda in state and local government) as well as the Governmental Accounting Standards Board's research on service, efforts, and accomplishments (SEA) reporting.[2]

We begin this chapter on the assumption that the first goal of performance budgeting is to select measures that reflect programmatic goals and align service activities with those goals. Starting any other way amounts to describing what the program is doing as opposed to examining what the program should be doing to advance its strategic and service delivery goals and to advance the overall mission of the organization. Programmatic planning is described in this chapter instead of in the previous chapter on planning for two reasons. First, planning at the programmatic level should occur with or without an organization-wide planning effort. Second, planning at the programmatic level establishes the context for a meaningful performance measurement system—the focus of this chapter.

The remaining sections of this chapter answer some of the more difficult questions associated with performance measurement in state and local government, questions often overlooked in advocacy of performance measurement. We believe our responses to these questions are balanced, though not always positive. Managers need to understand how a performance measurement system can advance program performance, can hinder program performance, or can accomplish nothing at all. Convenience statistics tend to fall into the latter two categories—they are counterproductive or accomplish nothing at all.

Our conclusion is simple. Performance measurement is here to stay in state and local government. The challenge is what to do with them. Successful performance management programs are goal-directed and multidimensional, like the four quadrants of the balanced scorecard. Programmatic planning determines the goals and reveals the dimensions.

Programmatic Planning

Because the amount of time invested in building a meaningful performance measurement system is directly correlated with the usefulness of the information derived from it, the importance of programmatic planning in state

---

Box 5.1

Example of Mission Statement

Fire Suppression

Fair—Fire suppression provides an environment of teamwork, with a commitment to excellence, compassion, and immediate community service.

Good—Fire suppression is responsible for the protection of life and property of the community through emergency response.

Best—Fire suppression provides protection of life and property of the community through emergency response with an environment of teamwork, commitment to excellence, and dedication to community service.

---

and local government cannot be overstated. Performance measures do not necessarily provide information that is ready for decision making; additional analysis is often required to convert performance statistics into real information. In other words, performance data are collected from the service delivery processes and are used to create performance measures that are required by the performance management system, which is created from programmatic planning. Information is created when the results of the performance measures are analyzed to support managerial decision making, including allocation decisions for performance budgeting.

The following sections on mission statement, program goals, objectives and measures, performance data, reporting process, and timing issues describe the programmatic planning process for building the infrastructure for performance measurement. Organizations often use one of two approaches to programmatic planning prior to initiating a performance measurement system—an entity-wide approach or a pilot-program approach. The entity-wide approach requires all programs in the organization to adopt performance measurement simultaneously. The pilot-program approach begins with a selected number of programs and adds new ones over time. The choice of approach usually reflects the organization's capacity for performance measurement.

Mission Statement

The planning function at the programmatic level begins with mission statements. The mission statement conveys the purpose for which the program

Figure 5.1 **Planning and Performance Measurement Worksheet**

I. Establish Link Between Mission, Goals, Objectives, and Performance Measures

Mission Statement	➤ A statement that conveys the purpose of the organizational unit; outlines the services provided; and describes what the unit is trying to achieve. It should answer the following questions: Why does the organizational unit exist? What does it seek to accomplish? ➤ *Example:* The mission of the transit authority is to link diverse parts of the city to help ensure the city's place as a center of commerce and recreation by providing safe, convenient, efficient, affordable, and environmentally sound transportation alternatives to its residents and visitors.
Goals	➤ Broad statement of purpose focusing on a major service ➤ *Example:* Provide convenient transportation alternatives
Objectives	➤ A specific action to implement/achieve a service delivery goal ➤ *Example:* Increase on-time rating of bus service by 10 percent
Performance Measure	➤ A direct measure of the achievement of an objective ➤ *Example:* Percent change in annual on-time rating for bus service

II. Distinguish Between Service Delivery Goals and Strategic Goals

Service Delivery Goal	➤ A goal directly related to accomplishing the mission of the organizational unit ➤ The goal should have at least one measurable objective as well as one related performance measure

Example of a service delivery goal, a related measurable objective, and a related performance measure:

Service Delivery Goal: Provide household recycling collection to residential customers
Objective: Maintain a participation rate in the household recycling program of 85 percent
Measure: Percent of eligible collection points participating in the household recycling program

Strategic Goal	➤ A management-type goal that would improve the ability of the organizational unit to meet its mission or the organization-wide mission ➤ Strategic goals assist programs with building internal capacity

Examples of strategic goals:

Strategic Goal: Develop a countywide approach to stormwater management
Strategic Goal: Implement neighborhood policing to increase police visibility
Strategic Goal: Purchase and implement a consolidated financial management system

exists. Although mission statements tend to remain static over time, they should be reviewed periodically for accuracy and completeness. Box 5.1 presents three mission statements for fire suppression, ranking them for comparison purposes. The first mission statement, that we labeled "fair," indicates that the purpose of fire suppression is to provide excellent, compassionate, and immediate community service. While this type of service should

III. Establish a Mix of Output, Outcome, and Efficiency Measures

Output Measure (Workload)	➢ Measure of the completed activity or effort, indicating the amount of work accomplished ➢ *Examples:* Financial transactions completed; number of clients served; and number of lane miles resurfaced
Outcome Measure (Effectiveness)	➢ Measure of how well a service is being provided (quality) ➢ *Examples:* Percent of financial transactions without error; average satisfaction score on survey given to citizens; and percent change in pavement quality index of asphalt roads
Efficiency Measure	➢ Measure of how inputs relate to outputs ➢ *Examples:* Transactions per full-time equivalent (FTE) employee; cost per ton of residential refuse collected; and cost per lane mile resurfaced

IV. Collect Background Information to Ensure Data Accuracy

Calculation of Measure	➢ Record the inputs and calculation methodology for each measure
Data Source(s)	➢ Describe the data collection system for each measure
Collector(s)	➢ Designate the responsible parties for collection of the data
Additional Information	➢ Provide other descriptive information, such as a definition of the measure, to further clarify the intent of the measure

Example of calculation, data source, and collector for a performance measure:

Measure:	Percent of financial transactions without error
Calculation:	number of financial transactions during FY 2002–2003 without error
	total number of financial transactions during FY 2002–2003
Data Source:	Performance Log in Financial System—code 11 for "number of financial transactions without error" and code 12 for "total number of financial transactions"
Collector:	Account Clerk

Source: Carla M. Pizzarella, research associate, Maxwell School of Syracuse University.

be a fundamental goal of every public program, it does not convey the actual purpose of the program and provides minimal information for creating service delivery goals.

The second mission statement, that we labeled "good," conveys the actual purpose of fire suppression, protecting the life and property of the community through emergency response. The mission statement we labeled "best" combines the previous statements, building on the strengths of each. Time invested in constructing the mission statement pays dividends in the performance measurement system at the program level. Once the mission statement is constructed, service delivery goals, objectives, and performance measures are then determined, creating a framework for a meaningful performance measurement system.

Program Goals (Service Delivery and Strategic)

Creating programmatic goals is the next step in the process. Goals are defined as statements of direction based on the mission of the program and the needs of community, including what the program expects to achieve in the future.[3] Figure 5.1 presents a worksheet to assist program managers with the planning process. The worksheet begins with an overview of the performance measurement system by describing mission statement, goals, objectives, and performance measures.

The next section of the worksheet shows service delivery goals and strategic goals. Service delivery goals are those goals directly related to accomplishing the mission of the program or unit. They normally are supported with at least one measurable objective as well as one related performance measure. They are static, remaining the same as long as the mission statement remains the same. The human resource/risk management division of the city of San Clemente, California, has three service delivery goals. Figure 5.2 shows that each service delivery goal stems from the mission statement, contains an objective, and uses a performance measure for tracking and reporting progress.

The third goal in Figure 5.2, recruit and retain qualified employees for the city, contains two quantifiable objectives along with the respective performance measures. The second objective, assure that 90 percent of vacancies are filled within 90 days, is supported by the measure *percent of vacancies filled within 90 days*. This is a key outcome indicator for human resources and the organization in general. Note that the measures are tracked by fiscal year. The first column represents an actual result of 95 percent of vacancies filled within 90 days. However, because the budget for fiscal year 2000–2001 was prepared during fiscal year 1999, actual data for an annualized result were not available for that fiscal year. To overcome this timing difference, the city reported the budgeted and projected percentages for fiscal year 1999–2000. Other solutions to timing problems with performance data would be: (1) report just the budgeted figure for fiscal year 1999–2000, (2) report the actual result for partial year data, or (3) report an annualized result based on partial year data.

Strategic goals at the programmatic level are those goals that are normally tied to management's philosophy for improving the capacity of programs or tied to organizational goals established in strategic or long-term planning processes. Unlike service delivery goals, strategic goals constantly change, responding to changes in organizational goals, new strategies for improving the operations of service delivery, new ways to expand the capacity of programs (e.g., technology), and fiscal constraints for new investment. The im-

Figure 5.2 **Examples of Service Delivery Goals**

Human Resources

Mission Statement

The mission of the Human Resources/Risk Management division is to attract and retain a qualified work force, improve organizational productivity and effective communications with employees regarding their rights, responsibilities, opportunities and benefits; to enthusiastically serve the City's customers with quick and effective service; to respond to the needs of the citizens; to advance the opportunities of applicants and employees to reach their full potential through fair and equal treatment; and to take proactive actions to solve personnel issues.

Service Description

The Human Resources/Risk Management division is responsible for the development, modification and management of all employee selection, classification, compensation, employee relations, employee safety and training. The division also has responsibility for administering all risk management programs including workers' compensation and general liability, and the City's volunteer program.

Performance Goals, Objectives and Measures

# Performance Goals, Objectives and Measures	1998-99 Actual	1999-00 Budget	1999-00 Projected	2000-01 Budget
Goal: Provide efficient and effective customer service to the public in the areas of human resources and risk management. Objective:				
1. Respond to 95% of public requests responded to within 5 days. Measure:				
% of public requests responded to within 5 days	97%	95%	95%	95%
Goal: Provide efficient and effective customer service to employees in the area of employee benefits, including retirement, workers compensation, training, wellness programs, labor relations and safety. Objective:				
1. 95% of all employee requests responded to within 3 days. Measure:				
% of all employee requests responded to within 3 days	98%	98%	95%	95%
Goal: Recruit and retain qualified employees for the City.				
1. Objective: Assure that 90% of employees successfully pass probation. Measure:				
% of employees successfully pass probation	95%	95%	95%	90%
Objective:				
2. Assure that 90% of vacancies are filled within 90 days. Measure:				
% of vacancies are filled within 90 days	95%	95%	90%	90%

Source: City of San Clemente, California, *Annual Budget & Capital Improvement Program Fiscal Year 2000–2001.*

portance of strategic goals is that they are the connection between organization-wide direction and programmatic direction. In other words, they are the linchpin between the two levels of planning in state and local government. This does not prevent program managers from using service delivery goals for making the connection to organizational goals, especially when goals at the organization-wide level involve the promotion of service productivity. Strategic goals simply provide more flexibility for this connection.

Figure 5.3 contains strategic goals for the Department of Health and Human Resources for the state of West Virginia. Their strategic goal to prioritize the allocation of limited staff is supported with the objective to focus on

Figure 5.3   **Examples of Strategic Goals**

Department of Health and Human Resources

Mission

The Department of Health and Human Resources (DHHR) promotes and provides appropriate health and human services for the people of West Virginia in order to improve their quality of life.

Goals/Objectives

Promote a department that is modern, professional, and accountable.

Enhance the exemplary management of the department.
- Achieve administrative and programmatic efficiency through automation.
- Enhance management and staff's abilities through interdepartmental communication, training, and continued education.
- Improve/maintain a sound fiscal policy through creative and legitimate financing of priority service delivery systems.
- Create and foster positive attitudes among staff through recruitment, rewards, working environment, and training so that customer service quality and efficiency is enriched.
- Emphasize accountability of staff and those with whom the department contracts services.

Prioritize the allocation of limited staff resources to best meet the administrative and programmatic needs of the department.
- Focus on the use of technology.

Implement and administer health care and welfare reform statewide.
- Focus on prevention and meeting basic needs.
- Assist individuals and families to become economically self-sufficient.
- Prioritize all services to be delivered to meet the basic health and human service needs of individuals and families within the limits of available federal and state funds.
- Evaluate the efficiency and effectiveness of the implementation of managed care.

Recommended Improvements
- Includes $601,600 for Vital Registration Document Imaging.
- Includes $1,426,383 for the West Virginia Birth to Three Program.
- Includes $3,070,000 for Court Order Related improvements.
- Additional $250,000 for Bateman/Sharpe Diverted Detainees.
- Additional $2,500,000 for Support Services Basic Living Skills.
- Additional $3,190,170 MR/DD Waiver.
- Includes $392,028 for Adult Family Care.
- Includes $445,025 for Customer Service Centers.
- Additional $20,000,000 TANF.
- Additional $100,000 for Board of Medicine for computer upgrades.

Source: State of West Virginia, *Executive Budget Fiscal Year 2003—Operating Detail.*

Figure 5.4   **Examples of Objectives and Performance Measures**

OBJECTIVE: To increase the % and number of calls for assistance successfully resolved from 75% / 1500 to 80% / 1600 by June 30, 2002.

STRATEGY: Continue outreach initiatives including housing fairs and PAC meeting participation.

MEASURE: # and % of calls for assistance successfully resolved	Actual FY 2000	Adopted FY 2001	Estimated FY 2001	Adopted FY 2002
	70%/1400	75%/1500	75%/1500	80%/1600

OBJECTIVE: To reduce the cost per successful resolution of call for assistance from $126 per resolution to $105 per resolution by June 30, 2002.

STRATEGY: Increase the productivity of Community Outreach Specialists. Implement call-tracking system within the department to increase the efficiency of response. Decrease the number of referrals that are not associated with the department.

MEASURE: Cost per resolution of call for assistance	Actual FY 2000	Adopted FY 2001	Estimated FY 2001	Adopted FY 2002
	$126	$105	$105	$95

Core Service: Lead Based Paint Abatement

GOAL: To improve the safety of housing stock by reducing the public health impact of lead.

OBJECTIVE: To abate 105 units that test positive for lead-based paint by June 30, 2002.

STRATEGY: Identify target housing, in collaboration with certified contractors, to give the program additional resources to achieve its goal.

MEASURE: # of units abated	Actual FY 2000	Adopted FY 2001	Estimated FY 2001	Adopted FY 2002
	0	20	20	85

Source: City of Durham, North Carolina, *FY 2001–2002 Budget*.

the use of technology. These goals are not only strategic, they are also tied to the long-range issues identified by the state at the organization-wide level, especially the goals of health care and welfare reform. Figure 5.3 also contains recommended improvements for the Department of Health and Human Resources, identifying the resources needed for implementation. Several of the recommended improvements impact the capacity of the department, including technology upgrades for process improvement. The state of West Virginia notes in its budget document that it is in the process of implementing a performance measurement system. Once implemented, performance measures can be used to track the impact of strategic goals as well as track service delivery goals and objectives at the program level.

Objectives and Measures

The next step in the planning process at the programmatic level is to establish measurable objectives, which are defined as something to be accomplished in

WORKLOAD MEASURES				
Units Completed:	Actual FY 2000	Adopted FY 2001	Estimated FY 2001	Projected FY 2002
homeownership	139	112	112	123
rehabilitation	90	102	102	112
rental housing	144	100	100	110
Code Enforcement Cases Brought Into Compliance:				
housing code	1458	1800	1800	1900
vehicles	961	1000	1000	1000
weedy lots	500	550	550	600
Community Life Court Cases				96
Lead Abatement Rehab Completions	0	20	20	85

CUSTOMER SERVICE STANDARDS			
Service	Standard	Estimate FY 2001	Projected FY 2002
Call for inspection	respond within 2 business days	100%	100%
Resolution of code enforcement cases	Vehicles - 8 business days	90%	90%
	Weedy Lots - 30 business days	85%	85%
	Housing - 117 business days	90%	90%
Request loans info	Mail information within 2 days	95%	95%
Applications for loans & grants	Written response within 30 days to complete application	100%	100%
Contractor payments	Process and pay requests within 10 days of receipt	95%	100%
Home Rehab	Complete rehab work within 60 days of contract	75%	100%
Lead Abatement	Within 45 days lead abate complete once contract executed	--	100%
Client Referrals	Within 72 hours	--	95%
Resource Referral	Within 72 hours	--	100%

specific, measurable, and time-limited stages.[4] Again, service delivery goals should contain at least one measurable objective that can be tracked with at least one performance measure. Figure 5.4 contains three objectives that are specific, measurable, and time limited. The objective, *to reduce the cost per successful resolution of call for assistance from $126 per resolution to $105 per resolution by June 30, 2002*, provides the program manager with information he/she needs to measure performance (the current cost per resolution, the desired cost per resolution, the time period in which the objective should be obtained), and develop strategies for program improvement.

Performance measures are selected after the objectives have been identified, understanding that not all performance statistics are tied directly to the selected objectives. Output or workload measures are normally identified first. They are critical for three reasons. First, output measures reflect operational accountability and provide the basis for annual budget requests in the form of projected workload. Second, output measures are used to create higher order measures of outcome and efficiency and are used as a baseline for process analysis. Third, they are used to place higher order measures into context, allowing program managers to track the performance of activities and processes from the standpoint of making daily management decisions.

Figure 5.4 contains a number of performance measures for review. The first measure is a combination of output and outcome, *the number and percentage of calls for assistance successfully resolved*. Performance results are then presented in four ways: actual, current year adopted, estimated, and future year adopted. This format is strongly encouraged by the Government Finance Officers Association's criteria for the Distinguished Budget Presentation Award. The second measure, *cost per resolution of call for assistance* is an efficiency measure. The third measure, *number of units abated*, is an output measure derived from the objective of *to abate 105 units that test positive for lead-based paint by June 30, 2002*. However, additional output (workload) measures and customer service standards are added to enhance accountability and data use.[5]

Performance Data

Though the terms are often used interchangeably, there is a difference between performance measures and performance data. Data are produced by the processes of service delivery and are used to calculate performance measures. Data collection systems are critical to performance measurement. The data collected must be relevant, reliable, and accurate. Program staff should participate in the selection of data to advance the relevant and reliable criteria. Data auditing should take place periodically to ensure accuracy. Every performance measure should contain a calculation methodology, the data sources needed for calculation, who is responsible for data collection, and the descriptive information necessary for measurement intent. This part of the planning process facilitates the audit process of performance statistics, and, more important, enhances the ability of state and local officials to use the information.

Reporting Process

To ensure that updated performance information is reported during the annual budget process (though not necessarily in the budget document), organizations need to construct a reporting process designed to accommodate both budgetary information and performance data. Chapter 3 offered an example of three organizations that expanded their annual budget processes to include performance data to ensure that performance statistics were available to support allocation decisions. One way to integrate performance data into the budget process is to expand operating budget worksheets to include performance worksheets. Figure 5.5 provides an example.

The performance worksheet is completed annually and forwarded to the

Figure 5.5   Performance Information Worksheet

Department: Program: Fund:

Program Mission Statement:

Program Service Delivery Goals:

Program Objectives: Associated Performance Measures

Output	FY 2001–2002 (Actual)	FY 2002–2003 (Budget)	FY 2003–2004 (Budget)
A.			
B.			

Outcome	FY 2001–2002 (Actual)	FY 2002–2003 (Budget)	FY 2003–2004 (Budget)
A.			
B.			

Efficiency	FY 2001–2002 (Actual)	FY 2002–2003 (Budget)	FY 2003–2004 (Target)
A.			
B.			

Strategic Goals:

Department: Program: Fund:

Measure	FY 2001–2002 (Actual)	Calculation	Data Source(s)

Explanatory Information:

budget office along with operating budget worksheets. The program's mission statement, service delivery goals, and objectives remain relatively static over time, as do the performance measures associated with them. The associated performance measures section is used to show what measures are used to reflect progress toward the quantifiable objectives. Remember, not all measures are tied directly to objectives; however, objectives are an excellent source for outcome and efficiency measures. The performance worksheet also contains strategic goals, which change constantly, and demonstrates that explanatory information is sometimes required to place the performance measures into context. This section can include a range of information, including a description of service delivery, definitions of performance data, and anomalies that caused performance variations from prior reporting periods.

Timing Issues

All government budget processes are driven by the fiscal year of operation. The most common fiscal year for states and local governments begins on July 1 and ends on June 30. Therefore, decisions have to be made well in advance of July 1 for preparing and adopting an annual operating budget. Performance budgeting requires that performance information be a part of budget deliberations that take place during the preparation phase of budget development. That means we need to reconcile the fact that the budget process is annual with the fact that some of the most critical performance information we need for decision making is not available annually. Improvements in programs and services do not always conveniently show up in the first or second year of operation. In fact, some of the more meaningful changes in processes and procedures may take several years to pay dividends. We may bias against long-term improvements if we make the decision on whether to continue funding new initiatives based on first year results, which is exactly contrary to what a performance budgeting system is supposed to achieve.

Placing performance measures in the budget document further complicates the budget cycle. Reporting performance on each program's budget page is a commendable activity. However, managers may struggle with the need to report measures that show improvement and the need to make decisions on measures that may not show improvement, at least in the short-run. If you pick up a budget that offers performance measures for each program, you will see that the measures often reported describe outputs (number of traffic citations issued) and efficiencies (cost per citation issued). Less frequently do they describe outcomes (percent fewer traffic accidents in the targeted zone). Managers may prefer to report outcomes, and they probably make their decisions based on outcomes. But the budget cycle requires that they report something annually and good judgment requires that they report something positive. So we see more output measures than outcome measures in most budgets, and we suspect the selection of the measure may have been partially influenced by an annual budget cycle and an administrative decision to report performance. The understandable pressure that managers feel to offer information to the public that reflects well on their programs and employees can be relieved by giving managers the discretion to choose the performance measures that appear in the budget document.

Measuring Performance

Now that we have demonstrated how the programmatic planning process should drive program priorities, we can move to what should be measured to be consistent with those priorities. But first we would like to start with the answers to a few hard questions about performance measurement. We contend that it is impossible to incorporate performance budgeting into a comprehensive management strategy unless managers understand performance measurement in more than a technical sense. In chapter 2, we traced the lineage of performance budgeting by using the tradition of bureaucratic reform in America. One reason for putting our readers through that history lesson was to explain why even the easy questions about performance measurement often get complicated. We wanted to show how the desire to be "reformed" could cause managers to adopt a new technique on paper but not in practice. No reform is more susceptible to "going through the motions" than performance measurement.

When Did Performance Measurement Begin?

The current incarnation of performance measurement at the federal level is generally traced back to the late 1980s, but some scholars were advocating the use of quantitative measures to improve service productivity and enhance effectiveness in states and local governments as early as the 1970s. The Urban Institute gets credit for being the first to advocate performance measurement to improve service productivity.[6] Its ideas about measuring the productivity of public services mirrored developments in the private sector. Corporate managers found year-end financial performance insufficient for decision making in an environment where customers had more options and were more discriminating than ever. They needed more flexible, outcome-based measures that would permit them to make process adjustments long before the annual financial reports were filed. Advances in information technology and data management made measuring and monitoring performance practical, and put productivity data in the hands of mid-level managers. Additional reports encouraging public managers to adopt performance measurement appeared in the late 1970s,[7] along with several articles in practitioner-oriented academic journals.[8]

By the mid-1980s the idea of performance measurement had drawn the attention of scholars interested in how measures could be incorporated into public management processes.[9] A few linked productivity improvement to the budget process.[10] The number of local governments measuring performance also was growing in the 1980s. A survey of 460 municipalities published in 1984 revealed that 68 percent of the respondents were measuring performance,[11] but other studies would suggest that number may be high.[12] Though performance measurement was not much more than a blip on the federal radar screen, localities were already trying it and a few states were working on ways to use performance measures to improve their budget processes. By the early 1990s, the idea of measuring performance as a way to enhance service effectiveness was well established and the public sector professional organizations were endorsing it enthusiastically. The Government Performance and Results Act, which required federal agencies to measure performance, was adopted in 1993.

Who Is Measuring Performance?

The answer seems to be practically everybody, at least as indicated by self-reported surveys of state and local government officials (one caveat is that local surveys are often aimed at larger jurisdictions). This is not surprising, as performance measurement is increasingly equated with administrative professionalism, a position taken by most all the public sector professional organizations. The enthusiasm for measuring service performance approached fervor in the late 1990s, prompting one journalist to observe, "governments that used to pay no attention to their own performance now seem obsessed with trying to measure everything in sight."[13]

Most of the attention to performance is devoted to administrative measures of service performance, but roughly a third of larger cities also measure citizen satisfaction—some comprehensively, and others with customer feedback cards for recently used services.[14]

The statistics are difficult to sort through because, as all survey researchers know, the way you ask the question determines the answer you get. A look at the numbers suggests that asking whether a state or local government measures performance or whether it uses performance measures can substantially affect the results. Previously, we reported that 68 percent of municipalities were measuring performance by the mid-1980s. But a 1998 study reported that 62 percent of the municipalities with populations greater than 25,000 did not use performance measures at all, and only 23 percent using performance data had centralized, performance monitoring systems.[15] How can both be right? The distinction is between "measure performance" and "use performance measures."

Another problem that confounds researchers is the extent to which performance measurement is used by all or selected programs in state and local government. Consider the manager who receives a survey asking this question: Does your organization collect and monitor performance data? There

Table 5.1

Types of Performance Measures Tracked and Reported

Types of performance measures	State budget offices (%)	State agencies (%)	City/county departments (%)
Input measures	80.9	63.1	70.2
Activity measures	81.3	60.1	70.5
Output measures	76.4	62.9	67.6
Outcome measures	47.1	51.9	46.9
Efficiency measures	42.3	33.6	44.1
Quality/customer satisfaction measures	23.9	24.8	43.1
Explanatory measures	25.0	23.2	26.9
Benchmarks	25.0	26.7	23.9

Source: Julia Melkers, Katherine G. Willoughby, Brian James, and James Fountain, *Performance Measures at the State and Local Levels: A Summary of Survey Results* (Norwalk, CT: Governmental Standards Accounting Board, 2002), 6.

are a number of appropriate answers. Yes, if the police department collects crime data and uses them to track patterns of criminal behavior. Or no, if only the police department collects and monitors data. Yes, if multiple departments collect data but do not monitor trends with them; or no, for the same reason. While most surveys are more carefully worded than our example, the point remains that one individual is asked to characterize a very diverse process of data management by checking off one of a very limited number of answer categories.

Asking a similar question a different way yields a more revealing answer. A recent study sponsored by the Governmental Accounting Standards Board (GASB) and the Sloan Foundation asked respondents what percent of their agencies or departments are measuring some aspect of performance and which aspect they are measuring. The results, shown in Table 5.1, provide a good "snapshot" of performance measurement in 2001. This survey also differs from previous efforts in that staff in state budget offices, state agencies, local budget offices, and local programs were surveyed, rather than one respondent from each jurisdiction (total of 489 responses, a 37 percent response rate).[16]

Still, there is considerable ambiguity associated with this survey. Respondents were asked whether the majority of their agencies or departments were measuring performance with the types of performance measures shown in Table 5.1. Again, the difference between collecting and using performance is unknown, and the respondents indicated only if a majority were or were not using the types of measures reported, rather than identifying the percentage of the departments or agencies that were using them.

By looking at all the survey data, and especially at this survey, we can form an answer to the question that we posed in the section: Who is measuring performance? Clearly, most states and larger localities are engaged in performance measurement. This supports earlier survey research that indicates widespread use of performance measurement. Table 5.1 also demonstrates that as the kind of measure used increases in difficulty (and presumed usefulness), the percentage of agencies and departments using it decreases—another indicator consistent with previous studies. Input, activity, efficiency, and output measures are all internal data. They are the result of action taken by service providers, as opposed to actions taken by recipients of services. That makes them easy to count and easy to track. Internal data may or may not be sufficient for outcome measures, which measure impact that programs and services have on their recipients. Citizen satisfaction measures and benchmarks are typically external data, the first from users of services and the second from other public service providers. Explanatory measures describe results when quantitative measures are impossible or impractical.[17]

Are Some Measures Better than Others?

We say no, not intrinsically, though some performance measures are certainly easier to collect and less prone to common problems. The relevant question for the manager is, "What do you want to know?" and "What will you do with the measures when you get them?" A prudent manager would probably not spend precious program resources to measure an aspect of his program's performance that he could not change. If the manager intends to use performance measures for decision making, he should gather the data that inform the decisions he wants to make. However, if the manager primarily uses the measures to append to the program's page in the annual budget document, he might want to select measures that either demonstrate the need for more resources or assure the reader that existing resources are being used efficiently. Most managers have discovered that if they want to use performance measures as the foundation for decisions about service delivery, the kind of performance measures needed are the most difficult to get.

It is helpful to have categories of performance measures and examine them in isolation and in comparison with each other. There are a half-dozen common groupings of performance measures, none necessarily more appropriate than any other. We have selected one grouping from the many to present here, mainly because it is clear and comprehensive and does not include input measures.[18] Input measures tell managers nothing about the actual performance of service delivery. Managers must track inputs in order to calculate efficiency measures, which are measures of performance. Keep in mind whether the data are internal or external, and the ease of collection when thinking about these categories.

Output Measures

The easiest of the four types to collect and analyze, output or workload measures, shows how much service the program is providing. Identifying output measures is sometimes very simple, but other times it is harder to decide what a unit of work looks like and what the best reference point for it would be. Take the case of the sanitation program. A unit of work has to involve garbage pickup, but how should it be measured? The city of St. Petersburg, Florida, sanitation program picked up garbage at 76,000 residential sites and 6,300 commercial sites in 2001.[19] Those are interesting and impressive numbers but they do not really get at the output of the program. For one thing, it would be hard to think about how output could be decreased or increased based on the action of sanitation workers. They have no control over the number of households and businesses from which garbage is collected. A better output measure would be the tons of garbage picked up per some meaningful unit of time (day/week/month). This reflects how much the sanitation program is producing and gives the manager information he/she can use to adjust the inputs (personnel, capital equipment) to improve outputs and to monitor progress over time. The criteria for this measure are the same as for any other—that they tell the manager something useful about how the program is performing.

Now consider the problem of determining good output measures for a state child protection agency. The Missouri Department of Children's Services, a division of Family Services, received 53,204 reports of child abuse or neglect in 2000. The caseworker assigned to each report had to determine if an incident of abuse or neglect had occurred or was occurring and what kind of service was appropriate for that finding. A finding includes: probable cause (case becomes a criminal matter), unsubstantiated, unsubstantiated but recommend preventative services, recommend family assessment, and other (which may include families that have moved out of state or cannot be located and false reports). The caseworker has a time limit of thirty days to evaluate the situation and make a finding.[20] A reasonable workload measure would be the number of findings (or case resolutions) per caseworker per thirty days. Managers might look for ways to increase the number of outputs (resolved cases) per worker per month.

The astute reader is already complaining that there is a world of difference between the sanitation program and the children's services program—between tons of garbage and a decision that affects a child's well-being. In fact, some readers may be questioning the appropriateness of any performance measure for children's services. We agree wholeheartedly that perverse incentives may attend to certain performance measures, and none are more susceptible to perverse incentives than outputs. We consider the matter of incentives, perverse and positive, at some length later in this chapter. But for now, we defend the collection and monitoring of workload measures even for the kind of services rendered by the children's services program. Just because the manager knows the workloads does not require him/her to (1) report them in the budget document or (2) press caseworkers to increase them. Managers need to understand the workload demands on caseworkers and how different caseworkers cope with them, for a variety of reasons. A good manager knows how to use workload information properly. The manager wants to know whether a drop in output from a productive caseworker resulted from a few very difficult and time-consuming cases. The manager also wants to know if an increase in output from a caseworker might indicate an inappropriately casual attitude toward investigation. Output or workload information is always relevant to a manager. His or her managerial skills dictate its appropriate use.

Efficiency Measures

One often sees efficiency treated as a value or ideal, especially when public services are being discussed. In fact, measuring efficiency is not comparing a program's efficiency with some ideal, but simply dividing the output measure by the input measure. In the case of St. Petersburg's sanitation program, the 280,000 tons of refuse it picked up in 2001 would be divided by the full-time equivalent positions assigned to collection to yield an efficiency measure (this measure has workload implications as well).[21] Other efficiency measures are expressed as unit costs. The cost per ton of refuse would be a common unit efficiency measure for refuse collection. The manager could monitor changes in efficiency over time as she adjusts outputs and inputs. Efficiency measures, like all performance measures, have to be treated with care. If the sanitation manager's cost per ton of refuse is rising because gasoline prices have driven up one of her primary operating expenditures, it signifies nothing about the manager's skills or her employee's output levels. It is always, however, useful information to have even when it has no action implication.

Now we turn to an efficiency measure for the children's services program. It is almost unseemly to suggest that efficiency criteria might be relevant to such matters, but managers need to know about efficiency for the same reasons they need to know about output. What they do with the information for decision making is an entirely different matter. Once again, unit costs are appropriate, and in the scenario we set earlier, the unit would be the report. When caseworkers are assigned a report, they have a routine for investigation that entails a review of computer records, phone calls, site visits, and other normal investigative techniques. All these activities have costs that can be quantified. The caseworker's logbook might be a valuable source of efficiency data. In it the caseworker would record the date and time of phone calls and perhaps the location and duration of visits. After the investigative costs are summed, the number of hours the caseworker spent on the investigation can be expressed as a salary cost. The computation could be either very detailed or approximate, depending on the manager's information needs.

The reader may wonder why on earth the manager would spend the time, effort, and money to collect such efficiency data when it is incomprehensible that the manager would tell the caseworker to try to keep investigative costs down so that the efficiency measure would be higher. In fact, the manager would reject such extensive data gathering efforts for exactly that reason because the cost of routinely gathering that information far exceeds the benefits for managerial decision making. However, the manager will make a reasonable effort to approximate an efficiency measure because the information may be useful for planning purposes. If the manager predicts a 4 percent growth rate in reports next year, what will those additional investigations cost? Using available and relatively unobtrusive data such as long distance telephone bills, fleet logs (where the caseworker signs out a car, notes the mileage and the destination), and perhaps overtime hours, the manager could calculate an efficiency measure accurate enough to support a budget request.

Outcome Measures

These are the heart of performance measurement because they capture the extent to which the service is meeting its service delivery goals. Another, perhaps better, name for these measures is "effectiveness measures." They require the manager to answer the questions, "What are my service objectives?" and "To what degree am I achieving them?" It sounds easy enough, but it is frightfully difficult for services that deal in vague or multiple objectives or that rely on personal contact between provider and citizen for service delivery. The difficulty of designing and collecting good outcome data explains why the figures in Table 5.1 drop about 20 percentage points between output and outcome measures. If we sorted out the percent of programs using outcome measures along service types, the actual percentages would probably be even lower. Let us go back to our two departments to explore the problem.

The St. Petersburg sanitation program might opt for an external outcome measure such as citizen satisfaction with curbside pickup. For service providers with clear objectives, for example, refuse collection, a customer satisfaction indicator has appeal. In addition to an outcome measure of its core objective, the sanitation program might have other objectives that are particularly amenable to outcome measures. The St. Petersburg department has a new community appearance division charged with removing graffiti and keeping vacant lots clear of debris.[22] The department could set an outcome goal, for example, of a two-business-day target for graffiti removal (which is not the same as number of graffiti sites cleaned, an output measure). Finally, St. Petersburg has an ambitious recycling program. In 2001 the program recycled 4,800 tons of newspapers, glass, and plastics, and turned 42,000 tons of yard clippings into free mulch.[23] An outcome goal for their recycling program might be a 3 percent increase in tons of recycled materials (internal measure) or a 3 percent increase in curbside recycling (an external measure). The manager should beware that meeting a recycling performance target has an impact on the output and efficiency measures. As more citizens participate in recycling, the tonnage of residential garbage might be affected.

How in the world can the Missouri Department of Children's Services measure outcomes? They can describe a desired outcome easily enough. A desired outcome is when the best interests of the child are served; when the caseworker's finding results in an appropriate action for the child and the family. But the problem is that we cannot calculate such an outcome except by rather arbitrary criteria. Even if we could refine the criteria for success would it provide the manager any useful information about how to achieve it? Some external outcome measures are just as problematic. It does not seem reasonable to ask either the child or the family from which the child may have been removed for an evaluation of service quality. It might, however, be reasonable to monitor the number of second reports of abuse or neglect in cases where families were left intact after investigation. Expressed as a percentage of total cases, that measure could be useful for managers and caseworkers. Another possibility might be the percentage of probable-cause cases that were successfully adjudicated by sentencing or sentencing alternatives. The obvious difficulty in the case of this service is the relationship between what matters and what we can count.

Productivity Measures

Productivity measures are the ratio of outcome to efficiency. They are the most useful kind of information for a manager, and, naturally, the hardest to obtain. First, all the problems surrounding outcomes need to be conquered, and then the appropriate efficiency measure must be chosen to yield a number that expresses the outcome achieved per unit cost. For our sanitation department's recycling program, let us assume there are 20,000 collection points (output measure). The cost per collection point is $2.50 (efficiency measure). The service goal is to increase the percentage of collection points engaged in recycling, an outcome. The productivity measure would be the number of collection points recycling divided by the cost of recycling. For example, if 45 percent of collection points are recycled, the productivity cost per participating collection point would be $5.50.

Things get tricky again when we look for a reasonable productivity measure for Children's Services. Recall one possible outcome measure, the number of second reports of abuse or neglect in cases where families were left intact after investigation. The relevant output measure might be the number of site visits by the caseworker after the report to assess the child's safety in the home. An approximate cost associated with each site visit would provide an efficiency indicator. If we divided the number of cases where there were no second reports by the cost per site visit we might have some reasonable proxy for productivity—in this case the productivity of site visits in achieving positive outcomes for families. A manager might want to have some indicator of the productivity of site visits for planning and budgeting purposes, even though no manager would encourage unneeded site visits or discourage needed site visits on the basis of such a productivity measure.

Which Performance Measures Do You Choose?

The reader has likely detected two patterns from the previous section on the types of performance measures. First, outputs and efficiencies were the easiest to measure for both refuse collection and children's services. That explains why managers often rely on outputs and efficiencies as their performance measures. They are more accurate and more reliable than outcome and productivity measures. Outputs and efficiencies also cost less to collect than outcomes and productivity measures, in fact, the government is probably already collecting output and efficiency data. They can simply be used to calculate performance measures and added to the department or agency's budget summary. Workload measures are especially appealing as performance indicators because they suggest that more resources may be required to continue to provide the current level of services.

The second pattern is that performance measures were easier all around for the sanitation program than for the children's services program. The reason may be obvious to students familiar with policy evaluation. When the goals are generally agreed upon and the technology is known, it is easier to determine the policy goals of the service provider and measure the provider's success in achieving them. The St. Petersburg sanitation department enjoys goal agreement across its programs, from recycling to graffiti removal, to vacant lot clearing, to curbside pickup. The means necessary to achieve these goals are not illusive (though the department might not know exactly why some people choose not to recycle).

When the goals are not agreed upon and the technology is not known, policy success is very difficult to evaluate. Some policy makers want the Missouri Department of Children's Services to emphasize keeping families intact except under the worst circumstances. Other policy makers want to reduce the likelihood of harm to children. Everyone wants the caseworkers to do the right thing for each child who comes to the attention of the program, but reasonable people can disagree on what the "right thing" is in any given case. To further complicate matters, no one knows how to achieve the goal of resolving the case in the best interest of the child. To be blunt, caseworkers do not know why some parents harm their children, so they do not know how to induce them to change their behavior. The caseworkers are well trained, and armed with the best research, but they have no checklist of factors that result in abuse situations and no formula for the number and duration of site visits required to prevent a second report. At the end of the day, the sanitation worker in St. Petersburg knows exactly what he/she has accomplished. At the end of the day, the Missouri caseworker probably longs for that kind of certainty.

We can generalize from these examples about the utility of different types of performance measures for different types of public services organizations. If we think of these measures as a continuum, with outputs on one end and productivity on the other, then service providers with a cause-and-effect relationship between their outputs and outcomes can measure performance at the outcome and productivity end of the continuum as shown in Figure 5.6. Service providers who do not know the cause-and-effect relationship between their outputs and outcomes will probably want to stay with measures of output and efficiency, venturing into the areas of outcomes and productivity very cautiously.

Another useful way to think about limitations on outcome/productivity measures is to consider the nature of the service being provided. If a private sector contractor could provide the service, it is more likely that meaningful outcome/productivity measures could be constructed, and managers could use them to build incentives into the production process to reward high-performing employees. On the other hand, if the service is a public good or service—one that the private sector would not provide because it would not be profitable—the likelihood of building a workable incentive system around good output/productivity measures of performance is not high.[24] Recall that

Figure 5.6   **Causal Knowledge and Type of Performance Measure**

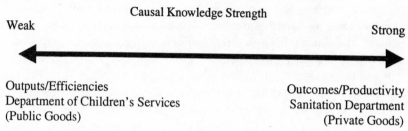

Causal Knowledge Strength

Weak   Strong

Outputs/Efficiencies   Outcomes/Productivity
Department of Children's Services   Sanitation Department
(Public Goods)   (Private Goods)

we said the children's services manager may find outcome and productivity data useful for a variety of purposes, excluding setting performance targets for caseworkers that would interfere with their best judgment on how to handle a report of child abuse.

In chapter 4, we noted that many public services are mandated, and the planning process must accommodate itself to them. Similarly, managers adapt their performance measures to the services and programs they are required to provide and to the way law or administrative rule dictates that they provide them. It would not make much sense to use performance measures to encourage innovation in service provision when innovation is constrained by law and administrative rules, as would be the case in the Department of Children's Services.

George Frederickson once commented that much of what passes for performance measurement amounts to "painting bull's-eyes around bullet holes."[25] He meant that service providers operate within a narrow range of discretion, so their performance measures reflect what they are already doing. This is part of a larger problem in "reinvented" or "entrepreneurial" public management where the manager actually has little maneuvering room for innovation. We can see the evidence of the "Frederickson effect" in the higher use rates of output performance measures relative to outcome measures. Most output measures are bullet holes around which targets have been painted. Outcome measures may be less susceptible to what we will call the "Frederickson effect" because they force managers to think about what their organization should be doing.

Problems with Performance Measures

Because many professional organizations have made an explicit connection between adoption of performance measurement and accountability to citizens, there has been an unfortunate tendency to accuse managers of not being very professional or accountable if they are reluctant to measure or to report their performance.[26] In fact, a good manager must consider the costs and benefits of performance measures and must be aware of some of the problems inherent to performance measurement. These things, done well and seriously, cost money and take time. Good managers struggle to improve productivity and enhance service effectiveness, but within the constraints of limited resources and perhaps limited attention to results by decision makers. No wonder they gravitate toward measures that cost little to collect and that do not challenge the mission of their organization—in other words, output and efficiency measures. Here are some real problems with performance measures that explain why managers sometimes approach performance measurement with trepidation.

Perverse Incentives

The identification of an outcome measure carries weight in the organization, and becomes a de facto incentive to improve performance on that outcome. Most agencies and departments have multiple missions. The users of performance information, including employees, elected officials, the media, and the public prioritize the ones that can be measured. There are no unobtrusive performance measures; what is measured determines what is done.[27] If sanitation workers know that the weight of the garbage is what is measured, they look for ways to increase weight that may or may not be related to the department's performance goal (one department watered down the garbage before weighing it). Other examples abound. Students and teachers alike know that the use of standardized tests as a way to measure educational performance has changed the way teachers teach and students learn. But educators and policy makers predicted the consequences of adopting that performance measure and they made a responsible decision to adopt it anyway.

Often the most perverse incentives come unexpectedly. Consider the case of a district attorney's office in a city we decline to identify. An outcome for a prosecutor's office is a successful prosecution, and so the performance measure was adopted with confidence. Attorneys analyzed their success rates and began to contemplate how they could improve them. A pattern quickly emerged. The surest successes were plea bargains, where the defendant pleads guilty to a lesser offense on the promise of a reduced sentence compared to what he/she might receive in a court trial. For the cases going to trial, the ones most likely to result in conviction were those where the defendant was represented by the public defender's office. The cases least likely to result in conviction were those where the defendant had the means to afford his/her own lawyer. Despite the best intentions of all involved, a two-tiered system of justice began to emerge in the city, one for affluent persons accused of a crime and another for poorer persons accused of a crime. This system would have been an affront to the ethics of all the attorneys involved had they been thinking about the consequences of their productivity rather than thinking about improving their productivity. Performance measures can do that.

Proxies

Most public programs and services cannot easily quantify successful outcomes. We cannot measure incidents of child neglect that did not occur because families received intervention services, though that is exactly what the children's services program would call a success. We cannot measure crimes prevented because police officers began more aggressive patrols, or, alternatively, began to spend more time in the community getting to know the citizens. Surely that was just the outcome that both kinds of police responses were designed to achieve. Proxy measures are usually developed to try to capture aspects of outcomes on the hope that the proxy is correlated with actual program outcomes. When the correlation is high, then what is measured tells the manager a lot about what is accomplished. When the correlation is low, the measure is, at best, useless. If employees try to maximize their performance on the proxy measure because it has been selected to stand for an outcome, but the relationship is weak, employee efforts may actually threaten rather than enhance the mission of the organization.

Causal Fallacy

Correlation is not causation.[28] Every student of statistics has been told that, yet we seem instinctually to leap from correlation to causation in the way we process information. If we take an action and get a result, we want to believe our action caused that result. If people who have a glass of red wine each day live longer than people who do not drink at all, the wine must produce longevity. But the relationship may be spurious, a result of another relationship that is masked by what we have chosen to correlate. In the wine example, it is much more likely that people who choose to drink one glass of red wine per day are affluent and have access to better health care throughout their lives.

As indicated before, the caseworker does not know why an adult neglects or abuses a child so the caseworker is powerless to prevent it. The sanitation manager does not know why some people refuse to recycle, so she does not know how to change their behavior. If a public education campaign increases recycling, perhaps there is correlation but there is no causation. Saturating reluctant recyclers with information is unlikely to bring about the desired result. In general, information about outcomes, when the manager can get it, does not reveal how those outcomes were achieved. "Unfortunately, many public employees, elected officials, and media people believe that regularly collected outcome information [means that] the government program and its staff were the primary causes of the outcomes. [O]utcome information provides only a score . . . whether one is winning or losing and to what extent . . . but it does not indicate why."[29]

We cannot conclude this section without another story. In another one of our anonymous cities, the police department created a "flying squad" of officers to combat street crime. The officers patrolled the toughest parts of the city in an unmarked car, looking for fights, muggings, and so forth. It worked; street crime in those areas went down. The chief called a press conference and there were hearty congratulations and much good cheer in the law enforcement community—until six months later, when the weather warmed up and it was comfortable enough for people to gather on the streets again. Street crime went right back to the pre-flying squad level. Ah, causality.

Managerial Control

This issue is related to causality and proxy measures, but is important enough to a manager to warrant a brief discussion of its own. Let us say the mayor charged the sanitation department manager with improving the city's residential recycling rate to 75 percent. Or that the governor charged the children's services manager to achieve a zero repeat report rate for a child placed back with the child's family after an investigation. The manager would pledge to do his/her best, but would remind the mayor and the governor that these goals are outside his/her "zone of control." The sanitation manager might well have some ideas about how to get defiant citizens to recycle, but they might not be appropriate or even legal. (Refusing to pick up other garbage unless the recycle bin was adequately stocked springs to mind.) The children's services manager might believe that once-a-week unannounced site visits with mandatory counseling might just get that all-important number to zero, but he/she probably does not not have nearly enough personnel or resources to implement the plan. These are two situations where the outcomes lay outside the manager's zone of control, but for different reasons. The first is causal knowledge; the second is resources. Our other two potential problems, perverse incentives and poor proxies, can place performance improvement outside a manager's zone of control. In the real world, the ability to identify a service outcome does not create the causal knowledge, resources, incentives, good measures, or managerial control to achieve it.

So What Are States and Local Governments Really Measuring?

The short answer to the question is that states and local governments are measuring aspects of programs and services that are amenable to measurement. Those would be the kinds of measures that rely on internal data that are either readily available or can be obtained at low cost. Examination of actual performance documents reinforces the conclusion that states and localities shy away from the more difficult and demanding task of measuring program outcomes.[30] Despite the proliferation of how-to manuals and other forms of assistance offered by professional associations, relatively few cities move beyond the compilation of workload data to real measures of program effectiveness. A survey of city and state auditors found respondents satisfied with the input and output data collected as a part of their performance management system, but not so satisfied with their measures of program effectiveness or efficiency.[31]

Therefore, the kinds of performance measures actually collected might provide useful information for managers, but do not usually capture the outcomes of the programs to which they may be applied, especially if the measures are static as the program changes to meet changing demands.[32] Generic or "cookbook" performance measures rarely meet the managerial needs of the organization[33] and cannot reflect the changing environment or service expectations for the organization. But even as performance measurement becomes institutionalized, localities have not typically moved beyond "cookbook" measures to program-specific measures.[34]

We know, theoretically, what characteristics performance measures should have. The best performance measures are valid, reliable, understandable, timely, resistant to perverse behavior, comprehensive, nonredundant, cost sensitive, program specific, and focused on aspects of performance that are controllable.[35] They should permit tracking performance results over time, but be updated regularly. They should capture outcomes that are impossible to quantify, be faster than a speeding bullet, leap tall buildings in a single bound, and so forth. The point is that managers may know the qualities of a good performance measure, but be unable to construct one because the criteria would eliminate most feasible choices. Compare GASB's criteria for a performance measure with GFOA's guidelines in Boxes 5.2 and 5.3. If you were a manager faced with such a daunting set of guidelines, you might measure inputs and outputs too.

What Are States and Localities Doing with the Results?

This is the question that bedevils the advocates of performance measurement. Many, perhaps most, argue that the process of measuring performance is helpful for managers, even if no productivity improvements are realized. We simply do not know how often managers change their delivery routines or purchasing behavior in response to the findings from performance data. It is the larger question of what kind of results we are talking about when we adopt performance measures to, as the American Society for Public Admin-

Box 5.2
GASB's Characteristics for Performance Information

Performance information should meet the characteristics of relevance, understandability, comparability, timeliness, consistency, and reliability. The application of these characteristics to performance information is discussed below.

Relevance
Performance information should include data that are essential to provide a basis for understanding the accomplishment of goals and objectives of the entity that have potentially significant decision-making or accountability implications. As with any other information provided in general purpose external financial reporting (GPEFR), performance information should be management's representations of the performance of the entity and its agencies, departments, programs, and services. Because the purpose of governmental entities is to establish and enforce laws, regulate activities, and provide services economically, effectively, and efficiently—not to earn profits—no single measure of performance is readily available to assist users in assessing accountability and in making economic, political, and social decisions. A broad variety of performance measures may therefore be required to meet the diverse needs of the different users; report on the many goals and objectives of different types of agencies, departments, programs, and services; and address the issues being considered for different decisions and levels of accountability.

Understandability
Performance information should be communicated in a readily understandable manner. It should communicate the performance of the agency, department, program, or service to any reasonably informed interested party. To enhance user understanding, different forms of reporting such as tables, charts, and graphs may be needed by different state and local governmental entities and for different agencies, departments, programs, and services.

Performance information should be concise yet comprehensive with regard to which (and how many) measures of performance are reported. Both conciseness and comprehensiveness in reporting performance measures are important because of the number, diversity, and complexity of state and local governmental agencies, departments, programs, and services.

(continued)

Box 5.2 *(continued)*

Performance information should be provided at the most appropriate level of aggregation or disaggregation. A balance should be achieved among the number of services reported, the performance measures reported, and the capability of users to understand and act on the information.

Performance information should include explanations about important underlying factors and existing conditions that may have affected performance. Explanatory information (including narrative explanations) should be reported with the measures of performance both for important factors that are substantially outside the control of the entity and for factors over which the entity has some control, which could affect performance. Narrative explanations about performance measures and any important factors that are known to have affected the reported results should be presented.

Performance information may be accompanied by a description of the way in which the performance measures should be used. This could include comments on the need to consider performance measures in conjunction with explanatory information, the need to consider the multiple aspects of performance when assessing results, instances where surrogate measures are being reported because of an inability to measure an outcome of a service, and the difficulty of using performance information to assess policy accountability. The descriptions could also contain additional information about performance measures that could assist users in understanding the reasons for the reported level of performance and actions planned or being taken to change results.

Comparability
Performance information should provide a clear frame of reference for assessing the performance of the entity and its agencies, departments, programs, and services. Performance measures, when presented alone, do not provide a basis for assessing or understanding the level of performance of an agency, department, program, or service. Therefore, performance information should include comparative information. This information may take various forms; for example, depending on the type of agency, department, program, or service being reported on, reported measures of performance could include comparisons with (a) several earlier fiscal years, (b) targets established by the entity such as targets established as part of the budgetary process, (c) externally established norms or standards of performance, (d) other parts or subunits of the same entity, or (e) other, comparable entities.

Timeliness
Performance information should be reported in a timely manner so that it will be available to users before it loses its capacity to be of value in assessing accountability and making decisions.

Consistency
Performance information should be reported consistently from period to period to allow users to have a basis for comparing performance over time and to gain an understanding of the measures being used and their meaning. However, performance measures also need to be reviewed regularly and modified or replaced as needed to reflect changing circumstances.

Reliability
For performance information to be of value to users, it is essential that it be reliable. To be reliable, the information should be verifiable and free from bias and should faithfully represent what it purports to represent. Therefore, performance information should be derived from systems that produce controlled and verifiable data. The value of a strong internal control structure has long been recognized when dealing with financial information. If performance information is to be considered for inclusion as part of the information required for GPEFR, it is important that the systems and methods used to gather and verify the information be subjected to analysis similar to that used for financial information systems.

Source: Governmental Accounting Standards Board, adapted from Concepts Statement No. 2 of the Governmental Accounting Standards Board, Service Efforts and Accomplishments Reporting; available at accounting.rutgers.edu/raw/seagov/pmg/perfmeasures/index.html.

istration says, "manage for results."[36] Fisher estimated that 75 percent of organizations that collect performance data do not use the results for decision making.[37] Why would local governments take the time and spend the money to develop and implement performance measures if they do not intend to use them? The answer may lie in the "me, too" nature of the reform tradition in public administration, especially when the reform carries the aura of increased efficiency and professionalism.[38]

Conclusion

Can performance measurement systems do for government what they, anecdotally, did for corporate America? The private sector can easily use perfor-

---

Box 5.3

**GFOA's Guidelines for
Performance Management**

The Government Finance Officers Association (GFOA) recommends that program and service performance measures be developed and used as an important component of long-term strategic planning and decision making, which should be linked to governmental budgeting. Performance measures should:

1. Be based on program goals and objectives that tie to a statement of program mission or purpose;
2. Measure program outcomes;
3. Provide for resource allocation comparisons over time;
4. Measure efficiency and effectiveness for continuous improvement;
5. Be verifiable, understandable, and timely;
6. Be consistent throughout the strategic plan, budget, accounting, and reporting systems, and, to the extent practical, be consistent over time;
7. Be reported internally and externally;
8. Be monitored and used in managerial decision-making processes;
9. Be limited to a number and degree of complexity that can provide an efficient and meaningful way to assess the effectiveness and efficiency of key programs; and
10. Be designed in such a way to motivate staff at all levels to contribute toward organizational improvement.

Source: GFOA Performance Management Initiative Adopted by Executive Board, March 2001, www.gfoa.org/services/rp/budget.shtml#2Relevance.

---

mance measures to create incentives for individual and departmental productivity. They do it by linking good performance to rewards. But we do not do that in the public sector, and not just because we do not have the money to reward high performers. Return to Box 5.1 to look at the distinction drawn between private goods and services and public goods and services. The closer the public service is to one that could be privately provided, the more successful any performance-based program is likely to be. The closer the service is to a purely public good, one that would not be provided by the private sector, the harder it is to capture outcomes with performance measures and the more problematic it is to create incentives for managers and employees to achieve them. The hardest part of a performance measurement system is not in derivation of indicators but in application of results. The problem is this: unless a government ties its performance measures *meaningfully* into its management systems—unless those measures are something more than decorations for the budget document—any performance management program will fail, and probably deserves to.[39]

Many observers assumed that performance-based management reform would have a fairly short shelf life for exactly those reasons. Others claimed the tenets of performance management amounted to little more than simplistic, often contradictory slogans that reinforced negative public opinion about government.[40] And finally, some scholars suggested that no managerial reform that actually changes how people think about what they do can be implemented overnight, especially in the public sector where laws and rules attend to almost every aspect of service delivery. It is helpful to distinguish between collecting and reporting performance data and using them for decision making. We are sure that the former has taken place, and we are beginning to see evidence of the latter.[41] The challenge is to offer managers a reason to move beyond collecting and reporting by offering them a comprehensive managerial framework that incorporates performance measurement in ways that inform decisions.

— Chapter 6 —

Benchmarking

In the previous chapter we contrasted performance data with performance information, drawing the distinction between measures that were ready to contribute to decision making and those that are useful only for monitoring certain aspects of service delivery. This chapter describes internal and external benchmarking, or comparisons of performance data between the past and present and between different jurisdictions. It describes how some external benchmarks can be used by program managers to look for opportunities for service delivery improvement by comparing their performance data with similar departments in other states or local governments.

Benchmarking has the potential to reveal best practices among programs and services and is a worthwhile endeavor for that reason. However, raw external benchmark data are rarely helpful for performance budgeting. It would be foolish for city council members in Nashville, Tennessee, to make budget decisions for their police department based on their department's clearance rate for Type I (felony) offenses relative to Knoxville and Memphis. Local priorities, local needs, local resources, and departmental performance determine the appropriate level of support for law enforcement.

However, what if benchmarking revealed an efficiency (cost per unit of output) gap between Nashville's and Knoxville's police departments? The chief would want to know what Knoxville was doing differently. When he found out, he might be able to change his service delivery system to take advantage of the efficiency enhancement, or he might not, depending on local law, political mandates, or fiscal constraints. However, if the chief concluded that the efficiency gain was feasible, he might establish that efficiency as a performance target, and monitor the department's progress toward it. Now, the performance data are performance information, suitable for decision making in the budget process.

The basis of all benchmarking programs is a comparison between two data points, with one of the data points designated as the benchmark. The traditional form of benchmarking in the public sector has been internal comparisons, where departments compare their current performance with their performance in prior reporting periods.[1] The Government Finance Officers Association (GFOA) refers to this form of benchmarking as process benchmarks, assessing how well core business functions or work processes contribute to the success of selected programs.[2] Process benchmarks provide a basis for continuous process improvement. Managers continually try to improve their service delivery performance rather than maintain the status quo, and they monitor their progress by looking at service delivery process improvement over time. Each time current performance is favorably compared to performance of the previous reporting period, it "raises the bar" for future standards. If there is no improvement over prior period's standard, the result is considered a static performance period (rather than a failure—there may be good reasons why improvement plateaus). It is not realistic to expect managers to overhaul their policies and procedures from one year to the next to achieve small improvements, but the idea of continuous process improvement requires them to look for opportunities on a continual basis.

More recently, benchmarking has come to mean comparing internal performance data with a different, external source. This allows an organization to analyze its performance against a comparable external organization, like a fire department in a city of similar size. External benchmarking in the public sector often takes one of two forms, corporate-style benchmarking or comparison of performance statistics as benchmarks.[3] The GFOA describes these forms of benchmarking as performance benchmarks, comparing the performance of service delivery from one organization to another in terms of efficiency and effectiveness.[4] The goal of external benchmarking is the search for best practices among similar service providers.

Another commonly used form of benchmarking is "targets" as benchmarks.[5] The GFOA calls this form of benchmarking "strategic benchmarks," where a government chooses some level of performance that a program, an organization, or even a community wants to achieve.[6] State and local governments often include targets in their budget documents for monitoring the progress toward goals and objectives for agencies, departments, divisions, and programs. Targets as benchmarks may take the form of internal or external benchmarking. It is internal benchmarking if targets are established for process improvement. It is external benchmarking if targets are tied to performance measures obtained from other organizations or to industry standards.

This chapter describes the four major forms of benchmarking and how benchmarking can support a performance budgeting program. It begins by introducing the link between benchmarking and performance budgeting, using fleet services for illustration. The following four forms of benchmarking are then presented: continuous process improvement, corporate-style benchmarking, comparison of performance statistics as benchmarks, and targets as benchmarks. It then discusses the organizational capacity required for benchmarking, including some common pitfalls to avoid and circumstances when benchmarking may not be appropriate. The chapter concludes with some general observations on how managers can select the right form of benchmarking for their programs to link performance to the budgetary process.

Benchmarking and Performance Budgeting

The relationship between benchmarking and performance budgeting begins with gathering the necessary data to begin one of the four forms of public sector benchmarking. Managers analyze these data to identify changes in the business practices of service delivery that will improve performance, justifying their recommendations based on the data. Managers then identify the resources they need for implementation. For example, a new staff position or an investment in technology may be necessary to achieve this new level of performance. Any new budget request that the manager makes based on performance standards enters the budgetary process for the coming fiscal year. What happens next—the deliberation of the budget request—is critical to performance budgeting. Whether it is approved or denied, if the decision about the new expenditure is based on performance, the criteria for performance budgeting has been satisfied. When the manager made his/her case based on performance, and the decision makers took performance into consideration in their deliberations, the organization was practicing performance budgeting, regardless of the outcome. Benchmarking supports a performance budgeting system by offering managers performance data that they can use to craft process improvements in service delivery.

If the data are reliable, if the benchmarking process is appropriate, and if the manager's conclusion about the relationship between a new investment in capital and performance improvement is correct, then would a council truly committed to performance budgeting not approve the expenditure? Not necessarily. Consider the case of the city of Blue Sky (Box 6.1).

The previous example raises three important points about performance budgeting in a political setting. First, council members made the decision not to fund the ten vehicles in the first fiscal year. This decision was made in part based on the performance of certain types of vehicles, realizing that annual cost of fleet maintenance would continue to be high as a percentage of the historical cost of the rolling stock. Second, the council members made a decision based on the financial performance of the organization, understanding that fund balance is extremely important to the fiscal stability of local government. Third, council members granted the appropriation for the ten vehicles in the following fiscal year's budget ordinance, basing their decision on the annual performance of certain types of vehicles.

Box 6.1

The City of Blue Sky

The fleet manager for the city of Blue Sky creates and tracks numerous performance statistics associated with the organization's rolling stock (vehicles). One measure, the annual cost of fleet maintenance as a percentage of the historical cost of the rolling stock, continues to increase despite efforts of cost control. The fleet manager constructs a questionnaire and sends it to five surrounding jurisdictions, requesting information on number of vehicles maintained by type, average miles driven per year by vehicle type, fleet replacement plan by vehicle type, annual cost of fleet maintenance, and historical cost of the rolling stock. The fleet manager recruits a budget analyst to assist with comparing the performance measures for the city of Blue Sky against the performance statistics collected from the five surrounding jurisdictions. The major finding is that the city of Blue Sky's replacement cycle is much longer for certain vehicle types as compared to the other jurisdictions. This explains why maintenance costs are higher—Blue Sky's police vehicles are older than those in the benchmark cities. Upon further review, the budget analyst determines that these types of vehicles also account for a large percentage of the annual cost of fleet maintenance.

The fleet manager constructs an alternative fleet replacement plan for the kinds of police vehicles that require the majority of the annual maintenance and repair work, using the performance data obtained from the benchmarking initiative for justifying the new business plan. In order to implement the business plan, ten vehicles must be purchased in the coming fiscal year. The fleet manager makes the budget request during the annual budgetary process, including information on the cost savings that will occur from a reduction in the annual maintenance and repair work. The budget request is denied as council members decide to focus on increasing the city's fund balance, responding to the new financial policy of maintaining a fund balance that is 15 percent of total expenditures. The fleet manager makes the same budget request the following fiscal year using updated performance information. Council members decide to appropriate the funds for ten vehicles based on the information that accompanied the request.

Council's answer was not "no" but "not yet," as other important goals compete with any request for new funding. When council decided that the fund balance was more important than the vehicle replacement the first year, they were still making their decision based on performance information, the amount saved from the change in fleet management versus the amount needed to meet the fund balance goal. They stayed true to their commitment to performance budgeting, even though they decided not to fund a change that would have improved performance the first year it was recommended. The test, if you will, is not whether the answer to a manager's recommendation is yes, but whether the deliberation about the answer was based on performance.

The link between benchmarking and performance budgeting is still in the developmental stage for state and local government. Public organizations tend to be proficient in creating, collecting, and reporting performance data. However, more work is needed in creating usable information for enhancing the utility of making sound business decisions from performance data, especially when the performance data are obtained from benchmarking projects. The information derived from performance measurement and benchmarking becomes the basis for expanding the budget process to include performance management as described in chapter 3.

Continuous Process Improvement

Few management initiatives have received more attention than total quality management (TQM), with the Deming-based version by far the most influential and widespread.[7] Driven by seven basic tenets, W. Edward Deming focused on improving quality through the experts (workers) who know best how to solve problems and improve processes.[8] Continuous process improvement, a core tenant of TQM, is often regarded as a stand-alone management initiative. Research on TQM in municipalities has shown that increasing employee productivity through continuous process improvement is a key reason for adopting TQM.[9] That same research also revealed that budgetary pressure is another common reason for implementing TQM. What can be extrapolated from this research is that municipalities approach continuous process improvement in the belief that budgetary decisions can be enhanced by process performance information.

There is an abundance of literature and training available on continuous process improvement; we will address its use in a performance budgeting program. Similarly, there are other management improvement aspects of TQM (product, organization, leadership, and commitment)[10] that we will not discuss so that we can focus on continuous process improvement as process benchmarks. However, the other factors associated with management improvement are important to performance budgeting as we discuss in chapter 8.

The basic methodology for continuous process improvement in state and local government follows these steps:

1. Management identifies a process for study;
2. A team is chartered to conduct the study, including workers directly involved in the process;
3. A flow chart of the existing process is created;
4. Performance data are obtained and tracked for the current process;
5. System techniques are used to analyze the process;
6. Recommendations for change are created from a review of the process and the data;
7. Resources are identified for implementing the recommendations;
8. Resources are requested during the budgetary process if additional resources are required;
9. Recommendations are implemented; and
10. Performance measures are used to monitor the success of the changes.

Note that the methodology for continuous process improvement includes process benchmarks in step four, obtaining and tracking performance data for the current process. This step establishes the baseline or the benchmark for the current process, providing the foundation for constructing the recommendations for change.[11] After the recommendations have been implemented, performance data are collected and compared to the baseline or to the benchmark for improvement. The process is continually monitored until the performance data reveal that the process has reached a new equilibrium stage at the higher standard. The baseline or the benchmark is then changed to reflect the performance of the new equilibrium stage, and the methodology for continuous process improvement is repeated.

The direct links to performance budgeting are found in steps 7 and 8. Implementing recommendations for process management requires resource adjustments, additional resources, or both. Performance budgeting is accomplished when these changes are tied to baselines or benchmarks for improving the efficiency and effectiveness of core business processes that support service delivery. Consider the case of the city of Big Bear (Box 6.2).

Is this an example of successfully linking continuous process improvement to the budget preparation process? Table 6.1 shows performance data presented in the annual operating budget for the city of Big Bear. Note that the number of customer inquiries during the application process by fiscal year is not presented as an outcome measure for the building codes division, even though the continuous process improvement team identified or "red flagged" it as a target for process improvement.

We simply cannot tell whether Big Bear is linking its continuous improve-

---

Box 6.2

The City of Big Bear

In 1994, the mayor and city council of Big Bear agreed to implement a continuous process improvement system in a few city departments. They wanted to see the relationship between a continuous process improvement system and productivity improvement in the selected departments. One of the units selected was the permit division of the Building Codes Department. The goal of the building permits unit was to decrease the number of customer inquiries during the building permit application process by decreasing the number of days from the time an application was made until the time the review was completed and a decision was made by the permitting review group to approve or reject the permit application.

A team from the budget office and the building permits unit assembled in August 1994 to track the current process, to collect performance data for creating a baseline, and to make recommendations. The team found that the high number of inquiries was directly linked to the high number of days for plans review. The benchmark was ten working days on average for reviewing submitted plans. Recommendations were created and implemented, requiring one additional full-time equivalent staff position. The performance data from the new process revealed that a plans review was now being finished on average in two working days. The number of customer inquiries during the building permit application process decreased.

---

ment process with a performance budgeting program. Reporting performance data in a budget document does not constitute performance budgeting. Performance data may be reported but not considered during budget deliberations or even added to the budget after all the allocation decisions have been made. Big Bear may or may not have made the connection between continuous process improvement and performance budgeting. The omission of customer inquiries as a performance measure would certainly raise suspicion, but council did authorize additional resources to the building codes division to implement the recommendations from the study team based on performance. Big Bear also tracks the average number of days for plans review, providing some indication of performance budgeting. ·

Overall expenditures increased by 4.3 percent in FY 1999–2000 for the building codes division, which might suggest an incremental rather than performance budgeting approach. However, state and local budgets may look incremental mainly because our examination of them is focused at the margins. As Rubin and others have pointed out, departments often shift and merge

Table 6.1

Building Codes Division

	FY 1998–1999	FY 1999–2000	FY 2000–2001	FY 2001–2002
Input				
Expenditures	$604,912	$630,925	$635,647	$640,494
Full-time				
personnel	16	17	17	17
Output				
Inspections:				
Building	3,860	5,008	6,946	6,235
Plumbing	3,209	3,529	3,513	3,343
Electrical	3,739	4,548	4,494	4,071
Mechanical	2,587	2,666	3,147	3,523
Permits:				
Building	1,283	1,234	1,134	1,192
Plumbing	582	723	575	547
Electrical	1,173	1,190	1,159	1,240
Mechanical	905	910	998	1,114
Outcome				
Permit valuation	$97,690,171	$59,399,146	$168,312,236	$108,087,718
Permit revenue	$653,598	$596,175	$695,016	$786,084
Working days/				
plans review	10	2	3	3

resources internally in ways that are not captured by budget totals.[12] We can conclude that the decision to fund the additional position is consistent with performance budgeting, responding to the team's recommendations derived from continuous process improvement.

Corporate-Style Benchmarking

There are two advantages for organizations that adopt corporate-style benchmarking. First, like continuous process improvement, it focuses on a single process, carefully analyzing the elements for success.[13] Second, unlike continuous process improvement, the recommendations for changing the business practices of the program are based in part on best practices from similar processes operated by other, comparable, organizations. Corporate-style benchmarking is appropriate when the goal is to increase the efficiency and effectiveness of service delivery based on service delivery techniques regarded as the best practices. Improvement may be achieved by providing more with less (efficiency) or by providing a higher quality of service (effectiveness). The best-practice benchmarks are then used as the basis for performance budgeting. Table 6.2 presents one way to approach corporate-style benchmarking in seven steps.

Table 6.2

Public-Sector Benchmarking in Seven Steps

Step 1. Determine which functional areas within your organization will benefit most from benchmarking	• The function makes up a high percentage of total cost • The function is a key service differentiator • The function appears to show room for improvement • The function is capable of being improved
Step 2. Identify the key performance variables to measure cost, quality, and efficiency for the functions you have selected	• Determine the specific variables of operation and performance • Performance variables range from compensation levels, administrative overhead, and labor productivity to procurement cycle times, client satisfaction, and service quality
Step 3. Pick the best-in-class organization for each benchmark item	• Best-in-class organizations are those that perform each function at the lowest cost or with the highest degree of quality or efficiency • Direct comparables are those entities, public and private, that perform services that are identical or nearly identical to those performed by your organization • Parallel comparables are one step removed from direct comparables, in that their menus of services overlap only partially with yours • Latent comparables are organizations that do not provide the same services as your organization, but may do so at some point in the future
Step 4. Measure the performance of the best-in-class organization for each function	• Published sources are the best place to start, but rarely will they take you the full distance • Data sharing is another potential source of valuable data • External interviews provide another means for data collection
Step 5. Measure your own performance for each benchmark item, and identify the gaps between you and the best-in-class	• Identify measures for collection • Assign responsibility for data collection • Identify sources for data collection • Determine timeline for data collection
Step 6. Specify actions and strategies to close the gap in your favor	• Analysis must contain specific, actionable recommendations • Analysis must be supported by senior management • Line employees must be involved
Step 7. Implement and monitor your benchmarking results	• Update and monitor results over time for lasting value from benchmarking process

Source: Kenneth A. Bruder and Edward M. Gray, "Public-Sector Benchmarking: A Practical Approach," *Public Management* 76 (September 1994): S9–S14.

The first step to corporate-style benchmarking is to determine which functional area will benefit from the analysis. Table 6.2 presents four criteria for making this decision. The third criterion recommends benchmarking for functions that appear to show room for improvement. This illustrates the need for performance measurement, providing the gauges (measures) for tracking the performance of processes. An additional criterion not included in step one is the feedback from line employees whose familiarity with processes can provide valuable information on the operating procedures they follow. The fourth criterion recognizes that formal policies in the form of statutes, ordinances, and resolutions may make it difficult to improve the process even when greater efficiency or effectiveness could be realized.

The second step requires strong analytical skills and a complete understanding of the process selected for study. The selection of variables from specific service dimensions is often determined by data availability, but new data are sometimes necessary to accurately measure the performance of the process. The information on performance measurement presented in chapter 5 offers an approach to the second step of corporate-style benchmarking.

Identifying organizations for comparing each benchmark item (step 3) and obtaining information on best practices for the process under study (step 4) are the most difficult steps in corporate-style benchmarking. Bruder and Gray offered three sources of external information: published sources, data sharing, and external interviews.[14] Professional organizations like the International City/County Management Association can be a source of external information as well. Regardless of the source, external interviews or site visits are often needed to supplement data for corporate-style benchmarking. It is difficult to understand the context of the external service provider's delivery process unless you talk to their employees or visit their organization to see the provider at work.

Step 5 is the stage of corporate-style benchmarking where performance comparisons are made between the internal measures designated as benchmark items and the external measures designated as the best practices. Step 6 is the link between this form of benchmarking and performance budgeting. The analysis must contain specific, actionable recommendations that require resource adjustments, new resources, or both. One goal of productivity improvement is to provide more output with equal or less input. If the new process is able to operate with less, then decision makers have the opportunity to reallocate the resources in the budgetary process or to reduce the overall budget. The reality is that the resources will in all likelihood be moved to other operations.

Just like continuous process improvement, corporate-style benchmarking involves updating and monitoring results over time. It requires a meaningful performance measurement system. It also supports the benefits of trend analysis where performance measures are tracked on a regular basis. It is important to understand that the management tools presented in this chapter have different advantages and disadvantages, but they are all related under the larger umbrella of performance management.

Comparison of Performance Statistics as Benchmarks

An emerging form of benchmarking for local government is comparison of performance statistics as benchmarks. The basic structure of this form of benchmarking begins with localities submitting performance and cost data for a variety of service areas to a central location. The staff members at the central location collect the data, may "clean" the data (check for accuracy), and calculate performance measures for each locality by service area. The information is then forwarded to the participating localities, allowing the participants to gauge their level of performance against other localities. The only nationwide project for this form of benchmarking is conducted by the Center for Performance Management, a division of the International City/County Management Association (ICMA project). There are several regional benchmarking projects currently in progress, including the North Carolina Local Government Performance Measurement Project (North Carolina project), Kansas City Metro Project, South Carolina Municipal Benchmarking Project (South Carolina project), and Northwest Municipal Conference Performance Measurement Program (Northwest program).

Table 6.3 summarizes three benchmarking projects that use comparison of performance statistics as benchmarks, noting their similarities and differences. The Northwest program and the North Carolina project collect and report performance measures only for municipalities. The ICMA project collects performance data for both municipalities and counties; however, it reports the information for cities and counties together by type of service provided.

All three projects focus on line services, such as police, fire, and public works (refuse collection is listed as a neighborhood service for the ICMA project). Unlike the North Carolina project, the ICMA project and the Northwest program include staff functions as part of their service areas under study. The major difference among the three benchmarking projects is that performance and cost data collected and reported for the North Carolina project are subject to a rigorous data cleaning effort as compared to the ICMA project.[15] Data comparability is handled by self-policing in the Northwest program.

The key to any benchmarking project based on comparison of perfor-

COMPARISON OF PERFORMANCE STATISTICS AS BENCHMARKS 165

Table 6.3

Benchmarking Projects

Characteristics	Northwest Municipal Conference Performance Measurement Program	North Carolina Local Government Performance Measurement Project	ICMA Center for Performance Measurement
Members	27 municipalities	14 municipalities	130 localities
Membership	Open to members of the Northwest Municipal Conference	Open to all municipalities in North Carolina	Nationwide membership
Services under study	Police, fire, community development, public works, and finance	Solid waste, police, streets, fire, and building inspections	Police, fire and emergency medical, neighborhood, and support
Services to members	Annual survey and Web-based data management	Annual collection forms, data management, annual reports, technical assistance, training	Annual survey, training, data management, annual reports, and customized reports
Decision making	Steering committee	Steering committee	Steering committee
Reporting data	Web-based	Annual report	Annual report/ Web-based
Comparability	Self-policing	Data cleaning	Reporting structure
Training	None	Annual training	Regional workshops

Source: Shayne Karanagh and W. Anderson Williams, *Designing Performance Measurement Systems* (Chicago: Government Finance Officers Association, forthcoming).

mance statistics as benchmarks is presenting performance and cost data that are accurate, reliable, and comparable in a format that can be used by the participating localities. Table 6.4 contains performance data taken from the FY 1998 data report published by the ICMA project, presenting three performance measures associated with crime investigations and clearance rates.

The measures are Uniform Crime Reporting (UCR) Part I violent and property crimes assigned per full-time equivalent (FTE) (workload or output measure), UCR Part I violent and property crimes cleared per sworn FTE (effectiveness or outcome measure), and cost per Part I crime cleared (efficiency measure).

The information produced by the ICMA benchmarking project has the potential to be extremely useful for making changes in business practices based on performance. But complications arise when organizations compare themselves with other organizations, and not just because localities have different levels of resources dedicated to programs of service delivery. For example, say the city of Ann Arbor decides to benchmark the performance of its police investigative unit against that of Lubbock. The performance data located in Table 6.4 show that Lubbock clears far more Part I crimes per sworn FTE police officer, and does so at a lower cost per crime. On the surface, this looks like a red flag for the Ann Arbor police department. But before we can conclude that investigators in Lubbock are both more efficient and more effective than in Ann Arbor, we have to ask a few questions about the investigative practices in those cities. First, how does the city of Lubbock assign violent and property crimes to the investigations division of the police department? Some jurisdictions assign only selected violent and property crimes to investigation while others assign all crimes to investigation. Second, once the crimes reach the investigations unit, how does Lubbock assign crimes to individual police investigators? Some cities use solvability factors, only assigning cases to investigators that have a reasonable chance of solution. Other cities assign all cases referred to the investigations unit to investigators, even when the probability of a clearance is very low. Finally, Ann Arbor will want to know what the definition of "cleared" is in Lubbock. Cleared by arrest? Cleared by reassignment to another unit? Cleared by "NFI" or no further investigation, indicating the case is cold and unlikely ever to be solved. True comparability of benchmarks is not often found on the surface of the data.

Another concern is that Table 6.4 reports crimes assigned per FTE in one column and crimes cleared per sworn FTE in another column. Terminology is extremely important with benchmarking projects, requiring an examination of clearances between FTE and sworn FTE. The cost per Part I crime cleared shown in Table 6.4 also needs further clarification. First, does the variable of crimes cleared only include the ones cleared by investigators or does it include Part I crimes cleared by total sworn officers? Second, what methodology was used for calculating the cost variable? Third, what is the definition of cleared and is it being used consistently across participating jurisdictions? These and other questions have to be identified

Table 6.4

Crime Investigations and Clearance Rates

Jurisdiction	State	Population of area served	Policy for assigning violent crimes to investigators	Policy for assigning property crimes to investigators	UCR Part I violent and property crimes assigned per FTE	UCR Part I violent and property crimes cleared per sworn FTE	Cost per Part I crimes cleared (dollars)
Austin	TX	601,360	Yes	Yes	34.7	5.8	13,759
Long Beach	CA	446,227	Yes	Yes	20.5	4.2	37,329
Riverside	CA	225,069	Yes	Yes	5.9	9.0	12,791
Lubbock	TX	196,679	Yes	Yes	30.4	12.8	5,966
Little Rock	AR	181,290	No	No	32.1	7.0	8,464
Ann Arbor	MI	108,758	Yes	Yes	6.8	4.1	21,587
Bellevue	WA	105,700	Yes	Yes	3.2	7.4	21,354

Source: International City/County Management Association, *Comparative Performance Measurement FY 1998 Data Report* (December 1999).

Notes: UCR = Uniform crime reporting; FTE = full-time equivalent.

and answered before the city of Ann Arbor can make changes to its business practices by using the performance and cost data from the city of Lubbock as benchmarks.

The North Carolina project follows a different procedure for collecting and reporting comparable performance and cost data, one that is intended to overcome comparability issues. However, the problems with comparability are not overcome in the North Carolina project, just mitigated. It requires an enormous amount of time by public officials to create a service definition, to collect accurate and reliable data, and to present performance measures that are materially comparable.

North Carolina Project

Local governments in North Carolina are required by state statute to operate on a fiscal year that begins on July 1 and ends on June 30. Therefore, all the participating municipalities conduct their annual financial audits during roughly the same period of time and follow the same budget calendar. This is not the case in all states. Participants in the South Carolina project, for example, have to contend with reconciling different fiscal years. This introduces a variety of deadline and production problems, and results in some of the jurisdictions receiving their performance and cost data reports after their annual operating budgets have been prepared and approved.[16]

The process for the North Carolina project begins with a steering committee meeting held in July of each year in conjunction with the North Carolina Local Government Budget Association Summer Conference. The purpose of the meeting is to review and finalize the process for collecting, cleaning, and reporting the performance and cost data. The meeting also is used to make last minute adjustments to the service areas under study and to discuss the various aspects of the North Carolina project, including how the performance and cost data are being used for service improvement and how the information is being linked to the budgetary process. The normal process is to mail the service profile forms (see Figure 6.1 for an example of a service profile form) and the accompanying accounting form (Appendix B) to all municipalities by mid-August.

The municipalities are given until mid-October to complete the information and to return it to project staff of the School of Government at the University of North Carolina at Chapel Hill, the central agency that compiles the results. Service managers normally complete the service profile forms, and budget and finance staff normally complete the accounting forms. Of course, the compilation of the performance and cost data varies from jurisdiction to jurisdiction. The collection process does not operate in a vacuum. Project staff at the School of Government is in constant contact with the participating units, providing direction and assistance as needed. The service profile and accounting forms are returned to the School of Government in various formats, including paper copies, files on diskette, and attachments to e-mails. Regardless of the format, a paper copy is always printed and filed for each unit and service.

Project staff members enter the data obtained from the service profiles and the accounting forms on spreadsheets. The accounting data are entered first, providing the first check between the data received and data entered. The final cost of each service area and the performance data contained on the service profile form are entered into a second spreadsheet where the performance measures are calculated. This format allows a comparison with prior year data, and, more important, allows a direct comparison between jurisdictions by line-item. These comparisons are critical in the data cleaning process.

Once data collection is complete, the spreadsheets are distributed to the municipalities for their review. Both steering committee members and service managers who prepared the service profile forms are responsible for reviewing the data, and ensuring that the information is accurate and complete. A data cleaning meeting is held sometime in early December. The purpose of the meeting is twofold. First, it allows project staff to ask questions that apply to all involved. This may require additional analysis if group consensus on data collection and definitions is not obtained. Second, the data cleaning meeting allows the municipalities to challenge the performance and cost data of other jurisdictions. This process often leads to additional questions and concerns that must be resolved before publishing the performance and cost data report.

Project staff members distribute draft copies of the performance and cost data report in early January. The difference between the draft report and the spreadsheets is that the former contains the graphs, the unit profile and service profile data, and the explanatory information for final review. Although changes are still being made during this period, only changes that will affect the materiality of the report are typically accepted. The final copy of the report is distributed to the participating units by the end of January.

However, the process is not over at this point. A steering committee meeting is scheduled as quickly as possible to begin preparation for the following fiscal year. Discussions are held regarding problems with the current service areas under study, the expansion of the North Carolina project by adding new services, and the use of the performance and cost data for service or process improvement. If new services are added, then meetings with service managers are held to define the service area and create the performance measures of workload, efficiency, and effectiveness.

Figure 6.1   **Service Profile Form**

CITY OF _____

HOUSEHOLD RECYCLING SERVICE

Definition: This includes both curbside collection of household recyclable materials from residences and certain other locations and the drop-off of such materials by citizens at recycling stations or centers. The recyclable materials collected are mainly aluminum and steel cans, plastics, glass bottles, newspapers, magazines, and cardboard. The curbside portion of this service involves regularly scheduled collection that utilizes containers small enough that residents and/ or workers can move or lift them. Excluded are collection of yard waste, leaves, and commercial recycling.

Briefly describe your city's recycling services in FY 2000–01. Include a listing of the different types of materials recycled in your city. (You may attach a separate sheet.)		

SERVICE DESCRIPTION		COMMENTS
1. Date Curbside Program		Provide date curbside recycling program was
Was Initiated		implemented in your city
2. Recycling Drop-Off Sites		Provide data for FY 2000–01.
a) No. drop-off sites		
b) Description of drop-off recycling service:		
3. Recycling Frequency FY 2000–01		Check or describe if necessary.
a) Weekly		
b) Every 2 weeks		
c) Other		
4. Recycling Fee FY 2000–01	$	Dollar amount and basis of any fee.
a) Revenue From Recycling		Is recycling fee included in solid waste fee?
		Include revenue collected by contractor and
		remitted to city
5. No. FTE Positions by Level of	No. FTEs	No. of positions in full-time equivalents. An FTE
Responsibility FY 2000–01		means a position based on 2080 hrs./ year.
a) No. collection FTEs		Include permanent & temporary positions. Supervisory
b) No. supervisory/ support FTEs		positions do not routinely participate in
		physical work. Support positions include
		clerical, administrative, etc.
6. Crew Composition: If your city provides recycling service with its own personnel, describe how many crews are used and how they are organized. For example, "four 3-person crews are used, each having 3 workers and 1 driver." Include brief explanation of organizational location of recycling program (a division in solid waste department, etc.)		

Source: William C. Rivenbark, ed., *A Guide to the North Carolina Local Government Performance Measurement Project* (University of North Carolina—Chapel Hill: Institute of Government, February 2001).

Data Cleaning

Data cleaning is a vital part of the North Carolina project. One of the primary goals of the North Carolina project is to produce comparable performance and cost data. Ensuring data comparability requires the combined efforts of project staff and participating municipalities. Both parties must carefully review draft results for this job to be done properly. As the data are collected, project staff immediately begin comparing the information to prior year data,

SERVICE DESCRIPTION		COMMENTS
7. Contracted Recycling		For FY 2000–01
a) $ amount of contracts		Total dollars paid to contractor
b) % of service contract/private		No. tons recyclables collected by contractors
		divided by total no. tons collected citywide
		Including by contract.
c) No. FTEs for contract supervision		No. FTEs used for contract supervision
		(FTE = 2080 hrs. per year) Include in costs.
8. Other FY 2000–01 Data		Complete for FY 2000–01 for both city-provided
a) No. collection points receiving		and contract service.
curbside recycling service		
b) No. tons collected - city		Include tons of recyclables collected by city crews.
c) No. tons collected - contractor		Include tons of recyclables collected by private hauler.
d) % of waste stream diverted by		Include all waste tonnage deposited in landfill or
recycling		incinerated plus yard waste/leaves in calculation
9. If the number of collection points for household recycling is different than residential refuse,		
please explain why.		
10. % Eligible Collection Points	%	Average for FY 2000–01. Please note below your
Participating in Recycling Program		definition of "participation"
a) Definition of "participation." Please provide data on the method used to calculate participation rate.		
11. No. Complaints in FY 2000–01	No.	Provide Data if available
a) Total no. complaints about		Total no. complaints about these services,
recycling service.		regardless of whether they are "valid"
b) No. "Valid" complaints about		Define "valid" complaint using your unit's
recycling service during the year		definition.
c) % valid complaints resolved		If available, includes trips to pick up
within one working day		missed collections.
12. State-confirmed Base Year	No. Tons	No. tons city solid waste disposed of in
Landfill or Incinerator Tonnage		city's "base year" as reported to state.
a) No. tons solid waste landfilled/		Provide if available.
incinerated in base year		
b) State-confirmed base year		State-confirmed base year used.
13. Please add any other comments about your recycling service which may be needed		
in order to understand your city's recycling program, such as council policies about		
recycling, unique contractual arrangements, etc.		

if available, and examining the data for reasonableness. Project staff then make direct comparisons among participating municipalities, which results in telephone conversations and e-mail between project staff and municipalities to reconcile performance and cost variances.

The next step of the process is to forward the spreadsheets containing the performance measures and the line-item costs to the municipalities for their review. This involves more phone calls and e-mail as the data continue to be cleaned. When data problems occur, most are found to have been caused by misinterpreting a definition or request, not providing all the information needed to calculate the performance measures, or omitting an indirect or capital cost. Another type of problem area arises when municipalities contract services to private vendors, especially when only a portion of the service is contracted. This often requires additional analysis to ensure that the measures are comparable.

Performance and Cost Data Reports

The original steering committee for the North Carolina project invested a great deal of time on the layout of the performance and cost data reports. A primary consideration was to present the data needed for comparison while avoiding unnecessary embarrassment for any participating jurisdiction performing below the level of its counterparts. One point drove the discussion. Local government administrators did not want the data displayed in a manner that provided a head-to-head comparison among the units, asserting that such displays could create political problems in their communities. Controversy could be stirred by misinterpreting the data or failing to understand the purpose of the North Carolina project, they maintained. They were especially concerned that direct comparisons of jurisdictions on one measure would not take into consideration the differences in service delivery that drive variances in performance. The service area of residential refuse collection provides an excellent example to illustrate this point. The units that provide backyard service are naturally less efficient than units with curbside service. On the other hand, backyard pickup represents a much higher level of service. Based on these considerations, the steering committee elected to avoid head-to-head comparisons by displaying the performance measures of individual units against an average as opposed to ranking all the participating units.

The performance and cost data reports published by the North Carolina project are partitioned by service area and by jurisdiction. A standard two-page layout is employed for illustrating a unit's performance and cost data for each service area. The first page of the layout, depicted in Figure 6.2, shows the results of workload, efficiency, and effectiveness measures. A graph presents each measure along with the group average for that particular measure. Each graph is labeled by type of measure and by the number of participating municipalities that provided the necessary data for calculation. The graphs show three years of performance data, including the measure and average for each fiscal year. The bar graphs show the bar and legend, data labels, and the actual performance measure.

The second page of the two-page layout, shown in Figure 6.3, contains four clusters of information. The first provides the city profile, presenting statistics like population, land area served, topography, median age, and unemployment rate. The second section shows the full cost profile by ac-

Figure 6.2   **Performance Measures for Residential Refuse Collection**

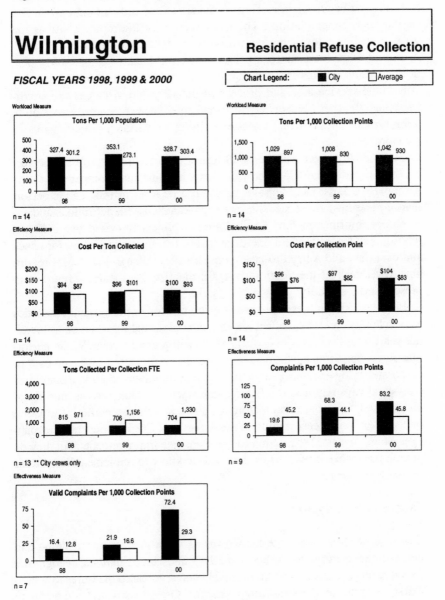

Source: William C. Rivenbark and Carla M. Pizzarella, *Final Report on City Services for FY 1999–00* (University of North Carolina—Chapel Hill: Institute of Government, February 2001).

tual dollars and by a percentage. The cost categories are personal services (salaries and benefits), operating costs (direct and indirect expenses), and capital costs (depreciation). The third section of the report contains the service profile data, or the data used to calculate the performance measures and other important statistics for the service area under study. The final section contains the explanatory information. It provides a description of the service area and process of delivery and discusses the conditions that affect service, performance, and cost. The explanatory information often provides the critical factors explaining the variances in performance measures.

The ICMA project and the South Carolina project use different layouts for their reports. The ICMA project uses a head-to-head comparison for its participating units, including the service profile information and the performance measures. These statistics are supplemented with definitions and explanatory information. The South Carolina project has used two different reporting styles, a standard one-page layout for illustrating its performance and cost data and a head-to-head comparison similar to the ICMA report. One key aspect of the South Carolina project is the use of survey data to present service quality.

Benchmarking projects that provide comparison of performance statistics as benchmarks are an excellent way to gather external information as localities search for best practices, with one very important caveat. While performance comparison benchmarking overcomes the most difficult part of corporate-style benchmarking, gathering external data, additional analytical work is always required to identify best practices. This may include direct contact with the other participating localities to obtain specific information on their service processes and business practices. The numbers tell the manager where to start in the search for performance improvements, but they do not tell the manager what he or she needs to know to implement them in his or her department.

Targets as Benchmarks

The state of Oregon became known for its work in strategic planning and benchmarking during the 1980s and 1990s and gained national recognition for using targets as benchmarks, or linking outcome-based measures to benchmarks that represent process improvement.[17] Oregon uses strategic planning to arrive at the benchmarks, the form of benchmarking that the GFOA defines as strategic benchmarks. However, targets as benchmarks can take two forms. Targets as benchmarks can take the form of internal benchmarking if the predetermined targets were established by trend analysis or, as in many

Figure 6.3 **Explanatory Information for Residential Refuse Collection**

Wilmington	Residential Refuse Collection
	Fiscal Year 1999–00

CITY PROFILE		EXPLANATORY INFORMATION
Population (OSP-99)	75,629	

Service Level and Delivery
Wilmington provides basic refuse collection service for residences once a week at curbside. Wilmington provides all collection containers and carts to its customers. Customers may use either a ninety-gallon or forty-gallon cart.

Land Area (Square Miles)	40.6
Persons per Square Mile	1,863
Topography	Flat; Coastal Plain
County	New Hanover
Climate	Mild
Median Family Income (HUD-98)	$44,700

A volume-based fee system is employed to finance residential refuse collection. This is designed to encourage residents to reduce the amount of refuse they generate. The city charged a monthly fee of $14.15 for a forty-gallon cart and a monthly fee of $17.15 for a ninety-gallon cart during FY 1999–00.

The city used the following crews during the fiscal year for residential refuse collection: three crews of one driver and two collectors, one crew with one driver and one collector, and two crews working in the central business district.

FULL COST PROFILE

Cost Breakdown By %
Personal Services	20.8%
Operating Costs	73.1%
Capital Costs	6.1%
TOTAL	100.0%

Twenty-nine collection routes were used during FY 1999–00, with an average of two trips per route per day to the landfill. The average distance to the landfill was 9.5 miles. The city collected 24,859 tons of residential refuse during FY 1999–00, at a cost of $100 per ton. The cost per ton does not include the disposal cost per ton of $32 for the landfill tipping fee.

Cost Breakdown By $
Personal Services	$	517,334
Operating Costs	$	1,816,504
Capital Costs	$	150,485
TOTAL	$	2,484,323

The city contracted 56 percent of the residential refuse service to private haulers during fiscal year 1999–00 at a cost of $1,326,619. While the cost and tonnage are included in the performance and cost data, the tons collected per collection FTE is based only on city workers.

SERVICE PROFILE
FTE Positions–Collection	15.5
FTE Positions–Other	3.5
Tons Collected	24,859
Residential Customers	23,853
(number represents collection points)	
Collection Location	Curbside
Collection Frequency	1 X Week
	(2 X week for fee)
Size of Crews	3 Person (3)
	2 Person/Downtown
Percentage of Service Contracted	56%
Service Fee	$14.15/Month–40 Gal.
	$17.15/Month–90 Gal.
Type of Equipment	4 Semi-Automated

Wilmington defines an automated packer as a truck that has an arm on it that the driver can operate from the cab. This arm grabs the trash cart and automatically dumps the garbage in the truck. A packer truck compacts the trash in the body of the truck. Rear loaders have hoppers in the rear that the carts are dumped into. There is a blade that sweeps into the hopper and moves the garbage back into the body of the truck. Semi-automated packers are packer trucks that have tippers on them to lift the carts.

Conditions Affecting Service, Performance, and Costs
The performance measure of tons collected per collection FTE represents city crews only.

Source: William C. Rivenbark and Carla M. Pizzarella, *Final Report on City Services for FY 1999–2000* (University of North Carolina—Chapel Hill: Institute of Government, February 2001).

cases, set arbitrarily rather than linked to actual achievement demonstrated elsewhere.[18] Targets as benchmarks also can take the form of external benchmarking if linked to best practices or to industry standards, relying on sources of performance data external to the organization.

The reality is that most public organizations typically use multiple processes for establishing targets. Managers rely on trend analysis, employee input, industry standards, organizations that provide similar services, political mandates, community/citizen input, and general leadership for setting benchmarks. Another consideration of targets as benchmarks is the amount of internal or external control a manager has over the success of a program for which he or she is responsible, a topic we mentioned in chapter 5. If success is linked primarily to external factors that are largely uncontrollable, managers must identify these factors when constructing meaningful targets. Setting a target for an objective directly linked to state and national economic conditions may be beneficial from senior management's perspective, but it is not beneficial for gauging the performance of line managers and supervisors. For example, the public works director can estimate the number of days of icy road conditions, but he cannot control the weather. A target expenditure for road sanding and salting is not fully under the control of the manager any more than the weather is. In a situation where internal control over success of programs is high, targets are an excellent way to monitor the performance of line managers and supervisors in addition to monitoring the overall success of the program.

Table 6.5 presents performance measures and performance targets taken from the approved 2001–2002 biennial budget for the city of Cincinnati, Ohio. (On a side note, proponents of biennial budgeting often cite the focus of planning, including performance, as a key reason for implementing a multiyear budget.) Table 6.5 presents two examples of measures that illustrate different levels of managerial control. The miles of sewer cleaned is an example of strong internal control, where management can make decisions on allocating internal resources to meet the performance target of cleaning 180 miles of sewer annually. Lowering the number of medical referrals for school-age children is driven both by internal programs and by external factors like the demographics of the community.

Organizations must be cautious when evaluating the performance of programs on the basis of performance targets. Table 6.5 shows a performance target of 3.3 minutes for the police department's response time, a critical outcome measure collected by most police departments. The assumption is that police managers will analyze their deployment and zone strategies and recommend improvements for decreasing the response time. These recommendations may or may not require additional resources. There is another

Table 6.5

Targets as Benchmarks, 2001–2002 Biennial Budget, Cincinnati

Function	Measure	2000 Actual	2001 Target
Police	Response time in minutes	3.4	3.3
Health	Medical referrals for school-aged children	6,290	4,000
Neighborhood services	Number of units for ownership created	77	70
Sewers	Miles of sewer cleaned	147.1	180
Transportation and engineering	Overage bridge rating	6.62	6 or better
Water works	Number of calls answered within thirty-five seconds	52.23%	70%

Source: City of Cincinnati, Ohio, *Approved 2001–2002 Biennial Budget.*

way to decrease response time, and it is costless. The quickest way to achieve the target is to change the definition of what types of calls require a response. For example, the police department could begin to count self-initiated calls as having a response time of zero, and recalculate the response time. In other words, changes in the collection or recording methodology alter performance information without changing performance results.

Table 6.5 also contains a measure for the water works function that is a prime candidate for continuous process improvement, linking two forms of benchmarking together. The number of calls answered within thirty-five seconds as a percentage of total number of calls received may be a function of process, organizational alignment, or responsibility. An analysis of the call response process is an excellent approach to closing the performance gap as reflected by the performance target before an additional position is approved for answering service calls.

Targets as benchmarks offer localities with internal performance management systems an approach to benchmarking without joining a formal benchmarking initiative like the one described in North Carolina, where comparison of performance statistics establishes benchmarks. The limitation of targets as benchmarks is the lack of relevant and comparable external data for setting performance targets.

Capacity for Benchmarking

An organization's ability to implement a meaningful performance measurement system and to adopt benchmarking for the advantages of comparison is

---

Table 6.6

An Organization's Readiness for Benchmarking

Pitfalls to avoid	• No context/no purpose • No high-level commitment • Insistence on perfection • Insistence on uniformity • No link to resource allocation, program evaluation, or employee evaluation
When not to measure	• Distrustful environment • Will not make a difference • Cost of measurement is high • Staff not properly trained • Problems with accurate/reliable data • No evaluation capacity
Uncooperative managers	• Total involvement from beginning • Patient pressure • Give a little in the beginning • Appeal to responsibility of accountability • Provide leadership

Source: Government Finance Officers Association National Training Seminar (2000).

---

directly linked to its organizational capacity. Organizational capacity, for this discussion, encompasses the following: leadership and vision, management and planning, fiscal strength and practices, and operational support.[19] Organizations that invest in management initiatives like performance measurement and benchmarking without the capacity to transform performance and cost data into meaningful information will not realize positive gains on their investments.

Table 6.6 presents criteria to assess an organization's readiness for benchmarking. Some of the criteria are directly linked to organizational capacity. Other criteria present issues that must be confronted regardless of capacity.

The area of "pitfalls to avoid" contains criteria for any new management reform. An initiative must have context and purpose, it must have high-level commitment, and it must be linked to other areas of the organization like resource allocation and program evaluation. Management's lack of attention in these areas will surely place any new initiative into the category of a passing fad. The two criteria directly aimed at benchmarking are insistence on perfection and insistence on uniformity. Performance data are never absolutely correct, and comparing two data points is often an art as much as a science.

The area of "when not to measure" is critical for benchmarking. A distrustful environment is especially dangerous when comparing performance of one organization against another. The most cited problem is "fudging" of the data. For example, an output (workload) measure for the building inspections function is number of inspections by type (building, electrical, mechanical, and plumbing). One way to increase the number of inspections by type and to increase the number of inspections by FTE inspector (efficiency or workload measure) is to include the number of reinspections, making the department "look better" as compared to other jurisdictions. Reinspections are a part of output and a part of outcome, but should be tracked separately for operational performance. In addition, managers must be aware when benchmarking will not make a difference given certain regulatory restrictions, for example, and when the cost of measurement is higher than the benefits of establishing benchmarks.

The remaining three criteria for "when not to measure" are also linked to organizational capacity. Before an organization embraces a management initiative like benchmarking, staff must be properly trained, accurate and reliable data must be obtainable, and analytical skills must be sufficient for evaluation. Professional organizations like GFOA provide seminars on performance measurement and benchmarking that address training and analytical needs. Accurate and reliable data are a function of process. Managers should review the processes that produce data and define the data needed for measuring operational performance. Maintaining employees with strong analytical skills is the most difficult criterion for most organizations. The most common approach is to hire individuals who already have the needed skills as job vacancies become available.

The third area, "uncooperative managers," is a self-explanatory matter beyond the scope of this chapter. However, one can increase managers' cooperation by involving them in a benchmarking initiative from the beginning and encouraging them to provide input in the benchmarking process. Senior managers also must be willing to "give a little" in response to line managers' concerns and needs, as the line manager probably understands the limits of the unit and the dimensions of the service delivery task better than the senior manager. In general, the best approach to uncooperative managers is to appeal to their sense of public accountability and personal responsibility to provide leadership for a positive change in their department. From a larger perspective, performance measurement and benchmarking should not be approached as a new management initiative that requires additional work for line managers and supervisors. Rather, measurement should be approached as part of performance management and as part of daily management practice in the public sector.

Conclusion

Benchmarking offers states and local governments a way to seek best practices through their performance measurement systems. The four forms of benchmarking presented in this chapter are continuous process improvement, corporate-style benchmarking, comparison of performance statistics as benchmarks, and targets as benchmarks. The first step to benchmarking, regardless of the form, is to compare two performance data points with one representing a benchmark. The second step is to analyze the operational variance between the two performance data points as represented by output, outcome, or efficiency and to create recommendations for improving the corresponding service dimension. Making changes to current business practices for improving performance often requires budgetary adjustments, setting the stage for performance budgeting.

Benchmarking is often used by localities on an informal basis, collecting benchmarks to analyze the operational performance of service delivery in response to particular requests or concerns. Council members may inquire about privatizing the garbage collection process or about consolidating the city's purchasing program with the county's purchasing program. Managers respond by collecting performance data from external organizations, both public and private, and from industry standards to document their success in service performance. This is a very rational behavior given the desire that we all have to protect the programs that we manage. But benchmarking works best when managers embrace it on a voluntary basis to improve service delivery and to accept operational accountability by tracking performance as compared to other operations.

The big question is what form of benchmarking should local government officials adopt for their operations? Table 6.7 presents the four forms of benchmarking discussed in this chapter and the advantages and disadvantages associated with each. The answer to the question is that managers should choose the form of benchmarking that reconciles with the purpose of establishing benchmarks. If a process is identified as in need of improvement, continuous process improvement may be the best choice. If a manager wants to collect external data from services provided by other organizations for comparison, performance statistics as benchmarks offer an excellent alternative. If improving community quality-of-life indicators such as teen pregnancy, underage drug and alcohol use, or homelessness is the ultimate goal, targets as benchmarks may be the better approach, as these problems may not respond directly to managerial initiatives.

Managers should be aware that each form of benchmarking comes with disadvantages as well. Strong analytical skills are required regardless of the

Table 6.7

Overview of Benchmarking Techniques

Technique	Advantages	Disadvantages
Continuous process improvement	• Focus on process improvement • Involvement of line employees • Produces recommendations for change	• Time required for team meetings • Focus on single process • Disconnect between team and responsibility for implementing changes • Required analytical skills
Corporate-style benchmarking	• Focus on process improvement • Focus on best practices • Produces recommendations for change	• Difficult to obtain information on best practices • Time consuming • Focus on single process • Required analytical skills
Comparison of performance statistics as benchmarks	• Focus on multiple service areas • Amount of data collected • High number of participants • Reported on an annual basis	• Time consuming • No attention to best practices • Requires follow-up studies • Comparability of data • Required analytical skills
Targets as benchmarks	• Based on goals of program • Relationship between objectives and performance • Often tied to industry standards	• Targets often set arbitrarily • No link to best practices • Lack of focus on process improvement • Required analytical skills

selection. Organizations must have the capacity to analyze the performance of selected services within the context of other internal and external business processes. To do so successfully often requires a combination of experience, education, and operational knowledge. Another disadvantage is the time and cost required to establish a benchmarking program, especially for corporate-style benchmarking and comparison of performance statistics as benchmarks. Finally, managers should not oversell the advantages of benchmarking.

Appendix B

North Carolina Local Government Performance Measurement Project

NORTH CAROLINA LOCAL GOVERNMENT PERFORMANCE MEASUREMENT PROJECT

Service: City:

TABLE I: DIRECT COST FOR FISCAL YEAR ENDED 2000–2001[a]

A. PERSONAL SERVICES

ACCOUNT	DEFINITION	FY2001 COST
1. Salaries and Wages–Permanent	Gross earnings of permanent employees subject to FICA and retirement regulations	
2. Temporary/Part-time salaries and wages	Gross earnings of all employees subject to FICA but not retirement regulations	
3. Overtime/holiday pay	For full-time permanent employees	
4. Longevity	Gross earnings of longevity paid to eligible employees	
5. Step Allowance–Law Enforcement	Payments to law enforcement officers under GS 143–166.42	
6. Step Allowance–Other	Payments for step allowance made to other employees	
7. Supplemental Retirement Income Plan–Law Enforcement	Payments to supplemental retirement plan provided for law enforcement officers under GS 143–166.50(e)	
8. Supplemental Retirement Income Plan–Others	Payments to supplemental retirement plan for other employees	
9. FICA/Social Security	Unit's share of Social Security taxes on wages	
10. Retirement Contribution	Payments into LGERS or own retirement fund for eligible employees	
11. Hospital/Medical Insurance	Unit's share of employee medical and hospitalization insurance	
12. Disability Insurance	Unit's share of cost of disability insurance	
13. Unemployment Compensation Contribution	Unit's cost for unemployment compensation on workers	
14. Workers' Compensation Contribution	Cost of workers' compensation: for self-insured, medical costs, compensation for lost job time for job-related accidents	
15. Deferred compensation/401K (if not charged to salaries/wages)	Unit's contribution to employee deferred compensation plans	
16. Other benefits	Cost of any other benefits not classified above	
Personal Services Subtotal		0

TABLE I: DIRECT COST FOR FISCAL YEAR ENDED 2000–2001

B. OPERATING EXPENSES

ACCOUNT	DEFINITION	FY 2001 COST
17. Operating Supplies	Includes the materials needed for the program to carry out its tasks and functions. For most units, several line accounts will be consolidated into this one category. Includes noncapital outlay equipment, tools, and software	
18. Purchases for resale	Cost of property or materials purchased for resale	
19. Training and Travel	Includes all travel and training related expenses for employees	
20. Maintenance and Repair–Equipment	Includes service and repairs to equipment and office machines. Includes maintenance contracts	
21. Fees and Licenses	Fees for recording deeds, maps, and so forth. Also, licenses permits, and so forth, needed by employees for performing their jobs	
22. Advertising	Includes advertising in all media	
23. Uniform purchase and rental	Includes uniforms and other personal gear purchased or rented for employee use. Includes safety shoes.	
24. Dues/memberships/subscriptions	Costs of dues paid for memberships in various organizations. Subscriptions to technical publications	
25. Telephone	Includes all direct costs or charges for local and long distance telephone services. May be provided by a telephone company, a unit's own internal service fund, or other charge back method	
26. Utilities	Includes all direct costs or charges for electric, gas, heating oil, water/sewer, or other utilities. May be provided by private utilities or by the unit's own utility systems	
27. MIS/Data Processing/GIS or other similar services	Includes all direct costs or charges for these services. May be provided by private companies, by consultants, by the unit's own internal service fund, or by another charge back method	
28. Professional or Contracted Services	Includes costs of contracted specialized services. May be retainer fees and other expenses associated with acquiring special expertise or other services by contract	
29. Contract Administration	Direct and indirect costs to the unit of administering service contracts, if not already captured in other accounts	
30. Property/Facility Maintenance	Includes all direct costs or charges for property or facility maintenance, custodial or janitorial service, repair or upkeep, whether performed by contract, by the unit's own internal service fund, or other charge back method	

31. Fleet Maintenance	Includes all direct costs or charges for fleet or vehicle maintenance whether contracted out, performed by the unit's own internal service fund, or other charge back method
32. Miscellaneous/Other	Any expenses incurred by a program unit not included in another category
33. Special program expenses	Expenses associated with only a specific program or department. These will vary from program to program, and from unit to unit. They differ from "miscellaneous/other" in that they are specific to one program and are for a specific purpose
Operating Expenses Subtotal	0

TABLE II: INDIRECT COST FOR FISCAL YEAR ENDED 2000–2001[b]

CENTRAL COST CENTERS	BASIS OF ALLOCATION	FY 2001 COST
1. Manager's Office: cost of general management function	No. of FTEs budgeted FY 2001	
2. Council: cost of governing board	No. of FTEs budgeted FY 2001	
3. Clerk: cost of clerk's office	Costs directly assigned to governing board	
4. Attorney/Legal: cost of attorney's office and other legal services	Attorney time allocated by function as a percentage	
5. Personnel/Human Resources: cost of personnel services	No. of FTEs budgeted FY 2001	
6. Budget and Evaluation: costs of city budget and evaluation function; includes program evaluation	No. of FTEs budgeted FY 2001	
7. Finance: cost of financial activities, including accounting, treasury, payroll, fixed assets accounting, cost accounting, and other financial functions; excludes billing and collection	No. of accounting transactions processed in FY 2001 (may be sample of several months)	
8. Revenue Billing & Collections: cost of activities relating to revenue collection, including meter reading, billing, collection of taxes, utilities, and privilege licenses	Percentage of actual expenditures for FY 2001	
9. Purchasing: cost related to purchasing function	No. of purchase orders processed in FY 2001 (may be sample of several months)	
10. Finance Professional Fees: cost of annual audit, cost allocation plan, and financial consulting	No. of accounting transactions processed in FY 2001 (may be sample of several months)	
11. Risk Management: cost of administration, claims processing, and safety	No. of FTEs budgeted in FY 2001	
12. Liability Insurance	No. of FTEs budgeted in FY 2001	
13. Property Insurance: cost of insurance on real property (land and buildings)	Percentage of insurance premium based on occupied square footage (real property) or on direct assignment where one program occupies an entire facility	

14. Insurance on Equipment and Vehicles: cost includes auto collision and comprehensive coverage	Percentage of insurance premium or cost based on no. of assigned vehicles or pieces of equipment in department or program
15. Central Support Services: stockroom/central supplies; mail services; printing/microfilming	No. of stock requisitions; postage charges (sample if necessary); no. of copies/printing/ microfilming (may be based on cost of contract)
16. Traffic Engineering	Percentage of staff time spent in FY 2001
17. Other Engineering	Percentage of staff time spent in FY 2001
18. Transportation Planning	Direct assignment to user programs/departments in FY 2001
19. Real Estate Management: cost relating to property management, sales, or acquisitions	No. of properties handled in FY 2001; No. of sales & acquisitions in FY 2001
20. Economic Development	Percentage of staff time spent in FY 2001
21. Communication Services: cost of interdepartmental radio services	No. calls taken (may be based on sample of 8 days)
22. City Planning: cost of development services, design review, and so forth.	Percentage of staff time spent in FY 2001
23. Departmental Overhead–Personnel: costs relating to administering a program at the departmental level	No. of FTEs assigned to program as Percentage of total no. FTEs in department
24. Departmental Overhead–Operating: costs at the departmental level relating to the operation of a program.	No. of FTEs assigned to program as percentage of total no. FTEs in department

Note: The following items may be budgeted and accounted for as direct costs, as indirect costs, or as direct and indirect costs. Please use the following items to account for those costs that are recorded as only indirect costs.

25. Telephone (local and long distance): operating cost for telephone services not allocated through a central services fund or other charge back method	Direct assignment to user programs/departments, or based on no. of communication instruments
26. Utilities: charges for electricity, gas, heating oil, water/sewer, or other utilities not allocated through a department or function	No. of square feet occupied
27. MIS/DP/GIS Services: charges not allocated through a central services fund or other charge back method	Estimated no. of hours of service provided, or by direct assignment to specific programs based on work orders
28. Property/Facility Maintenance: charges for property or facility maintenance, custodial or janitorial service, and repair or upkeep not allocated through a central services fund or other charge back method	Estimated no. of hours service provided, or by direct assignment based on work orders, or by no. of square feet maintained
29. Fleet Maintenance: charges for fleet or vehicle maintenance not allocated through a central services fund or other charge back method	Garage labor hours by program. Use full cost allocation
Subtotal Indirect Costs/Cost Centers	0

TABLE III: ALLOCATION OF CAPITAL EQUIPMENT FOR FISCAL YEAR ENDED 2000–2001[c]

EQUIPMENT CATEGORIES	BASIS OF ALLOCATION	FY 2001 COST
1. Equipment Use Allowance: used to allocate the capital costs of equipment and vehicles by year	Allocation is based on applying percentage to the historical cost of owned equipment, including equipment acquired by lease, installment purchase agreement, or other capital lease	
a) Furniture and Office Equipment	10 percent of acquisition cost	
b) Maintenance Equipment	12 percent of acquisition cost	
c) Autos and Light Vehicles	30 percent of acquisition cost	
d) Medium/Heavy Motor Equipment	16 percent of acquisition cost	
e) Data Processing Equipment	20 percent of acquisition cost	
f) Light/Misc. Equipment	10 percent of acquisition cost	
g) Other equipment that does not fit any of the above categories	For "one of a kind" assets. Please apply percentage based on (1) original estimated useful life or (2) your best judgment of useful life	
2. Equipment/Vehicle Rental Charges	Includes annual rental payments under operating or "time" leases for equipment and vehicles. Does not include capital leases or installment purchases	
Subtotal Capital Equipment		0

TABLE IV: ALLOCATION OF FACILITIES COST FOR FISCAL YEAR ENDED 2000–2001

FACILITIES	BASIS OF ALLOCATION	FY 2001 COST
1. Building Use Allowance: used to allocate the capital costs of buildings to departments or programs. Such buildings include those financed with lease or installment purchase agreements, certificates of participation, or other capital leases	The allocation for cost centers sharing a facility is square footage occupied with common space prorated. For cost centers wholly occupying a facility, direct assignment of cost is used. Building costs are based on 2 percent of the original construction cost	
2. Building Rental Charges	Includes annual rental payments on operating rentals of buildings. Does not include capital leases, installment purchases, or certificates of participation	
Subtotal Facilities		0
Total Cost		0

Source: William C. Rivenbark, ed., *A Guide to the North Carolina Local Government Performance Measurement Project* (University of North Carolina–Chapel Hill: Institute of Government, February 2001).

ᵃThe direct cost section is divided into personal services and operating expenses. Complete the cost items that apply only to the corresponding service area for fiscal year ended 2000–2001. Some cost items, like telephone and utilities, are listed under the direct cost section and the indirect cost section. Account for such items on the same basis as you record them in your jurisdiction.

ᵇComplete the cost items that apply only to the corresponding service area for fiscal year 2000–2001 and that have not been captured under the direct cost section. You may use your current indirect cost plan. However, please use the project's full cost plan rather than the A–87 plan. You may also use the project's basis for allocation for capturing any or all indirect cost items.

ᶜComplete the cost items that apply only to the corresponding service area for fiscal year 2000–2001, using your jurisdiction's fixed assets records. The basis of allocation should be applied to groups of fixed assets as opposed to individual fixed assets.

— Chapter 7 —
Audit and Evaluation for Performance Budgeting

The term "audit" in state and local government finance has traditionally referred to annual financial audits, conducted to determine if the financial statements issued by the government represent the actual financial position of the organization in accordance with generally accepted accounting principles (GAAP). Audits establish financial accountability, ensuring compliance with accounting rules and reporting on the material accuracy of external financial reports. At some point in modern accounting history, auditing was expanded to include both the accuracy of financial statements (financial accountability) and the performance of service delivery programs (operational accountability).[1] Today, auditors evaluate the performance of service delivery on the basis of economy, efficiency, and effectiveness.

Managers are concerned with economy, efficiency, and effectiveness, too, but their perspective differs from that of the accountant. Accountants are trained to apply certain performance standards or principles to all organizations. Managers are trained to maximize service performance subject to the fiscal, legal, and political constraints that come with the government they serve. We note this difference in perspective because it illustrates something about performance measures. The choice of performance standard affects the finding about service delivery. This chapter would be unnecessary if there were a single standard of service performance for all services provided by state and local government. But as long as Miami, Florida, and Homer, Alaska, face different service challenges, the foundation for auditing and evaluation for service improvement need to reflect those differences. One statement about auditing and evaluation can be applied to Miami *and* Homer: both require performance data to begin the auditing and evaluation process.

The "reinventing government"[2] initiative expanded the focus on operational accountability in state and local government, creating an environment where including performance measures in annual operating budgets became the norm for public organizations.[3] Reporting performance statistics in the

Box 7.1

Accuracy, Reliability, and Comparability

The terms accuracy, reliability, and comparability are used throughout this chapter. They have specific meanings for performance measurement. Accurate performance data are error free. Reliable performance data reflect the actual performance of service dimensions over time as opposed to reporting performance variation caused by changes in the of calculation methodology or the interpretation of definition. Comparable performance data are based on the same service dimensions and on similar service characteristics, permitting comparisons with other jurisdictions, industry standards, or internal performance targets.

budget document does not necessarily translate into performance budgeting. It does mean, at a minimum, that performance measures are being equated with operational accountability for service delivery. Until recently, however, performance measures were added to budget documents with minimal review for their accuracy, reliability, and comparability.[4]

Performance data auditing is not common in state and local government. However, the need for accuracy becomes paramount for managers when performance begins to impact the future of their programs. Some performance experts suggest that verifying the accuracy of performance statistics is the last step in a performance measurement process.[5] Because performance data form the basis of performance budgeting, performance auditing, and program evaluation, verifying data accuracy should be as important to a process as collecting and reporting data. A relatively new auditing technique known as performance data auditing is intended to provide state and local officials the assurance they need about the accuracy, reliability, and comparability of performance measures so they can use them with confidence during budget deliberations.

This chapter starts with overviews of financial auditing, performance auditing, and program evaluation, and provides context for the evolving technique of performance data auditing. The next section identifies major threats to the accuracy of performance data, including departmental changes, interpretation of definitions, reporting models, reporting capabilities, and functional boundaries. We illustrate two approaches to performance data auditing. The first approach—the Texas model—has a financial and performance auditing focus and is commonly conducted by internal auditors. The second approach—the North Carolina model—has a program evaluation focus and is designed for management, budget, and financial analysts. The chapter concludes with a discussion of how states and local governments can increase the accuracy of performance data.

Financial Auditing

Preparing financial statements is the responsibility of officials in the budget or finance office who oversee the financial management function for their governments. States and local governments are required by law to submit to annual financial audits to ensure that the statements were prepared in conformity with generally accepted accounting principles (GAAP). These standards of accounting and financial reporting are primarily established by the Governmental Accounting Standards Board (GASB).[6]

Table 7.1 presents the financial audit process, beginning with accepting an audit engagement and ending with the issuance of the auditor's report. The information shown in Table 7.1 is universal for conducting a standard financial audit and is governed by authoritative boards to ensure standardization and financial compliance. Both external and internal auditors can conduct financial audits. We focus this discussion on independent external auditors insofar as all states and most local governments are legally required to have an external audit of their financial statements.

It is difficult to describe the first step in the audit process without including the second and third steps because there is much overlap between them. It begins with the government sending out a request for proposals, or an invitation to bid, for a contract to perform audit services for a period of time. This contract, called the audit engagement, may be for one or more years. Not many governments rebid the audit engagement every year; three years is probably the average for local governments. The successful proposal will come from a firm that is fully qualified in governmental auditing. The firm should also have some knowledge about the government it will be auditing, including some notion of the audit strategy that would be appropriate for conducting the audit. The successful firm presents a comprehensive audit proposal that includes its qualifications and an audit strategy. This strategy includes its methodology for assessing the material accuracy of financial statements as described in Step 4. If internal control problems are found or if risk is high, the auditor must test more transactions for accuracy and draw larger samples for review. (Auditors do not check every financial transaction. They select a random sample of transactions to check based on standard methodology.)

Table 7.1

An Overview of Financial Auditing

Steps	Description
1. Accepting and establishing the terms of an audit engagement financial	A public organization normally issues a request for proposals for the annual audit. The selected proposal is combined with the contract to establish the terms of the audit engagement.
2. Knowledge of governmental unit and environment	The auditor should understand legal, political, and reporting requirements. The public entity should understand the auditor's administrative and operating characteristics.
3. Audit strategy—internal control and risk	Internal controls are a function of an entity's organizational, financial, and informational structures. Risk is a function of the environment in regard to error and fraud.
4. Setting materiality levels	Audits require testing percentages, analytical procedures, sampling, and qualitative considerations.
5. Planning, timing, and conducting the audit	Planning and timing are a function of prior experience with the client and experience of external auditors. Conducting the audit requires onsite work and scheduling considerations.
6. Audit samples, review of controls, and tests for compliance with laws and regulations	The core components of the audit, creating the necessary information for issuing an audit opinion.
7. Managing work papers	Documentation of audit work, including supervisory review and checklists.
8. Auditor's report and management letter	Issuing an unqualified opinion, a qualified opinion, a disclaimer, or an adverse opinion. An auditor may also issue a management letter, identifying financial control weaknesses that need to be addressed.

Source: American Institute of Certified Public Accountants, *Audits of State and Local Governmental Units,* 17th ed. (New York: Author, 2002).

Box 7.2

External and Internal Auditors

There are two types of auditors, external auditors and internal auditors.* External auditors are independent of the entities they audit and are normally governed by contractual relationships for conducting financial and performance audits. State and local governments bid competitively for audit services just as they do for other privately provided services. In recent years, there has been an increasing trend for external auditors to offer services beyond auditing to their government clients. An example of nonaudit services might be developing and implementing a new accounting system. However, recent changes by the U.S. General Accounting Office, as presented in its publication *Government Auditing Standards*, limit the extent to which external auditors can provide services beyond auditing.+ Conflicts of interest can arise when auditors or their firms are contracted to provide consulting or technical assistance to governments. The auditor may feel pressure to ignore transactions in which his or her firm has a financial interest.

Internal auditors, on the other hand, are government employees. Their activities have traditionally focused on proper internal controls for implementing and managing accounting systems. Today their audit objectives have expanded to include performance data auditing.± However, even internal auditors must take care to retain some level of independence to be effective. Conflicts of interest can still arise where auditors review their own work.§

*Stephen J. Gauthier, *Governmental Accounting, Auditing and Financial Reporting* (Chicago: Government Finance Officers Association, 2001).

+For more information on these changes, see Stephen J. Gautier, "GAO Limits Auditor Consulting," *Government Finance Review* 18 (April 2002): 36–37. The Government Auditing Standards, published by the U.S. Accounting Office, is commonly referred to as the "yellow book."

±Stuart S. Grifel, Stephen L. Morgan, and Paul D. Epstein, "Evolving Roles for Auditors in Government Performance Measurement," *PA Times* 24 (2001): 10.

§For more information on internal auditing, see Government Finance Officers Association, *Recommended Practices for State and Local Governments* (Chicago: Author, 2001).

The fiscal year of the public entity will partially dictate the planning and timing of conducting the audit in Step 5. Most governments operate on fiscal years ending on June 30, September 30, or December 31. The government and the auditor should discuss start dates after fiscal year end, dates for onsite visits, and when the auditor expects to issue the auditor's report. Circumstances that might create audit delays should be discussed, including plans for handling such delays caused by both parties involved. Step 6 of the audit process is the actual audit work of sampling financial data for materiality, reviewing controls for proper procedures and documentation, and testing for compliance with laws and regulations. An example of sampling financial data would be identifying a sample of accounts payable transactions, reconciling them with actual invoices and with account codes on the general ledger. Compliance with laws and regulations requires auditors to review ordinances, resolutions, and administrative financial policies to ensure that they are followed. For example, the written capital assets policy of a local government must be reviewed and reconciled with capital assets financial records so the auditor can issue an opinion about whether the local government is in compliance with its own policy. In fact, inadequate capital assets records are one of the main reasons for a public organization to receive a "qualified" audit opinion.

Auditors document their work during the audit process with work papers, which are the evidence for their findings and recommendations. Comprehensive and accurate work papers are extremely important to the process, and they form the foundations for supervisory review and the auditor's report. The auditor's report typically contains three paragraphs. The first describes the audit scope, including the responsibility of the auditor and the responsibility of management. The second paragraph provides information on the audit standards used for conducting the audit. The third paragraph sets forth the auditor's opinion and whether the financial statements are presented in accordance with generally accepted accounting principles (GAAP).[7] GAAP are the "rules" for governmental accounting; they are established by the GASB. Box 7.3 shows excerpts from the auditors' report for the city of Greenville, South Carolina, for period ended June 30, 1998. Greenville received an unqualified audit opinion.

There are four types of opinions issued by auditors: unqualified, qualified, disclaimer, and adverse. An unqualified opinion means that the financial statements are in conformity with GAAP. A qualified opinion means that the auditor has specific yet limited reservations concerning the financial statements' compliance with GAAP. A qualified opinion is the mildest form of an

Box 7.3

Independent Auditors' Report

The Honorable Mayor and Members of City Council
City of Greenville, South Carolina:

We have audited the accompanying general purpose financial statements
of the city of Greenville, South Carolina (the "City"), as of and for the year
ended June 30, 1998, as listed in the accompanying table of contents. These
general purpose financial statements are the responsibility of the city's
management. Our responsibility is to express an opinion on these general
purpose financial statements based on our audit.

We conducted our audit in accordance with generally accepted auditing
standards and the standards applicable to financial audits contained in
Government Auditing Standards, issued by the Comptroller General of the
United States. Those standards require that we plan and perform the audit
to obtain reasonable assurance about whether the financial statements are
free of material misstatement. An audit includes examining, on a test basis,
evidence supporting the amounts and disclosures in the financial statements. An audit also includes assessing the accounting principles used and
significant estimates made by management, as well as evaluating the overall financial statement presentation. We believe that our audit provides a
reasonable basis for our opinion.

In our opinion, the general purpose financial statements, referred to above
present fairly, in all material respects, the financial position of the city of
Greenville, South Carolina, as of June 30, 1998, and the results of its operations and the cash flows of its proprietary fund types and nonexpendable
trust fund for the year then ended in conformity with generally accepted
accounting principles.

Source: City of Greenville, South Carolina, *Comprehensive Annual Financial Report with Single Audit*, Period Ended June 30, 1998.

audit finding, but all governments want an unqualified opinion. A disclaimer
is issued when an auditor is unable to issue an opinion on all or parts of the
financial statements because he/she did not have enough information or documentation supporting the financial statements. Finally, an adverse opinion is
issued when the financial statements are not fairly presented in conformity

with GAAP.[8] That is, the government's financial statements do not comply with the norms of governmental accounting. An adverse opinion is rare, and it signals serious financial mismanagement or incompetence.

The processes for conducting financial audits and for issuing the final audit opinion are important to performance budgeting. Recall that one of the quadrants of the balanced scorecard approach to performance management described in chapter 4 was financial accountability or fiscal stability. Historical financial trends and future financial projections are critical to strategic planning because they form the foundation for analyzing the resources required to increase, decrease, or maintain current levels of service over projected time periods. The financial statements that support historical trends and future projects must be accompanied by unqualified audit opinions for these projections to be trustworthy.

Another connection between financial auditing and performance budgeting comes from the relationship between financial data and cost data. There is a growing consensus among public officials that governments must move beyond tracking only cash outlay expenditures associated with service delivery. The preferred method is to calculate the total cost of service delivery in the form of direct, indirect, and capital costs in order to track the true cost of providing governmental services (described in chapter 3). This move toward a total cost profile is one reason that GASB (the organization that establishes generally accepted accounting principles) implemented Statement No. 34, which changed the reporting model for general purpose financial statements.[9] Cost data are superior to financial data in calculating the unit cost of service delivery for several reasons, including privatization, managed competition, benchmarking, and cost recovery. The accuracy of cost data hinges on the accuracy of financial data, highlighting the fact that cost accounting systems are built from financial management systems. Once again, financial audits must verify that financial data are materially accurate so that cost systems can reveal the true cost of service delivery inputs, and so that performance budgeting can include consideration of service inputs and outputs/outcomes.[10]

Performance Auditing

Financial auditing is easier than performance auditing. Everyone can agree on how financial audits should be conducted and what they are supposed to accomplish. Performance auditing enjoys some consensus (but not unanimity) on what it is supposed to accomplish, but how to conduct a performance audit is the subject of some dispute in the public sector. In fact, we cannot all agree on what to call performance auditing, which is just as often referred to as an operational audit, a program audit, or a management audit.[11] There are no GAAP standards for performance audits (though some may be forthcoming, as we will discuss in chapter 8), but there are some established performance auditing techniques. From the traditional point of view, the purpose of performance auditing was to study and make recommendations on improving the economy and the efficiency of service delivery, economy meaning that the program is structured properly to accomplish its mission and efficiency meaning how inputs are used to maximize outputs.

Over time, the purpose of performance auditing expanded to include program auditing, which begins to take on the characteristics of program evaluation by assessing program effectiveness.[12] The purpose of performance auditing from a more contemporary perspective is to study and make recommendations on the economy and efficiency of service delivery and to determine the extent to which desired goals and objectives are being accomplished.[13] The following definition is particularly descriptive: *Performance auditing is the systematic and objective assessment of the performance of an organization, program, function, or activity by an independent auditor, who reports findings, conclusions, and recommendations to a party or group with legal responsibility to oversee and/or initiate corrective action.*[14]

A general process for performance auditing is presented in Table 7.2.[15] Note the similarities to the financial audit as we describe the process. The planning work conducted in the early stages of the audit determines how effective the findings and recommendations are for improving the program, activity, or process under study. The key to success in Step 1 is to construct a meaningful audit work plan with input from program managers, building commitment and identifying need, selecting individuals with the necessary experience and background to conduct the audits, and determining the audit objectives. Larger governments use their internal auditors to construct the work plan and build commitment for it; smaller governments may have to use external auditors. Audit staff cannot determine how the audit findings and recommendations will be used. Senior officials must decide whether performance audit findings are intended to make major decisions about program continuation or to make service or progress improvements. The answers to this question establishes the audit objectives and gives direction to all the participants.

Understanding management control, Step 2 of the audit process, is critical to conducting a performance audit and to the overall management of service delivery. Management control is the span of control or authority over the policies, procedures, and practices needed by personnel to carry out the basic activities and functions of providing governmental services. It also encompasses management's ability to accomplish goals and objectives. As management control increases, program effectiveness becomes a manage-

Table 7.2

An Overview of Performance Auditing

Steps	Description
1. Planning the audit	Includes establishing an audit work plan, identifying who will conduct the audits, determining the audit objectives, discussing the informational needs and evidence requirements, and agreeing on how conclusions will be presented
2. Understanding management control	The span of control over policies, procedures, and practices needed by personnel to achieve the objectives of the program
3. Conducting the performance audit	Obtaining evidence based on audit objectives and documenting work with detailed and comprehensive work papers
4. Specialized techniques	Obtaining evidence through statistical sampling, through interviews and questionnaires, and through actual review of processes and procedures
5. Reporting the audit results	Providing background information, audit scope, methodologies used, findings based on clearly articulated evidence, recommendations for change, and implementation guidelines
6. Follow-up system	An evaluation process used to ensure that the recommendations have been implemented

Source: Leo Herbert, *Auditing the Performance of Management* (Belmont, CA: Life-time Learning Publications, 1979).

ment responsibility. As management control decreases, the auditor must identify and control for other factors (internal and external) impacting program success that fall outside the manager's ability to enhance effectiveness.

Step 3 in the performance audit process is conducting the audit, using the specialized techniques shown in Step 4. The audit objectives guide this process. As the number of audit objectives increases, so does the amount of review work and documentation. Specialized techniques are often required given the amount of information subject to review, including employee interviews and actual review of program processes and procedures. Sampling may be required for large datasets that would be produced in service areas such as emergency communications. Before conducting the actual audit, however, the auditor should review the fieldwork standards for performance audits outlined in *Government Auditing Standards*.[16]

Step 5 of the audit process is to report the audit results. This requires peer review by managers of the program under study and others involved in the process. The ultimate goal is to offer recommendations and implementation guidelines that will actually be used to improve service delivery. Success often hinges on the detail found in the final audit report, including specific implementation guidelines. The final step in the audit process is the use of a follow-up system to ensure that the recommendations from the audit have been implemented. Previous research has demonstrated that more emphasis needs to be placed on this step regardless of the type of audit or evaluation conducted.[17]

Why would a government take the time and effort to conduct a performance audit and not implement the findings? Of course, the answer varies among governments, but common factors that contribute to management's failure to use audit reports include: (1) inadequate audit scope and independence, (2) finding development, (3) auditor relations, (4) reporting hierarchy, (5) recommendation development, (6) audit reports, (7) resources, and (8) politics.[18] Two factors of special interest are auditor relations and audit reports.

Auditor relations involve the interpersonal skills auditors need to communicate and work with program managers and line employees to get the performance information needed for the audit report. As audit veterans, we can attest that the manager who signals staff not to cooperate with auditors will have a valid reason for rejecting audit results. The results will be superficial or otherwise unhelpful, just as the quality of information that the auditor received was.

The new responsibility for audit reports lies squarely on the auditor. They should be well organized, clearly written, and specific enough to provide the necessary direction for improving service delivery. The importance of a well-written audit report goes beyond performance audit; it is applicable to program evaluations and performance data audits as well. The effectiveness of any audit or evaluation process is judged by the extent to which recommendations are used for service improvement. Managers and auditors share responsibility for good auditor relations.

Performance auditing and performance budgeting are separate processes with a common starting point: accurate, reliable, and comparable performance data. Both techniques use efficiency and effectiveness measures to support decisions such as staffing levels, process design, and technology investments. Given the correlation between the two and their dependence on performance data, performance data auditing naturally becomes the next step for governments committed to performance management.

Next we want to take a useful digression into program evaluation so that we can compare it with performance auditing. Readers with public administration backgrounds will be more familiar with program evaluation. Readers with accounting backgrounds are accustomed to calling what we are about to describe "program audits." There are process and purpose similarities between program evaluation and performance auditing. The major difference is that program evaluation often takes the perspective of the service recipient, relying on outcome impacts consistent with the goals of the program. Performance auditing takes the perspective of the service provider, and assesses effectiveness through the prism of economy and efficiency.

Program Evaluation

Modern program evaluation traces back to the social programs created in the 1960s by the federal government. As the number of social programs increased, so did the need for program evaluation to determine if the goals and objectives of such programs were actually being realized. Over the next three decades, evaluation was routinely employed by states and local governments as a way of gauging the effectiveness of their programs and services. However, modern evaluation has traveled two separate roads since the 1960s to arrive at its current status as an interdisciplinary approach for analyzing governmental services.

The purest approach to program evaluation was derived from evaluation research, adopted to the techniques and methodologies of social science research. The following definition of program evaluation reveals the social science perspective: *Program evaluation is the use of social research procedures to systematically investigate the effectiveness of social intervention programs that is adapted to their political and organizational environments and designed to inform social actions in ways that improve social conditions.*[19] There are significant advantages to this form of program evaluation. First, it is based on a systematic and repeatable model for the evaluation of social programs. Second, it is grounded in the proven techniques of social science research. Third, it focuses on the effectiveness of social programs and concentrates more on summative evaluation, providing feedback on the worth of the program to policy makers who will ultimately expand, maintain, or eliminate it. Summative evaluation shares an important feature with performance budgeting, given that it is intended to provide policy makers with information that directly affects resource allocation decisions. The only disadvantage of this approach is that it focuses primarily on social programs, which are more the province of federal and state governments and less so of local governments.

We describe the second road traveled by program evaluation as an ad hoc approach. The ad hoc approach uses multiple techniques for program

Table 7.3

Alternative Approaches to Program Evaluation

Approach	Description
Objectives-oriented	This approach focuses the evaluation on the extent to which a program is meeting its objectives.
Management-oriented	This approach is designed to provide management with critical information to enhance the utility of making decisions.
Consumer-oriented	This approach obtains feedback from the consumers or the service recipients on their perceptions of the program.
Expertise-oriented	This approach uses individuals with expertise in the field of study to analyze the worth of a program on the goals of the evaluation.
Adversary-oriented	This approach reduces the amount of bias in evaluation, introducing the views of both supporters and adversaries of the program.
Participant-oriented	This approach includes line managers in the evaluation process to obtain the necessary experience required for detailed analysis.

Source: Blain R. Worthen, James R. Sanders, and Jody L. Fitzpatrick, *Program Evaluation: Alternatives, Approaches, and Practical Guidelines*, 2d ed. (New York: Longman, 1997).

evaluation given the context for and goals of the evaluation. It includes components of summative evaluation for examining the merits of public programs for policy makers and elements of formative evaluation to provide program managers with information for improving service delivery.[20] Program evaluation under the ad hoc approach is found at all three levels of government and used for analyzing services as well as programs. Table 7.3 offers an overview of the multiple approaches to program evaluation.

The various approaches presented in Table 7.3 all have advantages and disadvantages that the individual or project team conducting the evaluation must consider. For example, the objectives-oriented approach is driven by the success of the program with respect to program objectives. The success of this approach, therefore, is correlated with the strengths of the objectives and the ability to track them reliably, assuming that they are tracked in the first place. Another example comes from the adversary-oriented approach, using supporters and adversaries of the program to assist with the evaluation or the interpretation of the results. The usefulness of this type of evaluation hinges on an individual with the kinds of interpersonal skills that it takes to bring adversaries and supporters to consensus.

Each technique of program evaluation offers slightly different versions of the general process. Some techniques require more work in the beginning stages, while others require detailed methodologies for gathering and analyzing data. Therefore, the general process presented in Table 7.4 is not intended to represent a comprehensive or a detailed description of program evaluation, but to offer an overview for discussing the link between program evaluation and performance budgeting.

The process of program evaluation begins with selecting a program to evaluate, determining the perception of the problem, defining the scope of the problem, and constructing evaluation objectives. These steps are the most critical to the success of the evaluation. Without a meaningful reason to conduct an evaluation, a well-defined scope, and definable objectives, evaluation is pointless. For example, several years ago a county government implemented a new program in an effort to reduce juvenile recidivism. Now some elected officials are questioning the effectiveness of the program. A program evaluation is planned, but the hard questions are still unanswered. Do the council members want the evaluation for informational purposes, or to make improvements to the program? Is the program on the political chopping block (will the results be used to decide whether to eliminate the program)? The answers to these questions directly impact the scope and the objectives of the evaluation.

The next three steps—select a study team, prepare a detailed study plan, and establish lines of communication—flow from the previous steps in the process, especially from Step 4 where the type of evaluation technique is selected after the objectives are identified. The importance of establishing lines of communication cannot be overstated given the number of employees involved in most programs at all levels of the organization. Returning to the juvenile recidivism example, the study team will need information from court administration, correctional facilities, and budget and financial staff. Each of these stakeholders has a different perspective, and probably different goals for the program.

Collecting, analyzing, and interpreting data are driven by the methodology selected for study and demand the greatest time and personnel resources. The major issue, however, is the accuracy of the performance data used during this step of the process. If the performance data have not been audited or verified previously, the project team may need additional time to audit the data for accuracy, reliability, and comparability depending on the scope of the program evaluation. Again, we return to our previous theme of accuracy of performance data as a foundation for evaluation.

Table 7.4

General Process to Program Evaluation

Steps	Description
1. Select a program to evaluate	May come from an annual work plan, a current problem or crisis, or a political request
2. Determine the perception of the problem	Feedback from the critical decision makers on the reason to conduct the evaluation and on the goal of the evaluation
3. Define the nature and scope of the problem	Helps identify the resources needed for the evaluation, responding to breadth of study and precision of results
4. Determine evaluation objectives	Information from this step used to identify purpose in regard to objectives and to select the type of approach for the evaluation
5. Select a study team	Function of the size of the organization and whether internal or external evaluators are used
6. Prepare a detailed study plan	Based on the preparation work presented in steps 1–4, a clear and comprehensive evaluation plan is constructed that describes the scope, methodology, and timetable
7. Establish lines of communication	Creating the ability to collect information in an efficient manner from all stakeholders involved
8. Collecting, analyzing, and interpreting data	Using the selected methodology from step 6 to guide the process and preparing for unintended consequences or unforeseen results
9. Reporting and using evaluation information	Using the information by implementing the recommendations based on the implementation guidelines contained in the final report

Source: Nicholas Henry, *Public Administration and Public Affairs*, 5th ed. (Englewood Cliffs, NJ: Prentice-Hall, 1992).

Reporting and using the findings and recommendations, respectively, create the opportunity for performance budgeting. Budgetary implications attend to every recommendation in the final report, setting the stage for performance budgeting in two ways. First, program managers can use the information as justification for budgetary requests or for reprogramming resources (changing the allocation of resources among activities) in completing their annual budget worksheets. Second, elected officials can use the information to move beyond horizontal decision making driven primarily by incrementalism—approving across-the-board increases and decreases—to vertical decision making based on program performance. Program evaluation, therefore, supports states and local governments that have made a commitment to performance budgeting.

Performance Data Auditing

One might reasonably conclude that data auditing is a support process for larger program performance assessment, and that would be true enough if most budget documents did not report performance measures for departments and units. As we noted at the beginning of this chapter, this trend of presenting performance measures in annual operating budgets is growing in state and local government because our professional organizations have encouraged governments to demonstrate operational accountability as well as financial accountability, and identified performance measurement as the means. Unfortunately, the professional organizations have not historically emphasized verifying the accuracy of performance data as much as reporting performance data. Governments routinely collect and report performance data. Whether the data are used for performance auditing, performance budgeting, program evaluation, or decoration for the budget document, periodic review is required to ensure accuracy, reliability, and comparability of the data.

Previous research has identified certain organizational factors that impact the integrity of performance data and revealed that data accuracy, reliability, and comparability problems can arise even in well-managed performance measurement systems.[21] We discuss these factors individually in this section because they are so widely applicable across governments. The factors are: complexity of process, organizational changes, interpretation of measures, reporting capabilities, and functional boundaries. Performance data auditing should not be viewed as a way to uncover misleading information and punish the individuals responsible. It should be viewed as a way to review the integrity of performance measurement systems, just as financial audits are used to review the integrity of financial management systems. Both are essential to good management in state and local government.

Complexity of Process

Performance statistics generally represent the performance of a particular aspect of service delivery with regard to output, efficiency, and outcome. Consider the workload measure *average caseload*, computed for social workers in the Children's Services division of the Department of Social Services. What does average caseload tell the reader? What service dimension is it supposed to address? The simple measure raises as many questions as it answers in the complex environment of social services to children. Complex processes require that data verification be conducted periodically to ensure that measures actually inform the intended service dimension. In our average caseload measure, we do not know whether it is based on daily, monthly, or annual averages; how "caseload" is defined; who meets the definition of a social worker (total budgeted social workers, social workers on the payroll at a specific point in time); or how workload data are tracked and reported for calculation (referrals, assignments). Such complexities of process can cause major variations in performance statistics that result from measurement techniques rather than actual program performance. When a slight change in how one of the many factors was calculated could have a profound change on the reported statistic, systematic data audits are necessary to ensure the integrity of the performance measurement system.

Organizational Changes

Governments evolve over time, with changes in the tenure of elected officials and administrative personnel, the policies and procedural changes that govern service delivery, and the resource realignments within the programs (e.g., the fire department increases its investment in fire prevention relative to fire suppression). Changes in personnel, structure, and resources require a review of performance data, or accuracy problems will occur. New personnel need training in performance measurement for tracking and reporting performance data, linking the measures to overall programmatic goals and objectives. Policy and procedural changes cause major variations in performance statistics if measures are not reviewed and adjusted to reflect the new service dimension. Resource realignment requires that measures be deleted, added, and changed to reconcile with new priorities. Performance data systems do not automatically adjust to changes in the service environment; they have to be adjusted. We do not assume that the financial system that served us adequately ten years ago is sufficient today. We should apply the same logic to operational integrity as we hold for financial integrity.

Interpretation of Measures

Interpretation of performance measures refers to how governments define the service dimensions being measured and how the performance data are defined for calculating the measures. As interpretations of the components of measures vary from one reporting period to another, variations occur in the performance measures that are not related to performance. For example, should average dispatch time in emergency communications include stack time (the amount of time an emergency call is held until a responding unit becomes available) or should average response time start once the call is ready for dispatch? Auditing performance data ensures that individuals responsible for data collection are using the appropriate methodology consistently to produce comparable indicators of service performance.

Reporting Capabilities

The ability to collect, track, and report performance data is a direct function of the reporting capabilities in an organization. Hopefully, the government has invested in an appropriate data management system to assist personnel with tracking performance data. A computer-aided dispatch (CAD) system for emergency communications is an excellent example. Other data management systems may include desktop databases and spreadsheets. Even manual systems are useful in capturing meaningful data. But as the reporting capabilities change over time, auditing the accuracy of performance data is critical for consistency. For example, if there is an error in constructing a formula in a spreadsheet, the error may be carried forward from year to year if the same format is simply copied over to use when new performance data are keyed. Data accuracy also is a function of the wholeness of the dataset. When partial year data or samples are used to construct measures that reflect annual performance because of limited reporting capabilities, audit work is a must for the integrity of the performance measurement system.

Functional Boundaries

The relationship between the need for auditing performance data and functional boundaries is twofold. First, functional boundaries for state and local government are often blurred, creating problems with calculating inputs required for calculating certain performance measures. Second, organizational performance as reflected by a single performance statistic often crosses multiple functional boundaries, creating problems with the tracking of performance data. Functional boundary problems are a common occurrence in police services, for example, where patrol officers may perform both patrol and investigative duties. The problem is compounded when these functional boundaries involve complex processes that are subject to change over time, as patrol and investigation do. Auditing of performance data allows police departments to track and document factors that impact both programs.

Other Factors

Our five factors are in no way an exhaustive list of circumstances that impact the accuracy of performance data. Other factors might include the size and scope of databases, the technical skills of employees responsible for tracking data, and the types of services the government provides. Variations in all these factors demonstrate the need for periodic auditing of performance data. The next section presents two models for auditing performance data, the Texas model for state governments and the North Carolina model for local governments.

Models for Performance Data Auditing

The Government Finance Officers Association (GFOA) uses "performance measurement verification" as its term for reviewing the accuracy and reliability of performance data, preventing confusion with performance auditing and drawing a distinction from financial auditing.[22] This is entirely justifiable insofar as financial improprieties can be punished by legal sanctions (like going to jail, in the most extreme case) while operational improprieties are punishable only by administrative censure.

We, however, use "performance data auditing" to describe the process of data verification. We borrow the following definition: *an activity that allows governmental officials to evaluate whether performance measures are providing meaningful and useable information, to gain a greater understanding of processes and programs, and to test for data accuracy, reliability, and comparability.*[23] The reason for the descriptive variation from GFOA is that auditing data is more comprehensive than verifying data reliability. Performance data auditing as we are about to describe it in the Texas and North Carolina models, is auditing. It encompasses a work plan, a methodology, and a statement of findings and recommendations.

Texas Model

The Texas model for auditing performance data follows a process very similar to financial and performance auditing, using internal auditors from the State Auditor's Office to conduct the audits. The objectives are: to examine the accuracy of performance measures, to determine how managers use performance information to manage operations, and to verify that adequate internal controls exist.[24] Agencies are selected for audit from a risk assessment process based on the following factors:[25]

1. Substantial changes in organizational structure and personnel;
2. Expressions of concern by legislators;
3. Patterns of unexpected performance;
4. Dollars appropriated to an agency;
5. Indications from previous audits that an agency has potential performance measure control weaknesses;
6. Frequency with which an agency's performance measures have been reviewed; and
7. Submission of self-assessment data.

Once the agency has been selected for audit, a set of key performance measures are selected for review as described in Step 1 of the process depicted in Figure 7.1. The state considers about 2,150 measures as key to its performance budgeting process from a total of approximately 7,600 measures used in conjunction with its strategic plan. These key measures are critical to the Governor's Office and the Legislature during the budget preparation process as they influence allocation decisions. Other measures are often selected as part of the audit if they are closely aligned with the statewide strategic plan or contain other significant characteristics such as providing a direct indication of whether programs are meeting their goals.

The next three steps in the process are the beginning of the audit work: determining if the agency can re-create the number reported, determining the method used by the agency to collect and calculate the performance data, and determining if the agency followed the measure definition. An interesting point these steps demonstrate is that a distinction is made between a performance measure and performance data in Step 3. The methodology used to collect the performance data, which in turn is used to calculate the final performance statistics, is reviewed to ensure that errors do not occur because of database or mathematical problems. Another interesting feature is the emphasis placed on measure definition in Step 4. Regardless of the accuracy of performance data, agreement on the measurement definition ultimately determines the reliability of the performance statistic.

The remaining steps in the process reveal the real strengths of the Texas model, providing the necessary detail for an effective audit. The auditor must review the types of records maintained in Step 5, including whether data are tracked manually or with an automated system. The internal controls are reviewed in Step 6, which requires that the auditor track the data flow from origination to final destination as a performance measure. The sample work outlined in Steps 7, 8, and 9 show basic auditing procedures used by all

Figure 7.1   **Auditing Performance Data: Texas Model**

STEPS IN A PERFORMANCE MEASUREMENT VERIFICATION

Step 1   Determine which of the department's measures to verify
Step 2   Determine whether the department can re-create the number reported in internal management documents and/or the annual budget
Step 3   Determine the method the department used to collect and calculate the performance data
Step 4   Determine whether the department followed the measure definition
Step 5   Determine whether the department keeps the data on a manual or automated system
Step 6   Determine whether adequate controls over performance measure data exist to ensure consistent reporting of accurate information
Step 7   Obtain a list of items to be sampled from the department
Step 8   Choose a sample
Step 9   Test the department's source documentation for accuracy
Step 10 Determine each performance measure's certification category

---

Source: Adapted from Texas State Auditor's Officer, *Guide to Performance Measure Management*: www.sao.state.tx.us/Resources/Manuals/prfmguide/perfguide.html.

auditors conducting financial audits. Once the population (all potential data observations) is obtained from the agency, a sample size of twenty-nine is selected for review as long as adequate controls exist; otherwise, the sample size is sixty-one. The performance measures created from the performance data are certified as long as the margin of error remains within plus or minus 5 percent for the sample.

The final step in the Texas model is to determine each performance measure's certification category. As in the case of financial audit findings, there are different categories of responses to certification. A measure is "certified" when accuracy is not in question. A measure is "certified with qualification" when the performance measure is accurate but the controls over data collection are questionable. "Factors prevented certification" is when documentation is unavailable for adequate review, which is similar to a disclaimer opinion in financial audits. The final category is "inaccurate," indicating that the measure is outside the margin of error of plus or minus 5 percent. This rating system for performance data auditing provides users with an understandable format for judging whether an agency's performance measures are within an acceptable range for making allocation decisions based on audit results.

Figure 7.2 contains an executive summary of a performance data audit conducted by the Texas State Auditor's Office on a sample of performance measures from eleven state agencies. The audit found that 54 percent of the measures reviewed were reliable (0 percent certified and 54 percent

Figure 7.2 Audit Summary for State Agencies in Texas

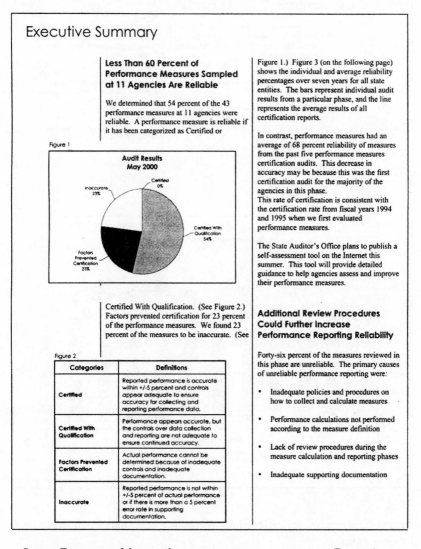

Executive Summary

Less Than 60 Percent of Performance Measures Sampled at 11 Agencies Are Reliable

We determined that 54 percent of the 43 performance measures at 11 agencies were reliable. A performance measure is reliable if it has been categorized as Certified or

Figure 1

Audit Results May 2000

- Certified 0%
- Inaccurate 23%
- Certified With Qualification 54%
- Factors Prevented Certification 23%

Certified With Qualification. (See Figure 2.) Factors prevented certification for 23 percent of the performance measures. We found 23 percent of the measures to be inaccurate. (See

Figure 2

Categories	Definitions
Certified	Reported performance is accurate within +/- percent and controls appear adequate to ensure accuracy for collecting and reporting performance data.
Certified With Qualification	Performance appears accurate, but the controls over data collection and reporting are not adequate to ensure continued accuracy.
Factors Prevented Certification	Actual performance cannot be determined because of inadequate controls and inadequate documentation.
Inaccurate	Reported performance is not within +/-5 percent of actual performance or if there is more than a 5 percent error rate in supporting documentation.

Figure 1.) Figure 3 (on the following page) shows the individual and average reliability percentages over seven years for all state entities. The bars represent individual audit results from a particular phase, and the line represents the average results of all certification reports.

In contrast, performance measures had an average of 68 percent reliability of measures from the past five performance measures certification audits. This decrease in accuracy may be because this was the first certification audit for the majority of the agencies in this phase.
This rate of certification is consistent with the certification rate from fiscal years 1994 and 1995 when we first evaluated performance measures.

The State Auditor's Office plans to publish a self-assessment tool on the Internet this summer. This tool will provide detailed guidance to help agencies assess and improve their performance measures.

Additional Review Procedures Could Further Increase Performance Reporting Reliability

Forty-six percent of the measures reviewed in this phase are unreliable. The primary causes of unreliable performance reporting were:

- Inadequate policies and procedures on how to collect and calculate measures

- Performance calculations not performed according to the measure definition

- Lack of review procedures during the measure calculation and reporting phases

- Inadequate supporting documentation

Source: For a copy of the complete report, see www.sao.state.tx.us/Reports/.

certified with qualification). The remaining measures were inaccurate (23 percent) or were placed into the category of factors prevented certification (23 percent). The executive summary shows the primary factors that caused 46 percent of the performance measures to be unreliable, including inadequate policies and procedures, calculations not performed ac-

Executive Summary, continued

To improve the reliability of their performance measurement systems, agencies should follow these procedures to prevent or detect reporting errors:

*   Review data submitted by field offices and third parties for accuracy and completeness.

*   Review the measure calculation for consistency with the measure definition and mathematical accuracy.

*   Review supporting documentation for accuracy and completeness.

*   Compare the final results submitted to the Legislative Budget Board with the summary documentation to ensure data-entry accuracy.

Please refer to the *Guide to Performance Measure Management* (SAO Report No. 00-318, December 1999) for additional information on improving performance measurement reliability.

Table 1 on the following page provides an overview of the current results.

Figure 3

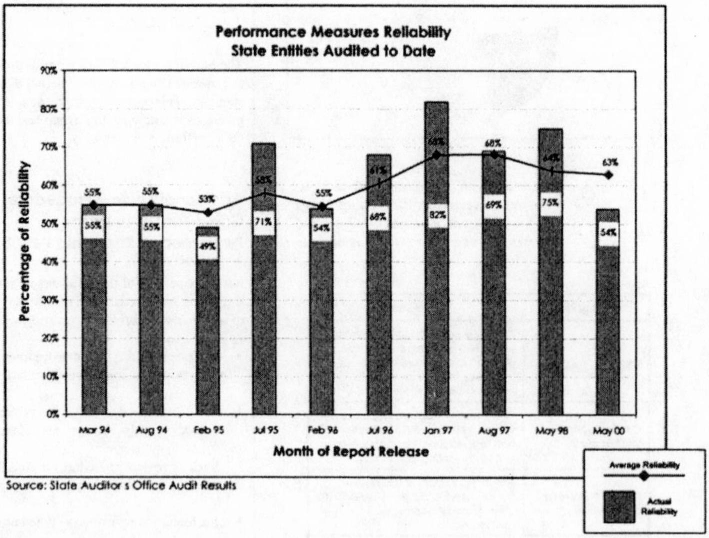

Performance Measures Reliability
State Entities Audited to Date

Source: State Auditor's Office Audit Results

cording to measure definition, lack of review, and inadequate supporting documentation.

A final point of interest comes from the graph in Figure 7.2 on the reliability of performance measures between 1994 and 2000. The graph shows that an average 63 percent of the measures reviewed were reliable during this period of time, which means that 37 percent were unreliable. These are very powerful findings given that the state of Texas has a very structured performance measurement system, which clearly supports our position that periodic performance data audits are necessary.

Executive Summary, concluded

Table 1

Name (Agency Number Order)	Current Audit Results						
	Certified	Certified With Qualification	Factors Prevented Certification	Inaccurate	Total Measures Audited	Reliability Percentage
Office of the State Prosecuting Attorney		2			2	100%
Securities Board		5			5	100%
Texas Aerospace Commission		1	4		5	20%
Office of Court Administration		1		1	2	50%
Telecommunications Infrastructure Fund Board		1	3	1	5	20%
Office of Consumer Credit Commissioner				5	5	0%
Finance Commission of Texas				1	1	0%
Research and Oversight Council on Workers Compensation		3			3	100%
State Office of Risk Management		5			5	100%
Optometry Board		4		1	5	80%
State Board for Educator Certification		1	2	2	5	20%
Totals	**0**	**23**	**10**	**10**	**43**	**n/a**
Percentage	**0%**	**54%**	**23%**	**23%**	**100%**	**54%**

Summary of Management Responses

The responses indicate that management generally agrees with the recommendations for improvement. Responses to the audit findings were provided by the audited entities' management and are included in the report after each agency's results and findings.

Summary of Audit Objectives and Scope

The primary objective of this audit was to determine the accuracy of key performance measures reported to the Automated Budget and Evaluation System of Texas (ABEST) database. We reviewed related control systems for adequacy. We also provided assistance to entities with collection and reporting problems. Performance information was traced to the original sources when possible.

North Carolina Model

The North Carolina model was derived from the benchmarking process we described in chapter 6. It was based on fourteen local government audits conducted by staff members of the North Carolina benchmarking project.[26] It goes beyond a data accuracy focus to include accuracy, reliability, and comparability, insofar as the performance data from the fourteen local governments are used to create performance benchmarks that are used by other local governments in the larger benchmarking project.

The performance data auditing process for the North Carolina model is presented in Table 7.5. Although it resembles the financial and performance

Table 7.5

Auditing Performance Data: North Carolina Model

Steps	Factors for success
1. Audit schedule	Considers the capacity for conducting meaningful audits, including time and personnel
2. Entrance conference	Includes managers and line employees
3. Scope of audit	Encompasses policy, process, definition, and data
4. Methodology	Includes data review, process analysis, and employee interviews
5. Findings	Based on scope and methodology of audit
6. Recommendations	Based on informational needs of managers and line employees
7. Implementation guidelines	Based on service dimensions and definitions for data accuracy
8. Exit conference	Includes managers and line employees
9. Audit report	Uses standard format similar to internal audit reports
10. Follow-up	Requires a process for review to ensure that recommendations have been implemented

Source: William C. Rivenbark and Carla M. Pizzarella, "Auditing Performance Data in Local Government," *Public Performance & Management Review* 25 (June 2002): 414–21.

auditing processes, the factors for success in each step of the process are more like program evaluation. In other words, the purpose of the review goes far beyond data accuracy and includes an evaluation of whether performance measures are providing meaningful and usable information, and explanatory information that describes the environment of service delivery. Another key point of the North Carolina model is that it is constructed for the use of management, budget, and financial analysts as opposed to external or internal auditors. Internal auditors can surely conduct this form of performance data auditing, but the fourteen governments in North Carolina varied in size; smaller jurisdictions rarely have internal auditors on staff.

The process begins with an audit schedule driven by the availability of resources to conduct the audit, mainly time and personnel. This step corresponds to the expertise-oriented approach to program evaluation. The entrance conference secures the involvement of managers and line employees.

This is where the scope of the performance data audit is agreed upon, including the objectives for conducting it. This may be the most important part of the process given that clear guidelines and objectives obtained from consensus building among the group create a productive environment for audit work. The methodology step includes data review, process analysis, and employee interviews, corresponding to the participant-oriented approach to program evaluation.

The findings and recommendations are based on the scope of the audit and on the informational needs of managers and line employees. The next step, implementation guidelines, enhances the usefulness of recommendations. It is not enough to simply offer recommendations and hope for implementation. Analysts who conduct these audits must provide detailed implementation guidelines and use follow-up review, the last step in the process, to ensure that the recommendations have been successfully implemented. The exit conference is used to build consensus on the findings and recommendations.

Figure 7.3 shows a sample performance data audit conducted by project staff of the North Carolina benchmarking project on emergency communications. One limitation of this example is that it does not contain implementation guidelines. It does, however, illustrate the entrance conference, scope, methodology, findings, recommendations, and exit conference. It also contains the revised performance measures based on accuracy, reliability, and comparability, and describes how they are being used to enhance the utility of making sound decisions about emergency communication.

The diagram in Figure 7.3 clearly demonstrates the need for performance data auditing for commonly reported emergency communication performance measures such as dispatch time. The steps involved in constructing the measure require a clear service definition, training on how to track the call data, training on how to calculate the measure, and audit work to ensure accuracy. Why bother? Because a measure like dispatch time does not reflect the level of detail needed to understand a functional area as complicated as emergency communications.

Conclusion

This chapter has presented information on the following three auditing and evaluation techniques, (1) financial auditing, (2) performance auditing, (3) program evaluation, and two auditing models (4) the Texas model of performance data auditing for state governments, and (5) the North Carolina model of performance data auditing for local governments. We have dedicated an entire chapter to audit and evaluation because a performance budgeting system rests on the accuracy of performance data. The bottom line is that per-

Figure 7.3   **Audit Summary on Emergency Communications in North Carolina**

ABBREVIATED AUDIT REPORT ON EMERGENCY COMMUNICATIONS

The scope of the performance measurement audit for emergency communications included the service profile form for that function, related performance and cost data in the Final Report on City Services for FY 1999–2000, and on-site interviews with emergency communications personnel for each participating unit. The audit was conducted during March and April 2001, concluding with an exit conference in May 2001.

Methodology

In February 2001, project staff developed a questionnaire and distributed it to each participating municipality. They used it to obtain initial information on how the municipality was collecting and reporting performance data. They then conducted on-site visits to detail how the participating municipalities were collecting and reporting data and to determine what their capabilities were for collecting and reporting other data. Project staff used the information from the on-site visits to generate the findings and the recommendations that follow.

Findings

1. A series of events occurs between the time a call requiring dispatch is placed and the time the call is dispatched. (For the steps in handling an emergency call, see Figure 1.) Variations such as routing patterns may exist across jurisdictions.

Figure 1. **Steps in Responding to Emergency Calls**

• Caller dials E-911 (or other number).

• Call is received by telephone company switching center and routed to Emergency Communications Center.

• Call rings in Emergency Communication Center.

• Call is answered by telecommunicator (beginning of talk time).

• Call is entered into CAD (computer-aided dispatch) system and routed, if necessary, to appropriate dispatcher.

• Call is ready for dispatch (and unit begins to respond if available).

• Call is held until unit is available to respond (if response is not immediate).

• Unit is assigned and responds to call.

---

2. Interpretation of the measure "Average time from receipt of call to dispatch, for calls resulting in a dispatch" has varied in the determination of when "receipt of call" begins:
   • For one jurisdiction, "receipt of call" begins when the call is registered by the telephone company.
   • In another case, "receipt of call" has been interpreted as being the moment when the telephone call is answered by the telecommunicator.
   • In most cases, "receipt of call" has been interpreted as being the moment when the call is first keyed into the CAD system.

Source: William C. Rivenbark and Carla M. Pizzarella, "Ensuring the Integrity of Crucial Data," *Popular Government* 67 (Winter 2002): 28–34.

3. Interpretation of the measure "Average time from receipt of call to dispatch, for calls resulting in a dispatch" has varied in the determination of when "dispatch" begins. The definition of "dispatch" and the reporting structures of CAD systems appear to differ from jurisdiction to jurisdiction:

- For at least one jurisdiction, "dispatch" represents the time when the telecommunicator makes the call available for dispatch. In this instance, "Average time from receipt of call to dispatch . . ." does not include "stack time" (the time the call was held).

- For other jurisdictions, "dispatch" represents the time when a responding unit has been assigned and is ready to take the call. In this instance, "Average time from receipt of call to dispatch . . ." does include stack time.

4. Interpretation of the measure "Average time from receipt of call to dispatch, for calls resulting in a dispatch" has varied slightly in the determination of which calls are included in "calls resulting in a dispatch":

- One jurisdiction includes only E-911 calls.

- Most jurisdictions include all calls resulting in a dispatch, which could be calls to E-911 or calls to another telephone number.

5. Variations exist in the tracking capabilities of units to arrive at "total number of incoming calls":

- One unit is able to track all non–E-911 calls but is unable to track E-911 calls, which are transfers from another center.

- Some units are installing a system to track the number of all incoming calls. These units have been either providing estimates or not providing the total number of incoming calls.

- Most units have a system that tracks the number of all incoming calls.

6. Variations exist in the types of calls included in the "total number of incoming calls." These variations are due to the different functions of each emergency communications center rather than differences in interpreting the question. Some units are primary centers; others are secondary. Some transfer calls to other units of government (for example, the sheriff or Emergency Medical Services); others receive calls that were transferred from another call center.

Recommendations

1. Add the measure "Calls dispatched per telecommunicator" to correspond with the existing measure "Calls answered per telecommunicator." The dispatch function is arguably the core element of emergency communications. Inclusion of this measure would provide an additional dimension of a telecommunicator's workload.

2. Replace the measure "E-911 calls only, answered per 1,000 population" with "Calls dispatched per 1,000 population." The number of calls dispatched provides a more comprehensive base of information than the number of E-911 calls. Calls dispatched can include calls that come through both the E-911 lines and other lines.

3. Replace the measures "Cost per call answered" and "Cost per E-911 call answered" with "Cost per call dispatched." Calls dispatched provide the most meaningful basis for cost information because call dispatch is the primary function of emergency communications.

(continued)

Figure 7.3 *(continued)*

4. Provide clear definitions of start and end times for the measure "For calls dispatched, number of seconds from receipt of call to dispatch." Reword the measure to read "For calls dispatched, number of seconds from CAD entry to dispatch." This measure would represent the interval from when the call is first keyed into the CAD system to when the call has been assigned and dispatched to a responding unit, including stack time if necessary.

5. Regarding "calls dispatched," include self-initiated calls except for administrative events, duplicates, or calls related to another call. Also include telephone responses and walk-ins.

6. Delete the measure "Sustained complaints per 100,000 calls answered" because of variations in definitions of "sustained" and "complaint" among jurisdictions.

7. If information is available only through sampling or estimation, write "N/A" (not available) on the service profile forms.

8. When possible, report raw service data on the service profile forms, allowing project staff to calculate the performance measures.

These recommendations are summarized in Table 1.

Table 1. Performance Measures for Emergency Communications

Existing	Proposed
• Total calls answered per 1,000 population	• Total calls answered per 1,000 population
• E-911 calls only, answered per 1,000 population	• Calls dispatched per 1,000 population
• Calls answered per telecommunicator	• Calls answered per telecommunicator
• Cost per call answered	• Calls dispatched per telecommunicator
• Cost per E-911 call answered	• Cost per call dispatched
• For calls dispatched, number of seconds from receipt of call to dispatch	• For calls dispatched, number of seconds from CAD entry to dispatch
• Number of seconds from initial ring to answer	• Number of seconds from initial ring to answer
• Percentage of calls answered within three rings (18 seconds)	• Percentage of calls answered within three rings (18 seconds)
• Sustained complaints per 100,000 calls answered	

Epilogue

During the exit conference in May 2001, police personnel reviewed and accepted the recommendations and the proposed performance measures contained in this report, and in July 2001 the project steering committee approved them. The service profile form for emergency communications was adjusted for data collection beginning in August 2001.

formance data are the lowest element in operational accountability in state and local government. But if the data are not accurate, then nothing above them works.

A comprehensive performance budgeting program requires managers to present, for every program under their jurisdiction, the following:

1. A mission statement;
2. Service delivery goals;
3. Performance objectives, which include expectations of achievement within a budget period;
4. Performance indicators, which include specific, measurable outcomes that result from program activity;
5. Performance criteria, which provide guidance and benchmarks by which results can be assessed;
6. Data elements, as well as data gathering methods and instruments, to facilitate accuracy and reliability;
7. Data review to ensure that information remains relatively stable and comparable over time in both form and substance; and
8. Data analysis to ensure that the performance measures are producing information, which forms the fundamental link to the budgetary process.[27]

These eight steps summarize the elements of performance budgeting from the highest element, the mission, to the lowest element, the data. These two elements and everything in between are necessary for a performance budgeting program to be successful.

We regretfully conclude that performance data are not thought of as the first step toward a mission-driven, outcome-focused service delivery system in most governments. Rather they are considered a way to represent operational accountability in the budget document and to be competitive for the Distinguished Budget Presentation Award sponsored by GFOA. Although we strongly support accountability and the efforts of GFOA, simply placing performance measures into the budget document may cause integrity problems over time if not properly managed.[28] When performance measures become part of the budget document, they are often considered to be facts, though we have shown that even well-structured processes suffer from accuracy problems. Recall that the performance data audit conducted by the state of Texas revealed that some data were accurate (54 percent), and others were not (47 percent).

To further increase the stakes of performance reporting, GASB is currently considering a proposal that would require state and local governments to report measures of performance in their general purpose external financial statements. Such a requirement would mandate performance data auditing to ensure that the performance measures reported in the financial statements are materially accurate. In other words, performance data would be subjected to the same level of audit review as financial data. That means the government must verify performance data as carefully as it verifies financial data.

Performance data auditing ensures the integrity of performance measures used to make allocation decisions, it reviews the effectiveness of performance measurement systems for operational accountability, and it sets the stage for conducting performance audits and program evaluations. As auditors and analysts verify performance data for accuracy, reliability, and comparability, they are also likely to raise some questions about service economy, efficiency, and effectiveness. Noting these concerns in the audit report permits governments to address both performance data issues and broader implications of service delivery at the same time. An integrated approach to performance data auditing reinforces another idea that is constant throughout these chapters: Performance budgeting is not a stand-alone system but the logical and appropriate extension of the collection, auditing, and reporting of the performance information that every public manager needs to make good decisions.

— Chapter 8 —

Capacity Building for Performance Budgeting

We began this book with a discussion of accountability. We concluded that accountability is important for the public sector, but there is no satisfactory measure of it. Specifically, we said that performance budgeting might be a strong indicator of accountability, but does not singularly constitute accountability. We are about to make a similar argument with regard to capacity. We can agree that governments should improve their capacity, but no one can say exactly how, or measure how much. Like accountability, capacity is context-specific. If accountability begs the question, "to whom?" then capacity begs the question "to do what?" We are about to assert that performance budgeting can enhance two kinds of public sector capacity, so we have to struggle honestly with the imprecise terms of organizational and managerial capacity. Included in the struggle is an acknowledgment that performance budgeting enhances accountability and expands capacity only when it is real. Real performance budgeting requires a commitment of time, resources, and leadership that some organizations cannot or will not make. In the absence of a commitment, performance measures are nothing more than window dressing.

Let us be frank. Sometimes new public management buzzwords like "performance" or "total quality" are attractive to governments dealing with intractable problems. They sound good, but they do not necessarily require the government to do anything differently, and thus avoid the conflict that comes from real change. In short, they are pseudo-reforms that relieve the pressure for reform without creating the problems associated with meaningful reform. An illustration might help explain why governments are drawn to pseudo-reforms.

Recently, a government finance director called one of your authors to ask about availability for some consulting work. The elected body passed an ordinance requiring a performance budget, and the finance director wanted to know what to do next. Full of enthusiasm for the opportunity to start a performance budgeting program from scratch, your author started talking about mission statements, strategic plans, outcome measures, and service delivery goals. The finance director listened patiently for a few minutes, then said, "Look, our budget hasn't balanced in three years. New taxes are off the table again this year, so we have to identify all discretionary spending and look for ways to balance the budget from cuts to those programs. I don't mean any disrespect, but this performance budgeting thing isn't real. We just need to put some performance stuff in the budget next year. Can you help us out with that or not?"

This government was not ready for performance budgeting, or anything else for that matter. It was in the middle of a political and fiscal crisis with no end in sight. The political leadership responded to the crisis by claiming that performance budgeting would solve it. In reality, performance budgeting exists within political and financial constraints and must accommodate them. As for the finance director, your author recommended a couple of budget documents to review for performance presentation. Because there was no money for data collection and analysis and no interest in using the results for decision making, it seemed a reasonable solution. The finance director was grateful and promised to get back in touch if the organization ever worked itself "out of this mess," commenting that it would be nice to actually have a system for measuring performance and using performance results in the budget process.

Political leaders respond to pressure from their constituents to keep taxes low and popular services high. To that end, they may postpone important capital improvements and take funds away from effective programs with low visibility while increasing funds to ineffective, high visibility programs even as they affirm their commitment to a management process that would preclude those choices. This is not necessarily a deceptive or disingenuous position. Elected *and* appointed officials can be absolutely committed to the public interest and still take the path of least political resistance. When citizens reward competent, innovative, and farsighted leadership with their support, we may see more of it. As it stands, we must accept that citizens have complicated and sometimes contradictory preferences for the services and programs provided by their government, and rely on good management practice and political leadership to promote their best interests. Performance budgeting encompasses good management practice and political leadership, so it is generally consistent with citizen preferences. But having better information about how public programs are performing will not make the path of least political resistance any less appealing, especially when hard choices about raising revenue or cutting programs must be made.

Context of Capacity

As chapter 2 indicated, there is something peculiarly American in the idea that the best way to change outcomes is to infuse the process that produced them with more rationality. Capacity-building activities are typically concerned with moving organizations away from patterns of decision making based on custom and toward decision criteria that are based on rationality—systematic analysis of relevant information. It is a normative construct that informed decisions are better decisions and that managers who make decisions on a rational basis are better managers.[1] However, we implicitly, if not explicitly, understand that ignoring citizen preferences does not enhance capacity, regardless of the sophistication of the data analysis supporting policy decisions.

For example, assume citizens in one neighborhood of Green Acres are upset because they believe that another, more affluent neighborhood, receives a better quality of police service than they do. Telling citizens that a top-notch performance budgeting program ties funding decisions for the police department to carefully selected, faithfully audited performance data probably will not change one citizen's attitude toward the police department. Consider how the budget process might work for the police department in Green Acres under our scenario. The police chief submits his budget request, using performance information to justify his request for new resources. The finance director reviews the performance information and the budget requests, and forwards her positive recommendation for the police department's budget to the city administrator, based on the performance information. The city administrator of Green Acres deliberates the police department's budget request, but is keenly aware that her decision is taking place in a politically charged environment. The mayor and city council want to deal with the political problem of a perception of unequal services and are willing to put resources in activities that advance this cause regardless of performance data or the recommendation of the manager and the finance director. It is, after all, their job to respond to citizen concerns about equity in service provision.

This scenario illustrates some different dimensions of capacity operating in Green Acres. The last aspect of capacity is beyond our scope in this book. Volumes have been written about political capacity and political leadership. It is important to keep in mind that the capacity of elected officials involves taking cues from public opinion about their preferred course of action as well as influencing public opinion toward a course of action that the elected official thinks is appropriate. Performance information can be useful for the elected official to explain or justify funding decisions about public services. But the other element of political capacity, the flow of public opinion to political action, explains why performance information cannot always determine funding decisions. When citizens cannot influence government action, there is no democracy. It matters whether performance information supports the chief's budget request, but it is not determinate. What matters more is what the citizens of that allegedly underserved neighborhood reveal about their perceptions of police service. If the elected leaders of Green Acres are not responsive to the concerns of this neighborhood, and if the appointed officials do not recognize that concern as legitimate and appropriate, Green Acres does not have a viable government.

The other two dimensions of capacity—organizational and managerial— are within our scope and are considered at length, separately and together. They are not independent of political capacity. In fact, political capacity is a part of organizational capacity because it permits the organization's activities to be directed and redirected toward changes in the policy environment that stem from citizen preferences. Political capacity also is tied to managerial capacity, though less directly, in that the political environment sets limits around the use of managerial tools for decision making.

Organizational Capacity

The literature on government capacity spends a lot of time defining the elements of capacity and struggling with the "capacity to do what?" question. One definition of organization capacity includes the ability to:

1. Anticipate and influence change;
2. Make informed, intelligent decisions about policy;
3. Develop programs to implement policy;
4. Attract and absorb resources;
5. Manage resources; and
6. Evaluate current activities to guide future action.[2]

These abilities are indisputably important, but they do not focus our attention on the two aspects of capacity that are related but not identical. Our examples—the finance director's fiscally stressed government and Green Acres—tell us that there is an aspect of capacity that management innovation cannot address and that it is not limited to political leadership. There is something about the environment in which management occurs that either enhances its effectiveness or constrains it. The manager must operate within that environment and accommodate management practice to it; he cannot make the environment accommodate the chosen management practice. We choose to define that environment as organizational capacity.

Actually, this is not a new definition. This externally determined definition of organizational capacity is decades old. Organizational capacity has been defined as the interaction of community expectations, community resources, and community problems.[3] This approach separates management capacity from organizational capacity in a way that permits performance budgeting to be evaluated in both contexts. We start with the three elements of organizational capacity.

Community Expectations

Governments do not make identical demands for political leadership or for administrative excellence. Organizations similar in all other respects may place very different expectations on their elected and appointed leaders. If a community is fractured over an issue or event, citizens will expect their leaders to resolve that dispute first and worry about service performance later. Another community may be extremely tax-resistant, preferring private contracting and other service delivery alternatives to traditional public services in order to keep property tax burdens low. Still another community may make high demands on their elected and appointed leaders to demonstrate excellence in service quality and quantity, and are willing to provide the resources necessary to achieve it. The community expectations variable reminds us that capacity is defined by the task to which it will be applied. A different type of managerial focus would be appropriate for each of the three scenarios, illustrating the point that organizational capacity suggests the dimensions of managerial capacity.

Community Resources

The resources variable is not limited to tax revenues, though different compositions of tax bases affect capacity. Some governments have a manufacturing base, some a service base, some are almost exclusively residential, and a few are still agricultural. Changes in the national and global economy will affect each of them differently. There are nonmonetary resources as well. One of the most important is an educated workforce. Another is a fully capitalized infrastructure on which to build a growing economy. Yet another is an active citizenry that votes, organizes advocacy groups, supports their nonprofit sector, and demands that their political and administrative leaders pay attention to their changing demands. All of these resources matter in assessing organizational capacity.

Community Problems

When the problems are simple, adequate levels of capacity may be small. When the problems are difficult, especially if they are intractable, a greater level of capacity is required to deal with them. However, the intractability of a problem is not evidence that the government or its leaders lack capacity. Consider the "border towns" in states along the Mexican border. Illegal immigration is technically a federal problem, but border town leaders will testify that it also is very much a local problem, and one they will never be able to solve. Other kinds of intractable community problems include racial and ethnic divisions, structural unemployment, or proximity to an unwanted or unsafe area (e.g., toxic chemical spill). Still other examples include location near flood-prone rivers, in "tornado alley," and coastal towns subject to hurricanes. In a sense these are not really problems as much as situations, as they can never be solved. Yet no one would assert that they have no influence on organizational capacity.

These three dimensions of organization capacity—expectations, resources, and problems—suggest that organizational capacity is dynamic and has a time dimension. Organizational capacity can grow, and it can shrink. The kinds of management strengths that elected and appointed officials bring to the government can be important in moving organizational capacity in or out, but they cannot define the boundaries of organizational capacity. We have all heard of cities that hired "hot shot" administrators to solve their problems and been bitterly disappointed when the miracle did not materialize. They were assuming, evidently, that managerial capacity could push organizational capacity out, expanding the city's ability to cope with its challenges. Managerial miracles happen, but they are more likely when optimism about a new administrator is combined with expectations for better governance, willingness to fund better governance, and a commitment to work with the new administration toward long-term solutions to persistent problems.

Managerial Capacity

We now turn to the issue of managerial capacity in the hopes of persuading the reader that performance budgeting can advance it. Unfortunately, we have no precise definition of managerial capacity that can help the reader discern the level of managerial capacity in an organization, nor even whether the organization has a sufficient level of managerial capacity to meet the demands placed on it by its citizens. There is some truth to the assertion that you know managerial capacity when you see it, in that capacity is specific to time, place, and circumstance as well as to the challenges that managers face in that time, place, and circumstance.

The best consensus definition of managerial capacity is tripartite. Managerial capacity is the capability to accomplish objectives in policy management, in resource management, and in program management.[4] Setting aside the capability portion for a moment, as it involves the tools of management we want to discuss, let us examine the areas of managerial capacity and what they entail. Policy management is essentially Gulick's POSDCRB, the description of the basic managerial functions.[5] It involves planning for programs by establishing goals and priorities, securing human capital and financial resources, guiding the implementation of policy, and ensuring meaningful evaluation of results. Resource management includes the management of information as well as personnel and capital allocated to the program. Program management is much like policy management, but at the level of the unit—agency or department—actually implementing the policy.[6] If you found the description of the three areas of management capacity vague and noticed overlapping functions, you have grasped the essence of managerial capacity. It is vague and slightly repetitive. There is one unifying theme, however; managerial capacity is expanded only when policy management, resource management, and program management are developed internally. That is, hiring consultants to manage these areas does not expand managerial capacity. Contracting outside the organization may be an excellent way to sharpen skills in all three managerial areas through expert advice and technical assistance, but it does not expand the managerial capacity of the organization. Before examining how managerial capacity can be expanded, consider how organizational capacity and managerial capacity might fit together visually.

A Combined Capacity Model

Based on the elements of organizational and managerial capacity just described, one can see the two concepts as concentric circles, with managerial capacity bounded by organizational capacity (see Figure 8.1).

The first feature you notice from the diagram is that managerial capacity exists within organizational capacity. We are suggesting by our depiction that organizational capacity determines management capacity in that the environment answers the question "capacity to do what?" Recall the anonymous finance director who wanted to look as if he were doing performance budgeting. The fiscal crisis created the environment in which the finance manager had to operate. He might be technically capable of setting up a performance budgeting system, and he indicated that he was interested in the idea, but he is no position to actually do performance budgeting. His organization lacks the capacity. The problems, the expectations, and the resources are interacting in such a way that the best they can do is add a few performance measures to the budget document while they looks for cuts in discre-

Figure 8.1 **Organizational and Managerial Capacity**

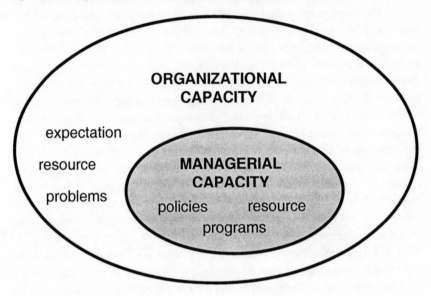

tionary spending. Eventually their political leaders will deal with the mismatch between resources and service expectations. When the crisis is over, perhaps their organizational capacity will permit their managerial capacity to expand.

Tools of Management

There is every reason to believe that organizations are expanding their managerial capacity through the adoption of one set, or, more likely, multiple sets of management tools. The International City/County Management Association (ICMA) began tracking the use of certain management tools in municipal government back in 1976.[7] Since then, follow-up surveys have shown that adoption of management tools has risen dramatically, especially in larger cities.[8] The list of management tools has expanded over time as well. The latest survey includes: program budgeting, zero-based budgeting, management-by-objectives, performance monitoring, productivity improvement, management incentive programs, productivity bargaining, program evaluation, financial trend monitoring, revenue and expense forecasting, strategic planning, and quality circles.[9] Today that list would surely include the balanced scorecard and performance budgeting.

Adoption of these tools does not necessarily move the managerial capacity circle out. What if a government went through a strategic planning process and constructed performance measures for every service and program? Strategic planning and performance measurement would be two important management tools. But what if the strategic plan were put on a shelf somewhere? What if departments submitted measures to the budget office, which ignored them during budget construction and added them to the budget document right before it went off to the printers? The point is that the presence or absence of adoption of strategic planning or performance measurement does not reveal anything about managerial capacity. It is possible, as we described in the opening paragraphs of this chapter, to adopt a management tool as "window dressing" while responding to policy problems the same way as in the past. There is also a further complication regarding the tools of management. Governments that adopt five of these tools do not have five times the managerial capacity of a government that adopts one. Therefore, the presence or absence of a tool like performance budgeting does not necessarily reveal much about capacity, nor does the number of management tools adopted by the government.

However, organizations can use tools like strategic planning, performance measurement, program evaluation, and performance budgeting to expand their managerial capacity. In our recommended model, the tools are used in concert. Strategic planning identifies organization-wide goals, and department plans identify strategies associated with those goals. Performance monitoring tracks progress toward those goals, and performance budgeting links resource decisions to goals and strategies by using performance data in budget deliberations. We admit that our model is predicated on the assumption that the best management decisions are mission and goal based, and supported by reliable and relevant information about progress toward those goals. We now turn to the issue of how public managers acquire the tools of management and use them to improve policy management, resource management, and program management, the three elements of managerial capacity.

Professional Organizations

Public managers are, as a group, very open to innovation, especially when it might enhance productivity.[10] They are accustomed to looking to the private sector for ideas that could be adapted to the public sector.[11] Perhaps a more accurate statement would be that their professional organizations are always looking for innovation and productivity-enhancing techniques, and looking to the private sector to find innovations that may be transferable to the public sector. Public managers look to their professional organizations to find the innovations and make them relevant and accessible to their government.

Professional organizations are responsible for a process called "diffusion of innovation" in public management, meaning that they share new ideas with their constituent members. They sometimes play the role of innovation advocate when the professional organization encourages members to adopt the new idea. Finally, professional organizations are teachers, providing the training and technical assistance their members need to adopt the innovation.[12] About 68 percent of local government professional organizations report that their mission includes promoting standards for their members.[13] These standards include new practices, as just described, as well as broader standards such as codes of ethics and statements of purpose. Most public sector professional organizations promote performance measurement as an ethical or purposive standard (accountability) as well as a management technique.

Professional organizations serve an important and commendable function in the profession, but they are not without their own motives and agendas. They are, after all, organizations, and any organization's first priority is self-maintenance. To that end, professional organizations often issue a resolution or opinion about an innovation that amounts to an endorsement, and then develop capacity within the organization to provide research, training, materials, and technical assistance to their memberships. We briefly describe several professional organizations along with the services they currently offer. We also summarize their position on performance measurement and performance budgeting. We then turn our attention to a standard-setting organization we have mentioned several times in earlier chapters, the Governmental Accounting Standards Board (GASB) and its initiative to establish a mandatory performance measurement reporting requirement for states and local governments.

NAPA

The mission statement of the National Academy of Public Administration (NAPA) identifies "improving the performance of governance systems" as its goal in the context of what many people define as the "new public management," or the nexus between government, nonprofit organizations, and the private sector. NAPA currently offers its members consulting and support service in eight program areas:

- *The Center for Human Resources Management* assists public sector customer organizations in improving performance and mission accomplishment through effective use of personnel.
- *The Management Studies Program* performs analyses of broad-scale structural, managerial, and performance problems and issues.

• *The Center for Improving Government Performance* focuses on implementation of the Government Performance and Results Act by offering expert advice on goal setting, performance monitoring, and regular reporting.

• *The Joint Center for e-Governance* explores the impact of the Digital Age on the transformation of the business of government and the governance of the system.

• *The Center for the Economy and the Environment* explores ways to mobilize private and public resources—in communities and at the state and national levels to protect the environment while building stronger regional economies.

• *The Center for Local and State Solutions*, through conferences, research, and a World Wide Web site, connects people across the country who are developing new and better ways to make government work.

• *The International Affairs Program* supports nations in developing their public management capacities, advises international organizations in their modernizing and streamlining efforts, and assists domestic agencies in organizing their international operations.[14]

NAPA adopted a resolution endorsing performance management in 1991, and created the Center for Improving Government Performance to assist federal agencies in the successful implementation of the Government Performance and Results Act of 1993 (GPRA) in September 1997. The GPRA is the federal government's formal adoption of performance measurement that required agencies to set goals for program performance and measure results. NAPA also created a consortium for federal agencies where participants identify common issues with GPRA implementation, share best practices, and "establish realistic expectations about GPRA implementation and its likely results."[15] Agencies pay a fee to participate in the consortium.

ASPA

The American Society for Public Administration (ASPA) has historically been the leader in public sector management innovation, having provided members information, materials, and consulting services on the latest trends in public management. Today ASPA offers federal agency employees a forum for the exchange of ideas and experiences with the balanced scorecard.[16] ASPA also offers members and nonmembers a considerable array of books and other resources, including consulting services and technical assistance on a wide variety of public management concerns. However, ASPA has been notable in its promotion of performance measurement.[17] ASPA's policy position on performance measurement, adopted by resolution in 1992, explicitly tied the practice to accountability to citizens and encouraged managers at every level of government to adopt performance management.

In 1996, ASPA created the Center for Accountability and Performance (CAP) to help its members and others learn the skills necessary to "manage for results." CAP fellows offer training services under the auspices of ASPA, and the organization sponsors symposia and offers a number of publications to help public managers begin or improve their performance measurement systems. The goals of CAP are:

• Demonstrate the value of performance measurement and management to line managers, staff, elected officials, and the public;
• Equip and motivate ASPA members to be learners of best practices and leaders of positive change;
• Identify successful practices in public sector performance management, both in the United States and internationally; and
• Act as a central information source for strategic planning, performance measurement, and best-practices research and techniques.[18]

While NAPA is more focused on federal agencies and employees, ASPA covers state and local government agencies and employees, along with a substantial set of performance measurement resources for the nonprofit sector.

ICMA

The International City/County Management Association (ICMA) traces its roots to the reform movement around the turn of the century. You may recall that the reformers advocated a council-manager form of government to improve the quality (or reduce the politics) of local government. ICMA became an educational as well as professional organization for city and county managers and continues in that role today. ICMA's declaration of ideals suggests the difficult balance it and all public organizations try to strike: between a representative and responsive democracy, and efficient and effective public management.[19] As we have pointed out a number of times, the most efficient solutions to budget problems are often at odds with public preferences.

In 1994, ICMA created a forum for the first comprehensive performance benchmarking project. This project stemmed from the pressing question of whether or not performance criteria could be standardized across localities or whether each locality needed its own performance statistics. Standardized measures were appealing because they permitted cross-jurisdictional comparisons or benchmarking, a topic that is covered at length in chapter 7. With a grant from the Alfred P. Sloan foundation, ICMA established the Center for Performance Measurement.[20]

A group of city and county managers gathered to identify best practices in local government police services, fire, and EMS services, neighborhood services, and support services. Each jurisdiction appointed a representative to a technical advisory committee to work out the details of defining indicators and collecting the data. Data definition proved a daunting task. The members took two years to look beyond the performance measures that were readily available to those measures that would best represent service quality.[21] The results were mixed. Data were simply not available from some member localities in the early stages, and not comparable in others. For example, there was no distinction between direct and indirect costs, and no standardization of fringe benefits, depreciation rates, or cost of living adjustments across participating local governments.[22] The first report, published in 1996, presented a quantitative performance ranking of participating jurisdictions, with some explanation of why the indicator might vary. High performers were identified, and information about the practices in the high performing jurisdictions was offered.[23]

ICMA continues to offer performance-related products and services to members and nonmembers through its Comparative Performance Measurement Program, including:

- Providing on-site training for new program participants;
- Coordinating meetings for both managers and departmental specialists;
- Refining data collection templates based on suggestions from program participants;
- Collecting and "cleaning" program data, to ensure the validity of interagency comparisons;
- Compiling information regarding best practices among program participants;
- Publishing an annual program report and CD-ROM; and
- Providing participants with raw data for customizing their own comparisons, graphs, and reports.[24]

NASBO

The National Association of State Budget Officers (NASBO) is an affiliate of the National Governor's Association dedicated to advancing best budgeting practices in state government. Their commitment to innovation in state budgeting is evident in their mission statement:

- Improve the quality and availability of information to state budget offices;
- Provide opportunities to share practices across states;
- Provide training and research information through publications and seminars; and
- Assist the National Governors' Association in the development and implementation of its policy positions.[25]

NASBO's position on performance measurement comes up short of advocacy, unlike most other organizations, but is consistent with its stated goal of monitoring state budgeting offices that are using performance measures, identifying best practices, and sharing those practices with its membership. In 1995, NASBO published an issue brief that stressed the uniqueness of each state and recommended a list of planning considerations that should precede a decision to adopt a performance measurement program:

- What is meant by performance measures?
- Will the initiatives be top down or bottom up?
- What will be the role of the legislature?
- Will the measures be integrated into the budget process?
- What technological tools are available?
- Where should the measures be developed and housed?
- Who will monitor the measures?
- Where will the measures be reported and how often?
- What are the potential barriers and what can be done proactively to address these barriers?[26]

GFOA

The Government Finance Officers Association (GFOA), founded in 1906, has been the primary resource for innovation and education among state and local public finance officers. GFOA has a "Best Practices in Public Budgeting" section that reflects current thinking about what budget professionals value in a budget process and in presentation. If you browse the "Best Practices" portion of the GFOA Web site you will find that its approach to budgeting is very similar to ours—it begins with establishing goals, then developing strategies to achieve the goals, measuring progress toward those goals, and making adjustments based on progress toward goals.[27] This reflects a consensus belief in our profession that budgeting is a management activity, and not some stand-alone function whose primary value is to approve spending limits.

On the education side, GFOA offers a certified public finance officers (CPFO) program to all public practitioners as well as a program of study for senior financial managers through its Advanced Government Finance Institute. Some of the seminars offered recently include change management, the effects of economic and demographic trends on financial management, technology issues, benchmarking and performance measurement, and competitive government and privatization.[28]

GFOA diffuses innovation and sets professional standards for public budgeters indirectly through its awards programs. Some of the innovations and standards are primarily technical, while others have a distinctly managerial focus. On the technical side, the Awards for Excellence in Government Finance include the categories of accounting, auditing, and reporting; budgeting and financial planning; cash management and investing; capital finance and debt administration; pensions and benefits; management and service delivery; enterprise financial systems; and technology.[29] The trend toward a management focus in budgeting is evidenced in the familiar Distinguished Budget Presentation Award program that recognizes governments whose budget documents meet GFOA's standards as a policy document, a financial plan, an operations guide, and a communications device. A similar award, the Certificate of Achievement for Excellence in Financial Reporting, is based on criteria for an annual financial report that meets accounting requirements and goes beyond them, reporting the general financial health of the government and changes in its financial outlook, among other things.[30]

Like other professional organizations, GFOA endorses performance measurement as a management tool to guide strategic planning and link program and service results to the budget. GFOA's position is, essentially, that performance measures are necessary but not sufficient for managerial accountability. In fact, GFOA has expressed concern that a focus on performance measurement to the detriment of other kinds of considerations in public policy making could actually be counterproductive. The GFOA position on the appropriate use of performance measures is contrasted with that of the Governmental Accounting Standards Board (GASB) in the next section. But to summarize, GFOA recommends that performance measures be linked to the budget process in a meaningful way and provides a two course sequence on designing performance measures and implementing performance systems in their training curriculum.

GASB: A Standards-Setting Organization

In 1990 the Governmental Accounting Standards Board (GASB), an organization that sets the standards for state and local government accounting and

Box 8.1

GASB's Position on Experimentation with Performance Measurement and Reporting

Performance measures presently are being developed and used by an expanding number of governmental agencies, departments, programs, and services. Currently used performance measures are being modified and replaced as improved information becomes available. Although progress has been made, more needs to be done to improve the art of performance measurement and reporting.

Before GASB considers establishing performance reporting standards for inclusion in general purpose external financial reporting (GPEFR), it is important that there be extensive experimentation in measuring and reporting performance. This experimentation should consider whether performance measures are developed that are relevant, understandable, comparable, timely, consistent, and reliable. Further analysis should explore how externally reported performance information is used and how it affects the quality, effectiveness, and efficiency of the agencies, departments, programs, and services being reported on.

Because performance reporting will expand the amount and types of information being reported externally, it is also important that the benefits and costs of specific performance measures be carefully considered. The Board recognizes both the importance and the complexity of comparing the benefits and costs of reporting performance information. Benefits and costs are affected by many factors including circumstances surrounding the gathering, reporting, and use of the information.

It is anticipated that experimentation will result in the development of specific performance measures for different aspects of various services. If GASB proposes to require reporting of specific performance measures, the benefits of those measures will need to be compared to the costs of gathering, verifying, and reporting the underlying data. In assessing the benefits and costs of a specific measure, consideration will be given to such factors as its particular value in measuring accomplishments, the extent to which it has gained general acceptance, its understandability to citizen and oversight groups, and the relative benefits of other, less costly measures.

Source: Governmental Accounting Standards Board, Adapted from Concepts Statement No. 2 of the Governmental Accounting Standards Board, Service Efforts and Accomplishments Reporting, accounting.rutgers.edu/raw/seagov/pmg/perfmeasures/index.html.

financial reporting, published *Service Efforts and Accomplishments Reporting: Its Time Has Come*, the first of a series of research reports that summarized the state of the art of performance measurement along with spotlighting best practices.[31] The report argued for the use of quantitative measures of service efforts and accomplishments as a means of improving service productivity and communicating to the readers of financial reports how the organization is using resources to accomplish its mission. Box 8.1 presents the GASB's position on performance measurement and its expectation for the research initiative it began with ICMA and the Sloan Foundation on performance reporting.

In a sense, this was an unexpected role for GASB, as it has historically been an arbiter of financial accountability rather than a leader in management innovation. That is, GASB establishes generally accepted accounting principles (GAAP) on which annual audits of state and local government financial reports are based. Each year, governments, just like private corporations, file financial statements, and those statements must be GAAP compliant, or report the required information, accurately and in the required way. Financial statements that are not compliant will not receive a favorable audit opinion, for which there are consequences. For GASB to take a position on performance measurement meant that its members, representatives of major accounting and financial management organizations, believed that performance measurement was tied to financial accountability. Some observers thought GASB's position was entirely justified and long overdue, but others worried about the consequences of reporting data that have been collected for internal (managerial) use to an external audience (citizens, bond rating firms).[32] If performance data were included in the financial statement, who would audit them and on what basis?

GASB itself paused over the same question when it issued Concepts Statement No. 2, Service Efforts and Accomplishments Reporting, in 1994. There are two remarkable features about Concepts Statement No. 2. First, it is a concept statement rather than a "statement." Statements are binding—they become part of GAAP and governments must comply with them or face the consequences at audit. This indicates that GASB was certain about why it should incorporate performance measures into financing reports, but they were not sure about how to do it. Second, they answered the why of performance measurement in a way that would change the profession, by saying it is appropriate to measure performance because it is a form of accountability, nonfinancial accountability, that, when combined with financial accountability constitutes complete accountability to citizens and other external consumers of the government's financial report. The key characteristics of an accountability system include, for example:

Box 8.2

GASB's Possible Approaches to Establishing Performance Reporting Standards

The establishment of performance reporting requirements might take many different approaches. For example:

(a) Reporting standards could require performance reporting for major agencies, departments, programs, and services of a governmental entity without specifying the particular performance measures that should be reported. In this case, the requirement could be that performance measures, with adequate explanatory information, be reported for all major goals and objectives of the agency, department, program, or service; and that comparisons over time and with established targets be reported.

(b) As an alternative, reporting standards could establish a minimum core set of performance measures for each major agency, department, program, or service, leaving the entity free to supplement that reporting with other measures as it deems appropriate. For this alternative, the GASB could draw on current practice to determine generally used measures for establishing the minimum set of performance measures.

(c) As another alternative, reporting standards could focus on one or more significant agencies, departments, programs, or services where relatively widely used performance measures already exist. The GASB could require reporting of a specific set of performance measures for these entities, with the requirement that other performance measures be reported for major purposes or goals and objectives for which performance measures have not been specified.

Source: Governmental Accounting Standards Board, accounting.rutgers.edu/raw/seagov/pmg/perfmeasures/index.html.

(a) focuses on outcomes, (b) uses a few selected indicators to measure performance, (c) provides information for both policy and program management decisions, (d) generates data consistently over time, and (e) reports outcomes regularly and publicly.[33]

Another decision about performance reporting that GASB must make coincident with Statement No. 2 is whether each government will determine the performance standards to which it will be accountable or whether GASB will identify standard performance measures for all governments to report. As shown in Box 8.2, GASB does not yet have enough evidence to make a determination on standardized measures. Standardized performance measures for all state and local governments could provide some very useful benchmarks, and perhaps raise performance in the service areas for which standardized measures are selected.

On the other hand, local governments differ with regard to their capacity, which calls into question the desirability of standardized measures. Community problems, resources, and expectations are externally determined, and the strategic plan for the organization should reflect them. Performance measures that do not reflect that plan are unlikely to advance accountability to citizens. The GFOA's position on the possibility that GASB will require performance reporting in the annual financial statements, and on the problems associated with standardized measures is shown in Box 8.3. We agree with GFOA's argument that any performance measurement program that is not driven by the mission of the organization will not advance accountability to citizens. We argue in the next section that, while performance budgeting can expand managerial capacity, a mandate to adopt any innovation such as that contemplated by GASB for performance measurement, does not necessarily expand managerial capacity.

Expanding Managerial Capacity Through Performance Budgeting

To review, we have defined managerial capacity as "in-house" capability sufficient to meet the external demands in policy management, in resource management, and in program management. We are now going to revert to our rather broad definition of performance budgeting as a managerial process to address the first of the three parts of capacity, policy management. We do this because performance budgeting begins with the identification of organization-wide goals through a strategic planning process and moves to the alignment of programmatic service objectives with those larger goals. If public policy is a set of decisions about what government should do, or not do, about a problem, then organization-wide goals set the boundaries of action by identifying priorities.

Managers certainly want to respond appropriately to unexpected demands for government action and avoid limitations on action that might result from a set of priorities established prior to the events that created the unexpected demand for policy action. However, there are two things to consider about making policy in uncertainty. First, there are relatively few completely unexpected events. Most policy demands are predictable; many come from within the organization rather than outside it. Second, when confronted with policy demands in the face of unpredictable problems, managers still want to evalu-

---

Box 8.3

GFOA's Policy Statement on Performance Measurement and the Governmental Accounting Standards Board (2002)

The Government Finance Officers Association (GFOA) has long been a zealous advocate of performance measurement in the public sector. Most recently, GFOA has undertaken a comprehensive strategic initiative designed to promote the expanded use of performance measurement by state and local governments.

GFOA routinely seeks opportunities to work with other groups to promote common goals; performance measurement has been no exception to this general rule. GFOA was a strong supporter, for example, of the National Advisory Council on State and Local Budgeting (Budget Council), which identified performance measurement as an essential component of a sound budgeting process. Likewise, GFOA has supported the research on performance measurement undertaken by the International City/County Management Association. GFOA, however, must go on record again, opposing in the strongest possible terms the efforts of the Governmental Accounting Standards Board (GASB) to play a role in the development of performance measurement in the public sector.

To be effective, performance measurement must be thoroughly integrated into a government's budgetary process. This natural relationship between performance measurement and budgeting was underscored in the Budget Council's Guidelines, and can be briefly summarized as follows:

A government uses strategic planning to identify its broad organizational objectives, which it then translates into specific goals and objectives.

A government frames its budgetary decisions on the basis of results and outcomes that are directly linked to these specific goals and objectives.

A government uses performance measures to monitor actual results and outcomes.

A government compares actual and projected results and outcomes and uses this analysis as a basis for identifying any adjustments that are needed.

Consequently, to be effective, performance measures must be specific rather than generic.

That is, a performance measure is only relevant to the extent it is clearly linked to the goals and objectives that a government sets for itself. Furthermore, inasmuch as goals and objectives reflect public policy, it is only to be expected that they will differ, sometimes substantially, from government to government.

GASB's involvement with SEA (Service Efforts and Accomplishments) is fundamentally incompatible with the understanding of performance measurement just described for several reasons:

Performance measures are inherently budgetary and managerial in character and clearly fall outside the purview of accounting and financial reporting, as those disciplines have traditionally and commonly been understood. The GFOA emphatically rejects GASB's attempt to assert its own self-imposed and ill-defined concept of "accountability" to justify the extension of its jurisdiction to virtually all aspects of public finance.

In the public sector, goals and objectives are the concrete realization and reflection of public policy. In a democracy, it is the unique prerogative of elected and appointed officials to set public policy. If GASB were to mandate the reporting of specific performance measures it would effectively be usurping this prerogative.

There is no such thing as a "neutral" performance measure. The selection of what to measure will inevitably drive performance. Therefore, it is unrealistic to believe that performance measures mandated by GASB would remain purely informational and somehow not have an effect on how governments manage their programs. Even were GASB to establish completely "voluntary" measures of performance for those governments that wish to use them, the very existence of benchmarks established by a national standard-setting body would put pressure on governments to conform their own performance measures to GASB's model measures.

GASB standards or recommendations would inevitably involve generic measures, which would break the crucial link between performance measurement and a government's specific goals and objectives.

The inclusion of performance measures as part of financial reporting inevitably would require at least some degree of involvement on the part of the government's independent auditor, resulting in additional audit costs. While we freely admit that data verification is essential if performance measurement is to be credible, we do not believe it should be necessary to involve independent auditors for this purpose. Internal auditing procedures should suffice.

GASB's expertise is limited to accounting and financial reporting. Expertise in accounting and financial reporting, while invaluable in many aspects of public finance, does not provide a sufficient basis for making decisions regarding how to measure the quality of services. Even if subject-matter experts were consulted, as the GASB promises, the fact remains that the ultimate decision would still be GASB's.

(continued)

Box 8.3 *(continued)*

GASB's efforts ultimately will not succeed in helping the cause of performance measurement. Real progress must come from governments themselves and the organizations that serve them. GASB's efforts, however, could succeed at diverting scarce resources from the board's proper mission of improving accounting and financial reporting. GFOA believes that both performance measurement and accounting will best be served by the GASB returning to its proper role as an accounting and financial reporting standard-setting body.

Approved by the Committee on Accounting, Auditing, and Financial Reporting and the Committee on Governmental Budgeting and Management, January 30, 2002. Approved by the Executive Board, February 15, 2002.

Source: Government Finance Officers Association, www.gfoa.org/services/policy/gfoapp1.shtml#plact12.

---

ate alternative responses in light of organizational priorities and goals. Performance budgeting demands such a focus and brings relevant information to predictable problems. Therefore, we assert that it expands policy management capacity.

The case for resource management capacity is fairly easy to make. Performance budgeting facilitates collection and analysis of data that senior managers and elected officials need to make informed allocation decisions. The budget office is where all the functions of the government organization are unified along one dimension. That dimension is resource flow from revenue sources to program expenditures. The budget office is the great leveler of otherwise incomparable activities (e.g., garbage pickup, crime prevention, mental health). Inputs and outputs are compared in order to generate some measure of the relationship between the level of resources directed at program activities and the accomplishments realized as a result of those activities. That said, promoting efficiency through cost control (minimizing the ratio of inputs to outputs) is typically not the budget office's primary concern, a point we will return to soon in the section about program management capacity.

Two final words about the budget office and resource management capacity. First, readers may have a perception that the budget process ends with adoption and the budget office goes on vacation until the process starts over later in the year. Most descriptions of the process do not describe what happens in the budget office between adoption and the budget message. But the budget office is where data are organized, audited, and retained for analysis in the current and future budget years. This process is ongoing, and it becomes the primary focus of the budget office during the budget cycle "lull," typically the period immediately after the budget is adopted. Budget analysts develop the technical and analytical skills they need to inform allocation decisions during this period. In states and in larger cities, budget analysts also develop program and policy specialties during this period by spending time with the people who administer the programs for which the analyst has budget responsibility. For example, a state budget analyst assigned to the corrections area might discuss emerging problems in corrections policy with corrections managers and staff while an analyst assigned to the city police department might learn about the police department's plans for a new crime prevention initiative. These interactions expand the resource management capacity of the budget office because they advance the analyst's understanding of program goals and constraints.

Because data analysis and trend monitoring are critical to the performance budgeting process, the budget office is the physical location of many state and most local government performance programs. Though detractors may see this as a way to expand the scope of influence of the budget office, it is actually a way to use the budget function to expand managerial capacity through resource management. In other words, performance budgeting is not a power grab by the responsible budget office, though we are sensitive to the department and agency managers who raise that concern. It is true that performance budgeting expands the scope of information that the budget office maintains for analysis and audit beyond financial data. It is not true that analysis and audit of performance data are the budget office's attempt to micromanage other agencies. To this charge we reply that the selection of the performance measures and how they are used for departmental decision making are not the budget office's decision. Similarly, department managers must take the responsibility for updating the performance information that the budget office collects, so that the information used for decision making reflect current service priorities and challenges.

The last aspect of managerial capacity, program management, offers an opportunity to demonstrate how performance budgeting can build capacity, and also to describe performance budgeting as a logical next step in the evolution of the budget office's role—from controlling program costs to enhancing program effectiveness. There is a consensus among budget scholars that the management role of the budget office has progressed far beyond the old notion of the "institutional no." The stereotype of the sour-faced analyst scrutinizing every nickel for wastefulness and turning down every request for more money on general principle is thankfully outdated.[34] However, budget analysts are not caped crusaders, fighting tirelessly for new spending for their programs, either. Their role is defined by how the budget office functions in their state and in their local government.

Budget scholars have long understood that state budget offices have different orientations, generally described as a control orientation, a management orientation, or a planning orientation.[35] Which orientation best describes a state budget office varies with the political, economic, and maybe even cultural traditions in state government. A recent study of state budget offices suggests that the control orientation still exists, especially in southern states, but the trend is toward a management orientation as budget officers increasingly see their role as facilitating the policy priorities of governors and assisting agency heads in realizing their goals.[36] We assert that a similar trend exists in local budget offices as well, based on evidence that city and county budget offices are increasingly adding management components to their traditional budget format, for example, performance and program budgeting and the alignment of budget priorities with organizational mission and departmental goals. That alignment represents expanded managerial capacity as the service priorities and the available resources are considered jointly rather than separately.

We hope we have demonstrated how performance budgeting can expand managerial capacity in policy, in resources, and in programs. In essence, we claim that adopting a performance budgeting approach can expand the inner circle, increasing the managerial capacity within the limits of organizational capacity. Below we suggest some implications for organizational capacity and performance budgeting. Two caveats bear repeating in conclusion.

First, collecting "cookbook" performance measures and reporting them in the budget document is not going to enhance managerial capacity one whit. It is a way to look "reformed" without having any commitment to a different decision-making process. Second, collecting and reporting performance measures and incorporating them into the decision process enhances managerial capacity, even when the decision is made on the basis of criteria that are not performance related.

Is it not interesting that we make such a distinction? What is the difference between doing things the same way as before without paying attention to performance data and doing exactly what you would have done before after paying attention to performance data? The answer lies in managerial capacity, the ability to bring useful and relevant performance information to decisions and to deliberate responsibly in the face of that information. If another set of values (political imperatives, resource constraints, other priorities) trump performance in the final decision, then the purpose of performance budgeting is still served and managerial capacity for good decisions is still enhanced.

Is Your Organization Ready for Performance Budgeting?

Why would every organization not be ready for performance budgeting, if it holds the promise of enhancing managerial capacity and may also increase organizational capacity? The answer is that performance budgeting is difficult and expensive. It takes time, it takes expertise, and it takes money to pay for both, along with some extra to buy the technology needed to make it possible. If money were the only issue, though, it would still be a bargain. The harder part of performance budgeting is the intangible inputs—leadership and commitment. We start with the easy requirements and then tackle the harder ones.

Despite the hopes of many local governments and more than a few states, performance budgeting does not begin with the decision to officially implement it. If nothing else, the federal government's decidedly mixed experience with the Government Performance and Results Act (GPRA) of 1994 tells us that.[37] Its advocates assumed that a transition to a performance-based system would be immediate and free. Qualified people would appear with the expertise necessary to design and implement the system, existing information technology would be adequate, the relevant data would be available, and the savings from poorly performing programs would allow successful programs to grow, while reducing the total cost of government.

In reality, the government must either hire new staff with expertise in performance measurement or spend considerable time and money training existing staff. Department managers and employees have to deliberate the adequacy and appropriateness of the measures that they currently collect, and invest in ways to gather new data that may be more relevant to department goals and priorities. And because performance budgeting is an information-driven system, the government may have to make a capital investment in information technology, for departments and also for the budget office. We argue that these are good investments in managerial capacity, but we do not claim that they are cheap. Good investments rarely are. If your government wants to do performance budgeting but does not want to make a financial commitment to training and staff development, it is not ready to do performance budgeting. Outside consultants are plentiful, but their value lies in preparing staff to implement and maintain a system. A performance system that you purchase "off the shelf" is a waste of money unless the only goal is to look different without changing. And there is absolutely no evidence that an investment in a performance budgeting system reduces the overall cost of government. Repeat: resource decisions based on performance may enhance operational accountability but they do not necessarily produce financial savings.

The other two necessary elements for performance budgeting—leadership and commitment—can be found in the federal story as well. When GPRA was implemented in federal agencies, some senior agency managers took a "wait it out" approach. They decided, understandably, that this reform was a passing fancy of the current administration and would be abandoned just as soon as a new administration took office. Their experience with various budgeting reforms, as you may recall from chapter 2, was that new presidents had new ideas that lasted only as long as the president's term. Some senior managers decided to worry about the "nuts and bolts" and ignore GPRA. On the other hand, other senior managers decided performance was "nuts and bolts" and that this new emphasis on results was powerful, appropriate, and real. For those managers and their agencies, it became real, it endured, and it changed the agency for the better.

We are most familiar with the stories of performance measurement in states and local government, where the same leadership choices were evident after a performance program was adopted. Some department managers decided it was just the latest new thing and ordered their staff to send the budget office some numbers. What numbers? Well, whatever other police departments, sanitation departments, economic development offices, and the like, were sending their budget offices, it did not matter. Other managers decided that this could be useful for them as managers and their departments. They put some care into the selection of performance measures and monitored the performance data they received. They made some changes as a result of the trends they encountered and what they learned from other service departments through comparing benchmarks. The difference was the same as in the federal government example. For managers who treated it as though it were real, it became real and it endured.

But managers are not the sole key to a successful performance program, though they are essential. Another key is the commitment of the elected officials and the chief administrators in state and local government. They offer the ingredient that is essential for a successful performance budgeting program—commitment to the principles of performance-based decision making. That commitment must endure even when economic downturns make cost control budgeting an attractive prospect. Elected and appointed leaders must resist the temptation to make across-the-board program cuts. They must refrain from protecting visible and popular programs regardless of their performance at the expense of high-performing less-visible programs.

We understand that this is a tall order, but caution government leaders that they cannot usually go back for a second bite of the apple. That is, only one commitment to performance budgeting is meaningful for managers and line employees. There is every reason to believe that public employees, like their private-sector counterparts, respond to incentives. If performance is offered as the incentive for the department, the program and the employees will respond to it. The question for the elected and appointed leaders to consider is not whether their organizations will begin to focus on performance, but whether they are prepared to respond to success appropriately. Appropriate responses include using performance information in budget and salary decisions. Inappropriate responses include rewarding programs that are able to increase their productivity with budget cuts (on the theory that they might be able to do even more with less), rewarding poorly performing programs with new resources (on the theory that they could improve if they had more), and "suspending" consideration of performance information until a political or economic crisis has passed. The first two responses constitute perverse incentives, and the second reveals that commitment to performance by top officials is based on convenience, not conviction.

We are not suggesting formulaic responses to performance data in this discussion of commitment, just as we have cautioned against them in the previous chapters. No reasonable leader cuts the police department budget during a crime wave. In fact, high-performing programs may sometimes face cuts while low-performing programs get more resources, all within a well-functioning performance budgeting system. The critical factor, recall, is the explicit consideration of performance information in the decision about how to make cuts or where to add resources on the part of top officials and a communication of that consideration to managers, who presumably will reassure line employees that performance is still relevant to budget decisions. Perhaps an example would be helpful for clarification.

In chapter 4 we described the use in Auburn, Alabama, of the citizen satisfaction survey in the budget process. We concluded, justifiably, that the notion of a citizen-based outcome measure of performance was progressive and appropriate. But there is more to the story. City officials noted that citizens rated animal control quite poorly for several years in the late 1980s. Council responded by providing more funding for animal control, and, by the mid-1990s, citizen ratings for animal control had improved to "good" or "excellent."[38] Does this story about how a performance indicator was used to influence budget deliberations illustrate a success of performance budgeting or a failure?

Clearly, the animal control department improved its performance, based on the strongest type of service performance indicator—outcomes as citizens experience them. Council might never have understood that citizens were dissatisfied with their animal control service and the appropriate attention and resources might not have been directed toward the department of animal control without the survey. Insofar as we have claimed that when performance information is institutionalized into the budget process and used for decision making, then the story is a success for performance budgeting.

The goal of any performance program is to improve the service quality of departments. Sometimes poorly performing departments get more funds, especially when the service they provide is a high citizen priority. What matters is that the department of animal control was held accountable for improving performance after receiving new resources, and it demonstrated remarkable success. Top leaders must pledge their commitment to managers to refrain from formulaic responses to performance data even as they pledge to make it a part of every deliberation, lest a few departments become anointed "winners" in the performance competition. Otherwise, the race is on among departments to find the performance measure that demonstrates the highest success for whatever the department is currently doing in order to be competitive for funds.

To review, there are four components of a successful performance budgeting system:

1. Commitment by top elected and appointed officials to the principles of performance-based decision making, during good times and bad, in all funding decisions.
2. Leadership by department or agency managers to develop meaningful measures of service performance that align with the organization-wide goals and reflect the department's strategies for achieving those goals, and to create appropriate incentives for employees to achieve them.
3. Recognition that performance budgeting requires expertise that can be achieved only through employee training and continuing education. Consultants can help governments develop an internal capacity for performance budgeting, and guidebooks can suggest a range of performance measures to consider for relevance and appropriateness, but you cannot buy a performance budget system—you have to build it.
4. Performance budgeting is not easy or cheap. There are some considerable start-up costs, one of which is staff with the skills to use performance budgeting to produce the kind of data that managers at all levels need for decision making. If there were no efficiencies or enhancements to effectiveness associated with performance budgeting, it would have little to recommend it as a management tool. These efficiencies and productivity improvements are not realized in the short term when compared to the start-up cost.

Performance Budgeting and Organizational Capacity

We are now ready to make the case that performance budgeting can expand organizational capacity. Recall the three components of organizational capacity: community expectations, community resources, and community problems. While different communities make different demands on the elected and appointed leaders, an expectation for good public services and a qualified staff to deliver them is common to all communities. As we suggested earlier, expectations may take the form of a high tax/high service mix, a low tax/low service mix, or something in between. A focus on productivity and performance from community leaders can raise community expectations of service quality. If community leaders invest in the tools of management, human and capital resources and make a commitment to incorporating performance information into their decisions, managerial capacity can meet higher expectations and expand organizational capacity.

The second component of organizational capacity is community resources. Recall that we defined resources as much more than the tax base of the community, including the ability of managers to respond to changing economic conditions and changes in citizen service needs and preferences. It is easy to see how an organization that constantly monitors and updates its performance will be prepared to respond to change, if it does not become so enamored with the measures that it ignores the outcomes they are supposed to reflect. Moreover, the focus on outcomes that is critical to a successful performance budgeting system invariably includes external assessments of citizen/customer satisfaction, and reporting service performance progress to citizens. This orientation was evident in the balanced scorecard approach to performance budgeting that we outlined in chapter 4. Performance budgeting can enhance the readiness of services to respond to changing service demands, and enhance the role of citizen-based assessments of service quality in service planning. Progress in readiness and responsiveness expands community resources and increases organizational capacity.

The most difficult test of performance budgeting in expanding organizational capacity lies is the third component, community problems. As we said in chapter 1, performance budgeting will not solve a financial crisis, will not take the politics out of budgeting decisions, will not reduce the influence of interest groups, will not prevent poor managerial decisions, and will not refocus citizen priorities. How then can we claim it might expand organizational capacity to solve community problems?

The answer is that we will join the chorus of budgeting reformers in history who asserted that more information is always better than less, and better quality information brought to deliberations over policy problems enhances the quality of decisions that result. This is a normative position shared by rationalists everywhere, and is especially popular with budgeting types, as our chapter 2 demonstrated. Performance budgeting does not need to solve problems to advance organizational capacity; it only needs to inform them in a consistent and meaningful way that enhances the quality of the information at the decision maker's disposal. But performance budgeting does not merely illuminate policy alternatives. It brings to the arena an element of accountability to citizens for the activities of government along with the information, and we assert that both of those values enhance the problem-solving capability of government and expand organizational capacity.

Conclusion

We leave you with an answer that we did not know we had until this manuscript was almost finished. A very competent, very cynical budget officer accused performance budgeting of being just another "buzzword" signifying nothing more than the current fashion in public management. He said he thought the whole notion was useful primarily to consultants selling performance management seminars and workbooks, and to elected officials as a way to dodge the hard choices between raising taxes and providing adequate public services. (He also mentioned that performance budgeting might be useful for a couple of hard-luck, public finance professors trying to sell a book.) Give me one reason, he said, why this is more than a blip on the public management radar screen.

The answer was out before the thought was fully formed: Say's law. At least the common understanding of the idea attributed to the French economist Jean-Baptiste Say (1767–1832) that "supply creates its own demand." We are on an irreversible path toward information-driven decision making in both the public and private sectors. Why do we demand information and analysis before we make management decisions that we used to make based on experience, instinct, or some other basis? Because it is there. The ability to inform every decision with relevant data demands that every decision be informed. After all, we have hired experts and invested in technology on the belief that the people and the machines add value to our organizations. We will not ignore the fruits of that investment when we make decisions that determine the future of the organization, public or private. Certainly our job in the public sector is complicated by the nature of the goods and services we produce, but our decision to embrace various management tools mirrors that of the private sector, and our decision to use them for decision-making mirrors the private sector. Public and private organizations use data analysis to make decisions because it is available and because doing so is consistent with our philosophical affinity for rationality. The bottom line is this. We may call it something else in a decade, but the principles of performance budgeting are here to stay.

Notes

Notes to Chapter 1

1. V.O. Key, Jr., "The Lack of a Budgetary Theory," *American Political Science Review* 34 (1940): 11–37.

2. Aaron Wildavsky, "Political Implications of Budgetary Reform," *Public Administration Review* 21 (1961): 183–90.

3. Laurence E. Lynn, Jr., Carolyn J. Heinrich, and Carolyn J. Hill, "Studying Governance and Public Management: Challenges and Prospects," *Journal of Public Administration Research and Theory* 10 (2000): 233–61.

4. See David Swindell and Janet M. Kelly, "Linking Citizen Satisfaction Data to Performance Measures: A Preliminary Evaluation," *Public Productivity and Management Review* 24 (2000): 30–52; Janet M. Kelly and David Swindell, "A Multiple Indicator Approach to Municipal Service Evaluation: Correlating Performance Measurement and Citizen Satisfaction Across Municipalities," *Public Administration Review* 62 (2002): 610–21; and Janet M. Kelly, "Citizen Satisfaction and Service Performance Measures: Is There Really a Link?" *Urban Affairs Review* (2003) forthcoming.

5. Albert Gore, *From Red Tape to Results Creating a Government That Works Better and Costs Less: Report of the National Performance Review* (Washington, DC: U.S. Government Printing Office, 1993).

6. Luther Gulick and Lyndall F. Urwick, *Papers on the Science of Administration* (New York: Institute of Public Administration, 1937), 10.

7. Kurt M. Thurmaier and Katherine G. Willoughby, *Policy and Politics in State Budgeting* (Armonk, NY: M.E. Sharpe, 2001).

8. Janet M. Kelly and William C. Rivenbark, "Reconciling the Research: Performance Measurement in Local Government," *Public Administration Quarterly* 26 (2002): 218–33.

Notes to Chapter 2

1. Arthur M. Schlesinger, Jr., *The Cycles of American History* (Boston: Houghton Mifflin, 1986).

2. Woodrow W. Wilson, "The Study of Administration," *Political Science Quarterly* 2 (1887): 197–222.

3. Norton E. Long, "Public Policy and Administration: The Goals of Rationality and Responsibility," *Public Administration Review* 56 (1996): 149.

4. Steven G. Koven, *Public Budgeting in the United States* (Washington, DC: Georgetown University Press, 1999).

250 NOTES TO CHAPTER 2

5. Frederick Taylor, *The Principles of Scientific Management* (New York: Norton, 1911).

6. Frank J. Goodnow, *Politics and Administration* (New York: Macmillan, 1900).

7. Jane Dahlberg, *The New York Bureau of Municipal Research* (New York: New York University Press, 1966), 5.

8. Jonathan Kahn, *Budgeting Democracy* (Ithaca, NY: Cornell University Press, 1997).

9. Ibid., 20–21.

10. Frederick A. Cleveland, *Organized Democracy* (New York: Longman, 1913).

11. Ibid.

12. Dalhberg, *The New York Bureau of Municipal Research*, 31.

13. William H. Allen, *Efficient Democracy* (New York: Dodd, Meade, 1907).

14. Henry Bruere, "The Bureau of Municipal Research," *American Political Science Association Proceedings* 5 (1912): 111.

15. From *Plunkitt of Tammany Hall*, recorded by William Riordan (1905) (New York: E.P. Dutton, 1963).

16. Kahn, *Budgeting Democracy*, 82–83.

17. Ibid., 61–62.

18. Irene S. Rubin, *Class, Tax and Power* (Chatham, NJ: Chatham House, 1998), 40.

19. David Bernstein, cited in Kahn, *Budgeting Democracy*, 89.

20. Kahn, *Budgeting Democracy*, 119.

21. Ibid., 94.

22. Frederick C. Mosher, *Basic Documents of American Public Administration, 1776–1950* (New York: Holmes and Meier, 1976).

23. Ibid., 106.

24. Christopher Hood, *Administrative Argument* (Aldershot, UK: Dartmouth Press, 1991).

25. Petri E. Arnold, "Reform's Changing Role," *Public Administration Review* 55 (1995): 407–17.

26. Ronald C. Moe, *The Hoover Commission Revisited* (Boulder, CO: Westview, 1982).

27. Paul Appleby, "The Role of the Budget Office," *Public Administration Review* 17 (1957): 156–58.

28. Luther Gulick and Lyndall F. Urwick, *Papers on the Science of Administration* (New York: Institute of Public Administration, 1937), 10.

29. Allen Schick, "The Road to PPB: The Stages of Reform," *Public Administration Review* 26 (1966): 255.

30. Allen Schick, "A Death in the Bureaucracy: The Demise of Federal PPB," *Public Administration Review* 33 (1973): 146–56.

31. Aaron Wildavsky, "Rescuing Policy Analysis from PPBS," *Public Administration Review* 29 (1969): 189–202.

32. E.O. Harper, F.A. Kramer, and A.M. Rouse, "Implementation and Use of PPB in Sixteen Federal Agencies," in *Perspectives on Budgeting*, ed. Allen Schick (Washington, DC: American Society for Public Administration, 1980), 91–102.

33. Arnold, "Reform's Changing Role."

34. Allen Schick, *Capacity to Budget* (Washington, DC: Urban Institute Press, 1990), 33.

35. Peter F. Drucker, *The Practice of Management* (New York: Harper, 1954).

36. R. Rose, "Implementation and Evaporation: The Record of MBO," in *Perspec-

tives on Budgeting, ed. Allen Schick (Washington, DC: American Society for Public Administration, 1980), 107.

37. Arnold, "Reform's Changing Role."

38. Thomas P. Lauth, "Zero-Based Budgeting in Georgia: Myth and Reality." In *Perspectives on Budgeting*, ed. Allen Shick (Washington, DC: American Society for Public Administration, 1980), 114–32; Arnold, "Reform's Changing Role."

39. Stephen Kelman, "The Grace Commission: How Much Waste in Government?" *Public Interest* 78 (1985): 62–82.

40. Robert D. Behn, "Cutback Budgeting," *Journal of Policy Analysis and Management* 4 (1985): 155–77.

41. Ibid., 168.

42. David Osborne and Ted Gaebler, *Reinventing Government: How the Entrepreneurial Spirit Is Transforming the Public Sector* (Reading, MA: Addison-Wesley, 1992).

43. National Performance Review, *Creating a Government That Works Better and Costs Less* (Washington, DC: Government Printing Office, 1993).

44. James Q. Wilson, "Reinventing Public Administration," *Political Science and Politics* 27 (1994): 667–73.

45. The National Performance Review was retitled the "National Partnership for Reinventing Government" in 1997.

46. James R. Thompson, "Reinvention As Reform: Assessing the National Performance Review," *Public Administration Review* 60 (2000): 508–21.

47. National Performance Review, *Creating a Government That Works Better and Costs Less.*

48. James Thompson and Vernon Jones, "Reinventing the Federal Government: The Role of Theory in Reform Implementation," *American Review of Public Administration* 25 (1995): 183–99.

49. Donald Kettl, "Building Lasting Reform: Enduring Questions," in *Inside the Reinvention Machine: Appraising Governmental Reform*, ed. Donald Kettl and John DiIulio, Jr. (Washington, DC: Brookings Institution, 1995), 9–83.

50. Allen Schick, *Budget Innovation in the States* (Washington, DC: Brookings Institution, 1971).

51. Julia Melkers and Katherine Willoughby, "The State of the States: Performance-Based Budgeting Requirements in 47 Out of 50," *Public Administration Review* 58 (1998): 66–73.

52. National Association of State Budget Officers, *Budget Processes in the States* (1997), available at www.nasbo.org.

53. Ibid.

54. Melkers and Willoughby, "The State of the States."

55. Ibid.

56. Meagan Jordan and Merl M. Hackbart, "Performance Budgeting and Performance Funding in the States: A Status Assessment," *Public Budgeting and Finance* 19 (1999): 68–88.

57. Cheryle A. Broom and Lynne A. McGuire, "Performance-Based Government Models: Building a Track Record," *Public Budgeting and Finance* 15 (1995): 3–17.

58. Michael Connelly and Gary Tompkins, "Does Performance Matter: A Study of State Budgeting," *Policy Studies Review* 8 (1989): 288–99.

59. Thomas P. Lauth, "Performance Evaluation in the Georgia Budgetary Process," *Public Budgeting and Finance* 5 (1985): 67–82.

60. Gloria A. Grizzle and Carole D. Pettijohn, "Implementing Performance-Based

Program Budgeting: A System-Dynamics Perspective," *Public Administration Review* 62 (2002): 51–62.

61. Julia E. Melkers and Katherine G. Willoughby, "Budgeters' Views of State Performance-Budgeting Systems: Distinctions Across Branches," *Public Administration Review* 61 (2001): 54–64.

62. Jordan and Hackbart, "Performance Budgeting and Performance Funding in the States," 75.

63. Robert D. Lee, "A Quarter Century of State Budgeting Practices," *Public Administration Review* 57 (1997): 133–140, 153.

64. Naomi Caiden, "Public Service Professionalism for Performance Measurement and Evaluation," *Public Budgeting and Finance* 18 (1998): 40.

65. Theodore H. Poister and Gregory Streib, "Performance Assessment in Municipal Government," *Public Administration Review* 59 (1999): 325–35.

66. Gregory Streib and Theodore H. Poister, "Performance Measurement in Municipal Governments," in International City/County Management Association, *The Municipal Yearbook* (Washington, DC: 1998), 9–15.

67. Ibid.

68. The GFOA membership database generally reflects the size distribution of cities in the United States. Roughly 54 percent of all cities are in the size range 2,500–9,999, 37 percent in the size range 10,000–49,999, and 9 percent in the size range 50,000 and above. Our sample drew 54 percent of respondents from the lowest range, 37 percent from the middle range, and 9 percent from the high range.

69. Evan Berman and Xiao Hu Wang, "Performance Measurement in U.S. Counties: Capacity for Reform," *Public Administration Review* 60 (2000): 409–20.

70. Ibid.

71. Ibid.

72. Warren Bennis, *An Invented Life: Reflections on Leadership and Change* (Reading, MA: Addison-Wesley, 1993).

73. James Q. Wilson, *Bureaucracy: What Governments Do and Why They Do It* (New York: Basic Books, 1989), 95–96.

74. J. Thomas Hennessey, Jr., "Reinventing Government: Does Leadership Make the Difference?" *Public Administration Review* 58 (1998): 522–32.

75. Ibid., 529.

76. V.O. Key, Jr., "The Lack of a Budgetary Theory," *American Political Science Review* 34 (1940): 1137–44.

77. Verne B. Lewis, "Toward a Theory of Budgeting," *Public Administration Review* 12 (1952): 47.

78. Charles E. Lindblom, "The Science of Muddling Through," *Public Administration Review* 19 (1959): 79–88.

79. Ibid., 87.

80. Charles E. Lindblom, "Still Muddling, Not Yet Through," *Public Administration Review* 39 (1979): 517–26.

81. Aaron Wildavsky, "Political Implications of Budgetary Reform," *Public Administration Review* 21 (1961): 183–90.

82. Aaron Wildavsky, *The Politics of the Budgetary Process* (Boston: Little, Brown, 1964).

83. See especially Lance T. LeLoup, "The Myth of Incrementalism: Analytical Choices in Budgetary Theory," *Polity* 10 (1978): 488–509.

84. Wildavsky, "Political Implications of Budgetary Reform," 187.

85. Ibid.

86. Executive Office of the President of the United States, *Weekly Compilation of Presidential Documents* 29 (September 13, 1993): 1703.

87. Beryl A. Radin, "The Government Performance and Results Act (GPRA): Hydra-headed Monster or Flexible Management Tool?" *Public Administration Review* 58 (1998): 307–15.

88. I.S. Rubin, *The Politics of Budgeting*, 4th ed. (New York: Chatham House, 2000).

Notes to Chapter 3

1. National Advisory Council on State and Local Budgeting, *Recommended Budget Practices* (Chicago: Government Finance Officers Association, 1999).

2. National Association of State Budget Officers, *Budget Processes in the States* (2002), available at www.nasbo.org.

3. It should be noted that some jurisdictions have a balanced budget ordinance that permits a surplus budget to be adopted.

4. Governmental Accounting Standards Board, *Basic Financial Statements and Management's Discussion and Analysis for State and Local Government* (Norwalk, CT: Author, 1999).

5. For more information on how budgetary compliance is handled for proprietary funds, see: Robert J. Freeman and Craig D. Shoulders, *Governmental and Nonprofit Accounting*, 5th ed. (Upper Saddle River, NJ: Prentice-Hall, 1996).

6. While fiduciary funds typically are not directly involved in the budget preparation process, they can have major impacts on operating budgets. Expanding on the pension fund example, a state or local government may be required to substantially increase its contribution to the pension plan if an actuarial assessment shows that the plan is underfunded. This contribution would normally come from general fund revenue, causing an impact on general fund service provision.

7. Stephen J. Gauthier, *Governmental Accounting, Auditing and Financial Reporting* (Chicago: Government Finance Officers Association, 2001).

8. Donald Axelrod, *Budgeting for Modern Government* (New York: St. Martin's Press, 1988).

9. Leon E. Hay and Earl R. Wilson, *Accounting for Governmental and Nonprofit Entities*, 9th ed. (Boston: Irwin, 1992).

10. David N. Ammons, *Tools for Decision Making* (Washington, DC: CQ Press, 2002).

11. National Association of State Budget Officers, *Budget Processes in the States.*

12. Salomon A. Guajardo, *An Elected Official's Guide to Multi-Year Budgeting* (Chicago: Government Finance Officers Association, 2000).

13. See the Village of Sauk Village, Illinois, *FY 2002–2003 Annual Budget*, for additional information on its budget process. The village also embraces components of performance budgeting, including goals, objectives, and performance measures by program.

14. See the State of West Virginia, *Fiscal Year 2003 Executive Budget*, for additional information on its budget process. The state is also implementing a performance measurement system to complement its budget process.

15. Jane McCollough and Howard Frank, "Incentives for Forecasting Reform among Local Finance Officers," *Public Budgeting and Finance Management* 4 (1992): 407–29.

254 NOTES TO CHAPTERS 3 AND 4

16. William Earle Klay and Gloria A. Grizzle, "Forecasting State Revenues: Expanding the Dimensions of Budgetary Forecasting Research," *Public Budgeting and Financial Management* 4 (1992): 381–405.

17. Irene S. Rubin, *The Politics of the Budgetary Process*, 4th ed. (New York: Chatham House, 2000).

18. For additional information on the state of Washington's budget process, see www.ofm.wa.gov.

19. For additional information on Fairfax County's budget process, see www.fairfaxcounty.gov/dmb.

20. Fremont J. Lyden and Ernest G. Miller, eds., *Planning Programming Budgeting*, 2d ed. (Chicago: Markham, 1972), 7.

Notes to Chapter 4

1. Florence Heffron, *Organization Theory and Public Organizations* (Englewood Cliffs, NJ: Prentice-Hall, 1989).

2. See Evan M. Berman and Jonathan P. West, "Productivity Enhancement Efforts in Public and Nonprofit Organizations," *Public Productivity and Management Review* 22 (1998): 207–19; and Frances Stokes Berry and Barton Wechsler, "State Agencies' Experience with Strategic Planning: Findings from a National Survey," *Public Administration Review* 55 (1995): 159–68.

3. Charles M. Mottley, "Strategic Planning," in *Planning Programming Budgeting*, ed. Fremont J. Lyden and Ernest G. Miller, 2d ed. (Chicago: Markham, 1972).

4. Ibid.

5. Government Finance Officers Association, *Recommended Practices for State and Local Governments* (Chicago: Author, 2001).

6. Government Finance Officers Association, *Recommended Practices*.

7. National Advisory Council on State and Local Budgeting, *Recommended Budget Practices* (Chicago: Government Finance Officers Association, 1999).

8. Harry P. Hatry, "Performance Measurement: Fashions and Fallacies," *Public Performance and Management Review* 25 (2002): 352–58.

9. Dee Ann Ellingson and Jacob R. Wambsganss, "Modifying the Approach to Planning and Evaluation in Governmental Entities: A 'Balanced Scorecard' Approach," *Journal of Public Budgeting, Accounting and Financial Management* 13 (2001): 103–20.

10. Kim Soonhee, "Participative Management and Job Satisfaction: Lessons for Management Leadership," *Public Administration Review* 62 (2002): 213–41.

11. Roger M. Schwarz, *The Skilled Facilitator* (San Francisco, CA: Jossey-Bass, 1994).

12. Gerald R. Kissler, Karmen N. Fore, Willow S. Jacobson, William P. Kittredge, and Scott L. Stewart, "State Strategic Planning: Suggestions from the Oregon Experience," *Public Administration Review* 58 (1998): 353–59.

13. Ibid.

14. See Dakota County, Minnesota, *2002 Annual Plan and Budget Report*.

15. Information about the planning process is based on a telephone interview with Heidi Welsch, senior management analyst, Office of Planning, Evaluation, and Development, Dakota County, Minnesota, May 5, 2002.

16. Craig Clifford, "Linking Strategic Planning and Budgeting in Scottsdale, Arizona," *Government Finance Review* 14 (1998): 9–14.

17. Hatry, "Performance Measurement."

18. Ibid.

19. Salomon A. Guajardo and Rosemary McDonnell, *An Elected Official's Guide to Performance Measurement* (Chicago: Government Finance Officers Association, 2000).

20. The information used to describe the process used by the city of Charlotte, North Carolina, was taken from: "Budget and Evaluation," *FY 2001 Year-End Report*, Charlotte, NC.

21. Robert S. Kaplan and David P. Norton, "The Balanced Scorecard—Measures That Drive Performance," *Harvard Business Review* (January–February 1992): 71–79.

22. Ken W. Brown, "The 10–Point Test of Financial Condition: Toward an Easy-to-Use Assessment Tool for Smaller Cities," *Government Finance Review* 9 (1993): 21–26.

23. See Johnson County, Kansas, *Capital and Operating Budgets 2001*.

24. For more information on management controls, see the General Accounting Office—Electronic Codification of Governmental Auditing Standards (1999), available at www.gao.gov.

25. Joseph Rosse and Robert Levin, *High-Impact Hiring* (San Francisco, CA: Jossey-Bass, 1997).

26. Robert S. Kaplan and David P. Norton, *The Balanced Scorecard: Translating Strategy into Action* (Boston: Harvard Business School Press, 1996).

27. Elaine Sharp, "Citizen-initiated Contacting of Government Officials and Socioeconomic Status: Determining the Relationship and Accounting for It," *American Political Science Review* 76 (1982): 109–15.

28. Rita Mae Kelly, "An Inclusive Democratic Polity, Representative Bureaucracies, and the New Public Management," *Public Administration Review* 58 (1998): 206.

29. See Harry P. Hatry et al., *How Effective Are Your Community Services?* (Washingon, DC: Urban Insitute Press, 1977); and Thomas I. Miller and Michelle Miller, *Citizen Surveys: How to Do Them, How to Use Them, What They Mean* (Washington, DC: International City/County Management Association, 1991).

30. Roger B. Parks, "Linking Objective and Subjective Measures of Performance," *Public Administration Review* 44 (1984): 118–27.

31. Stephen L. Percy, "In Defense of Citizen Evaluations as Performance Measures," *Urban Affairs Quarterly* 22 (1986): 66–83.

32. Mark S. Rosentraub and Lyke Thompson, "The Use of Surveys of Satisfaction for Evaluations," *Policy Studies Journal* 9 (1981): 990–99.

33. See Brian Stipak, "Citizen Satisfaction with Urban Services: Potential Misuse as a Performance Indicator," *Public Administration Review* 39 (1979): 46–52; and Karin Brown and Philip B. Coulter, "Subjective and Objective Measures of Police Service Delivery," *Public Administration Review* 43 (1983): 50–58.

34. Robert L. Lineberry, *Equality and Urban Policy: The Distribution of Municipal Services* (Beverly Hills, CA: Sage, 1977).

35. William E. Lyons, David Lowry, and Ruth Hoogland DeHoog, *The Politics of Dissatisfaction* (Armonk, NY: M.E. Sharpe, 1992).

36. Lyke Thompson, "Citizen Attitudes About Service Delivery Modes," *Journal of Urban Affairs* 19 (1997): 291–302.

37. Mark A. Glaser and John W. Bardo, "A Five-Stage Approach for Improved Use of Citizen Surveys in Public Investment Decisions," *State and Local Government Review* 26 (1994): 161–72.

38. Stipak, "Citizen Satisfaction with Urban Services," 51.

39. Brown and Coulter, "Subjective and Objective Measures of Police Service Delivery."

40. Stephen L. Percy, "In Defense of Citizen Evaluations as Performance Measures," *Urban Affairs Quarterly* 22 (1986): 81.

41. Kaplan and Norton, *The Balanced Scorecard*, 75.

42. Thomas I. Miller and Michelle Miller, "Assessing Excellence Poorly: The Bottom Line in Local Government," *Journal of Policy Analysis and Management* 11 (1992): 612–23.

43. Julia Melkers and John Clayton Thomas, "What Do Administrators Think Citizens Think? Administrator Predictions as an Adjunct to Citizen Surveys," *Public Administration Review* 58 (1998): 327–34.

44. David J. Watson, Robert J. Juster, and Gerald W. Johnson, "Institutionalized Use of Citizen Surveys in the Budgetary and Policy-Making Processes: A Small City Case Study," *Public Administration Review* 51 (1991): 232–39.

45. Wendy L. Hassett and Douglas J. Watson, "Citizen Surveys: A Component of the Budgetary Process," *Journal of Public Budgeting, Accounting and Financial Management*, forthcoming.

46. Lyons, Lowery, and DeHoog, *The Politics of Dissatisfaction*.

47. Ibid.

Notes to Chapter 5

1. David N. Ammons, *Municipal Benchmarks* (Thousand Oaks, CA: Sage, 2001); and Harry P. Hatry, *Performance Measurement* (Washington, DC: Urban Institute Press, 1999).

2. Harry P. Hatry, James R. Fountain, Jr., Jonathan M. Sullivan, and Lorraine Kremer, *Service Efforts and Accomplishments Reporting: Its Time Has Come* (Norwalk, CT: Governmental Accounting Standards Board, 1990).

3. Salomon Guajardo and Rosemary McDonnell, *An Elected Official's Guide to Performance Measurement* (Chicago: Government Finance Officers Association, 2000).

4. Ibid.

5. It should be noted that these additional output measures and customer service standards are for the Department of Housing and Community Development, which includes the core service area of community development.

6. Harry P. Hatry and Donald M Fisk, *Improving Productivity and Productivity Measurement in Local Government* (Washington, DC: Urban Institute Press, 1971).

7. Rackham S. Fukuhara, "Productivity Improvement in Cities," in *The Municipal Yearbook* (Washington, DC: International City Management Association, 1977), 193–200; and Harry P. Hatry et al., *How Effective Are Your Community Services?* (Washington, DC: Urban Institute Press, 1977).

8. Stan Altman, "Performance Monitoring Systems for Public Managers," *Public Administration Review* 39 (1979): 31–35; and Harry P. Hatry, "The Status of Productivity Measurement in the United States," *Public Administration Review* 38 (1978): 28–33.

9. See Paul D. Epstein, *Using Performance Measurement in Local Government* (New York: Van Nostrand, 1984); and Joseph S. Wholey, *Evaluation and Effective Public Management* (Boston: Little, Brown, 1983).

10. See Gloria A. Grizzle, "Performance Measures for Budget Justification: Developing a Selection Strategy," *Public Productivity Review* 8 (1985): 328–43; Glen H. Cope, "Local Government Budgeting and Productivity: Friends or Foes?" *Public Productivity Review* 41 (1987): 45–47; and Richard E. Brown and James B. Pyers, "Putting Teeth into the Efficiency and Effectiveness of Public Services," *Public Productivity and Management Review* 48 (1988): 735–43.

11. Theodore H. Poister and Robert P. McGowan, "The Use of Management Tools in Municipal Government: A National Survey," *Public Administration Review* 44 (1984): 215–23.

12. Daniel E. O'Toole and Brian Stipak, "Budgeting and Productivity Revisited: The Local Government Picture," *Public Productivity Review* 12 (1988): 1–12.

13. Jonathan Walters, "Benchmarking or Bust," *Governing* 7 (1994): 33.

14. Theodore H. Poister and Gregory Streib, "Performance Assessment in Municipal Government," *Public Administration Review* 59 (1999): 325–35.

15. Gregory Streib and Theodore H. Poister, "Performance Measurement in Municipal Governments," in *The Municipal Yearbook* (Washington, DC: International City/County Management Association, 1998), 9–15.

16. Julia Melkers, Katherine G. Willoughby, Brian James, and James Fountain, *Performance Measures at the State and Local Levels: A Summary of Survey Results* (Norwalk, CT: Governmental Standards Accounting Board, 2002).

17. The research on performance measurement by the Governmental Accounting Standards Board also contains information on how state and local governments are using performance measures. For more information, see: www.seagov.org/index.html.

18. Ammons, *Municipal Benchmarks*.

19. City of St. Petersburg, Florida (2002), www.stpete.org/sanit.htm.

20. Missouri Department of Social Services, Division of Family Service, Child Abuse and Neglect in Missouri (2001), www.dss.state.mo.us/re/pdf/cancy00.pdf.

21. City of St. Petersburg, Florida (2002), www.stpete.org/sanit.htm.

22. Ibid.

23. Ibid.

24. John Topinga, "Moving from Measuring Outcome to Measuring the Performance of People at the Local Level," paper presented at the Southeastern Conference on Public Administration, Baton Rouge, LA, October 2001.

25. George H. Frederickson, "Painting Bull's Eyes around Bullet Holes," *Governing* 12 (1992): 13.

26. Janet M. Kelly, "Why We Should Take Performance Measurement on Faith (Facts Being Hard to Come By and Not Very Important)," *Public Performance and Management Review* 25 (2002): 367–80.

27. Brian J. Cook, "Politics, Political Leadership and Public Management," *Public Administration Review* 58 (1998): 225–30.

28. Allan Drebin, "Criteria for Performance Measurement in State and Local Government," *Governmental Finance* 9 (1980): 3–7.

29. Harry P. Hatry, Craig Gerhart, and Martha Marshall, "Eleven Ways to Make Performance Measurement More Useful to Public Managers," *Public Management* 76 (1994): S17.

30. See Gloria A. Grizzle, "Linking Performance to Funding Decisions: What Is the Budgeter's Role?" *Public Productivity Review* 10 (1987): 33–44; and Susan A. MacManus, "Intergovernmental Dimensions of Urban Fiscal Stress," *Publius* 14 (1984): 1–82.

31. H. Perrin Garsombke and Jerry Schrad, "Performance Measurement Systems: Results from a City and State Survey," *Government Finance Review* 15 (1999): 9–12.

32. David Affholter, "Outcome Monitoring," in *Handbook of Practical Program Evaluation*, ed. Joseph S. Wholey, Harry P. Hatry, and Katherine Newcomer (San Francisco, CA: Josey-Bass, 1994), 96–118.

33. Larry L. Decker and Paul Manion, "Performance Measures in Phoenix: Trends and a New Direction," *National Civic Review* 76 (1987): 119–29.

34. Mark A. Glaser, "Tailoring Performance Measurement to Fit the Organization: From Generic to Germane," *Public Productivity and Management Review* 14 (1991): 303–19.

35. See Ammons, *Municipal Benchmarks*; Harry P. Hatry, "Performance Measurement Principles and Techniques: An Overview for Local Government," *Public Productivity Review* 4 (1980): 312–39; and Hatry, Gerhart, and Marshall, "Eleven Ways to Make Performance Measurement More Useful to Public Managers."

36. American Society for Public Administration, Center for Accountability and Performance, www.aspanet.org/cap/about.html.

37. Ronald Fisher, "An Overview of Performance Measurement," *Public Management* 76 (1994): 2–8.

38. Hatry, Gerhart, and Marshall, "Eleven Ways to Make Performance Measurement More Useful to Public Managers"; and Jonathan Walters, "Benchmarking or Bust," *Governing* 7 (1994): 33–37.

39. David N. Ammons, "A Proper Mentality for Benchmarking," *Public Administration Review* 59 (1999): 106–7.

40. Richard C. Kearney, Barry M. Feldman, and Carmine P.F. Scavo, "Reinventing Government: City Manager Attitudes and Actions," *Public Administration Review* 60 (2000): 535–47.

41. Patria de Lancer Julnes and Marc Holzer, "Promoting the Utilization of Performance Measures in Public Organizations: An Empirical Study of Factors Affecting Adoption and Implementation," *Public Administration Review* 61 (2001): 693–705.

Notes to Chapter 6

1. David N. Ammons, *Municipal Benchmarks*, 2d ed. (Thousand Oaks, CA: Sage, 2001).

2. Salomon A. Guajardo and Rosemary McDonnell, *An Elected Official's Guide to Performance Measurement* (Chicago: Government Finance Officers Association, 2000).

3. David N. Ammons, "Benchmarking as a Performance Management Tool: Experiences among Municipalities in North Carolina," *Journal of Public Budgeting, Accounting and Financial Management* 12 (2000): 106–24.

4. Guajardo and McDonnell, *An Elected Official's Guide*.

5. Ammons, "Benchmarking as a Performance Management Tool."

6. Guajardo and McDonnell, *An Elected Official's Guide*.

7. James E. Swiss, "Adapting Total Quality Management (TQM) to Government," *Public Administration Review* 52 (1992): 356–62.

8. Donald F. Kettl, "Building Lasting Reform: Enduring Questions, Missing Answers," in *Inside the Reinvention Machine*, ed. Donald Kettl and John J. DiIulio, Jr. (Washington DC: Brookings Institution, 1995), 9–83.

9. Evan M. Berman and Jonathan P. West, "Municipal Commitment to Total Qual-

ity Management: A Survey of Recent Progress," *Public Administration Review* 55 (1995): 57–66.

10. Kettl, "Building Lasting Reform."

11. Richard J. Fischer, "An Overview of Performance Measurement," *Public Management* 76 (1994): S2–S8.

12. Irene S. Rubin, "Budget Theory and Budget Practice: How Good the Fit?" *Public Administration Review* 50 (1990): 179–89.

13. Ammons, "Benchmarking as a Performance Management Tool."

14. Kenneth A. Bruder and Edward M. Gray, "Public-Sector Benchmarking: A Practical Approach," *Public Management* 76 (1994): S9–S14.

15. Charles K. Coe, "Local Government Benchmarking: Lessons from Two Major Multigovernmental Efforts," *Public Administration Review* 59 (1999): 110–23.

16. For more information on the North Carolina project, see William C. Rivenbark, ed., *A Guide to the North Carolina Local Government Performance Measurement Project* (University of North Carolina at Chapel Hill: Institute of Government, 2001).

17. Gerald R. Kissler, Karmen N. Fore, Willow S. Jacobson, William P. Kittredge, and Scott L. Stewart, "State Strategic Planning: Suggestions from the Oregon Experience," *Public Administration Review* 58 (1998): 353–59.

18. Ammons, "Benchmarking as a Performance Management Tool."

19. Patricia Fredericksen and Rosanne London, "Disconnect in the Hollow State: The Pivotal Role of Organizational Capacity in Community-Based Development Organizations," *Public Administration Review* 60 (2000): 230–39.

Notes to Chapter 7

1. Katherine Thompson, "Performance Auditing: What Is It?" *Government Accountants Journal* 45 (1996): 14–18.

2. David Osborne and Ted Gaebler, *Reinventing Government* (New York: Penguin Group, 1992).

3. It should be noted that this expanded reporting technique for budget execution in regard to defined work programs, results to be accomplished, and resources required to finance them is not a recent phenomenon. In fact, it has been a part of state and local government for well over fifty years. For more information, see A.E. Buck, "Techniques of Budget Execution," *Municipal Finance* 21 (1948): 8–11.

4. W. Anderson Williams, "Trusting the Numbers: The Power of Data Verification," *Government Finance Review* 18 (2002): 18–21.

5. Katherine Barrett and Richard Greene, "Truth in Measurement," *Governing* 13 (2000): 86.

6. Leon E. Hay and Earl R. Wilson, *Accounting for Governmental and Nonprofit Entities*, 9th ed. (Boston: Irwin, 1992).

7. Stephen J. Gauthier, *Governmental Accounting, Auditing and Financial Reporting* (Chicago: Government Finance Officers Association, 2001).

8. Ibid.

9. Governmental Accounting Standards Board, *Basic Financial Statements—and Management's Discussion and Analysis—for State and Local Government* (Norwalk, CT: Author, 1999).

10. As early as 1944, proponents of cost accounting were advocating its advantages for managing public services. They also agreed that the cost system should be a subsidiary to the general accounting system, it should operate independently from the

general ledger, and it should be consistently balanced to control the subsidiary accounts. For more information, see H.M. Kimpel, "Cost Accounting for Municipalities," *Municipal Finance* 16 (1944): 30–32.

11. Thompson, "Performance Auditing."

12. James R. Nobles, Judith R. Brown, John A. Ferris, and James R. Fountain, "AGA Task Force Report on Performance Auditing," *Government Accountants Journal* 42 (1993): 11–25.

13. Robert J. Freeman and Craig D. Shoulders, *Governmental and Nonprofit Accounting* 5th ed. (Upper Saddle River, NJ: Prentice Hall, 1996).

14. Nobles et al., "AGA Task Force Report on Performance Auditing."

15. For more information on the specifics of performance auditing, see Leo Herbert, *Auditing the Performance of Management* (Belmont, CA: Lifetime Learning Publications, 1979).

16. General Accounting Office, *Electronic Codification of Government Auditing Standards* (Washington, DC: Author, 1999).

17. Richard C. Brooks and David B. Pariser, "Audit Recommendations Follow-Up Systems: A Survey of the States," *Public Budgeting and Finance* 15 (1995): 72–83.

18. Thompson, "Performance Auditing."

19. Peter H. Rossi, Howard E. Freeman, and Mark W. Lipsey, *Evaluation: A Systematic Approach*, 6th ed. (Thousand Oaks, CA: Sage, 1999).

20. The information on summative evaluation and formative evaluation is based on: Blain R. Worthen, James R. Sanders, and Jody L. Fitzpatrick, *Program Evaluation: Alternatives, Approaches, and Practical Guidelines*, 2d ed. (New York: Longman, 1997).

21. William C. Rivenbark and Carla M. Pizzarella, "Auditing Performance Data in Local Government," *Public Performance and Management Review* 25 (2002): 414–21.

22. Williams, "Trusting the Numbers."

23. Rivenbark and Pizzarella, "Auditing Performance Data in Local Government."

24. State Auditor's Office, *Guide to Performance Measure Management* (State of Texas: Author, 2002): www.sao.state.tx.us/resources.

25. Ibid.

26. For more information on the auditing process, see: Rivenbark and Pizzarella, "Auditing Performance Data in Local Government"; and William C. Rivenbark and Carla M. Pizzarella, "Ensuring the Integrity of Crucial Data," *Popular Government* 67 (2002): 28–34.

27. Thompson, "Performance Auditing."

28. See the Government Finance Officers Association's Web site for more information on the budget presentation award, www.gfoa.org.

Notes to Chapter 8

1. William A. Giles, Gerald T. Gabris, and Dale A. Krane, "Dynamics in Rural Policy Development: The Uniqueness in County Government," *Public Administration Review* 40 (1980): 24–28.

2. Beth Walter Honadle, "A Capacity-Building Framework: A Search for Concept and Purpose," *Public Administration Review* 41 (1981): 575–80.

3. John J. Gargan, "Consideration of Local Government Capacity," *Public Administration Review* 41 (1981): 652.

4. Ibid.

5. Luther Gulick and Lyndall F. Urwick, *Papers on the Science of Administration* (New York: Institute of Public Administration, 1937), 10.

6. Gargan, "Consideration of Local Government Capacity," 650.

7. Rackham S. Fukuhara, "Productivity Improvement in Cities," in *The Municipal Year Book* (Washington DC: International City Management Association, 1977), 193–200.

8. Theodore H. Poister and Robert P. McGowan, "The Use of Management Tools in Municipal Government: A National Survey," *Public Administration Review* 44 (1984): 215–23.

9. Theodore H. Poister and Gregory Strieb, "Management Tools in Municipal Government: Trends Over the Past Decade," *Public Administration Review* 49 (1989): 240–48.

10. Poister and McGowan, "The Use of Management Tools in Municipal Government."

11. Poister and Streib, "Management Tools in Municipal Government."

12. Richard D. Bingham, Brett W. Hawkins, John P. Frendries, and Mary P. LeBlanc, *Professional Associations and Municipal Innovation* (Madison: University of Wisconsin Press, 1981).

13. David N. Ammons, "The Role of Professional Associations in Establishing and Promoting Standards for Local Government," *Public Productivity and Management Review* 17 (1994): 281–98.

14. National Academy of Public Administration, Center for Improving Government Performance, www.napawash.org/ program_concentrations/index.html.

15. Ibid., www.napawash.org/pc_government_performance/performance.html.

16. American Society for Public Administration, Balanced Scorecard Interest Group, www.aspanet.org/bscorecard/index.html.

17. American Society for Public Administration, *Encouraging the Use of Performance Measurement and Reporting by Government Organizations* (Washington, DC: Author, 1992).

18. American Society for Public Administration, Center for Accountability and Performance, www.aspanet.org/cap/about.html.

19. International City/County Management Association, "Declaration of Ideals," www.icma.org/go.cfm?cid=1&gid=2&sid=4.

20. International City/County Management Association, Center for Performance Measurement, www.icma.org/go.cfm?cid=1&gid=3&sid=101&did=104.

21. Mary Kopczynski and Michael Lombardo, "Comparative Performance Measurement: Insights and Lessons Learned from a Consortium Effort," *Public Administration Review* 59 (1999): 124–34.

22. Charles Coe, "Local Government Benchmarking: Lessons from Two Major Multigovernment Efforts," *Public Administration Review* 59 (1999): 110–23.

23. International City/County Management Association, *Comparative Performance Measurement: FY 1995 Data Report* (Washington, DC: Author, 1996).

24. International City/County Management Association, Center for Performance Measurement, www.icma.org/go.cfm?cid=1&gid=3&sid=101&did=104.

25. National Association of State Budget Officers, "About NASBO," www.nasbo.org/About_Nasbo.html.

26. National Association of State Budget Officers, "Performance Measures Resources," www.nasbo.org/Publications/information_briefs/performancemeasures_1995.html.

27. Government Finance Officers Association, "Best Practices in Public Budgeting," www.gfoa.org/services/nacslb/.

28. Government Finance Officers Association, GFOA's Advanced Government Finance Institute, www.gfoa.org/services/institute.shtml.

29. Government Finance Officers Association, GFOA Awards for Recognition, www.gfoa.org/services/awards.shtml.

30. Ibid.

31. Harry P. Hatry et. al, eds., *Service Efforts and Accomplishments Reporting: Its Time Has Come* (Norwalk, CT: Governmental Accounting Standards Board, 1990).

32. Richard E. Brown and James B. Pyers, "Service Efforts and Accomplishments Reporting: Has Its Time Really Come?" *Public Budgeting and Finance* 18 (1998): 101–13.

33. Adapted from Concepts Statement No. 2 of the Governmental Accounting Standards Board, Service Efforts and Accomplishments Reporting (1994), available at accounting.rutgers.edu/raw/seagov/pmg/citizen/index.html.

34. Irene S. Rubin, *The Politics of Public Budgeting*, 4th ed. (New York: Chatham House, 2000), 12.

35. Allen. Schick, "The Road to PPB: The Stages of Reform," *Public Administration Review* 26 (1966): 243–58.

36. Kurt M. Thurmaier and Katherine G. Willoughby, *Policy and Politics in State Budgeting* (Armonk, NY: M.E. Sharpe, 2001).

37. Beryl A. Radin, "The Government Performance and Results Act (GPRA): Hydra-headed Monster or Flexible Management Tool?" *Public Administration Review* 58 (1998): 307–15.

38. Wendy L. Hassett and Douglas J. Watson, "Citizen Surveys: A Component of the Budgetary Process," *Journal of Public Budgeting, Accounting and Financial Management*, forthcoming.

Index

About the Authors

Janet M. Kelly is the Albert A. Levin Professor of Urban Studies and Public Service in the Maxine Goodman Levin College of Urban Affairs at Cleveland State University. She earned a Bachelor of Science in Economics and a Master of Public Administration from the College of Charleston, and a Ph.D. in Political Science from Wayne State University. She teaches courses in public and nonprofit financial management in the graduate programs in public administration and urban studies at Cleveland State University. Her research interests include intergovernmental fiscal relations, performance measurement and performance budgeting in state and local government, and financial administration for small nonprofit organizations. She has published a series of scholarly articles on performance measurement in *Public Administration Review, Urban Affairs Review, American Review of Public Administration*, the *Journal of Urban Affairs, and National Civic Review.* She regularly contributes to *Government Finance Review* and provides training for the Government Finance Officers Association.

William C. Rivenbark is an assistant professor in the School of Government at the University of North Carolina at Chapel Hill. He earned a Bachelor of Science in Business Administration from Auburn University, a Master of Public Administration from Auburn University at Montgomery, and a Ph.D. in Public Administration from Mississippi State University. His responsibilities in the School of Government include teaching the public budgeting and finance course for the Master of Public Administration Program, providing technical assistance and training on the topics of performance and financial management, and conducting applied research for state and local government. He also provides training for the Government Finance Officers Association. He has been published in the following academic and professional journals: *Government Finance Review, International Journal of Public Administration, Journal of Public Affairs Education, Journal of Public Budgeting, Accounting and Financial Management, Popular Government, Public Administration Quarterly, Public Finance Review*, and *Public Performance & Management Review.*